Challenging to change: dialogues with a radical baptist theologian

Challenging to change: dialogues with a radical baptist theologian

Essays presented to Dr Nigel G. Wright on his sixtieth birthday

Introduction by David Coffey

Edited by Pieter J. Lalleman

WIPF & STOCK · Eugene, Oregon

Wipf and Stock Publishers
199 W 8th Ave, Suite 3
Eugene, OR 97401

Challenging to change
dialogues with a radical baptist theologian
By Lalleman, Pieter J. and Coffey, David
Copyright © 2009 by Lalleman, Pieter J. All rights reserved.
Softcover ISBN-13: 978-1-7252-8769-3
Hardcover ISBN-13: 978-1-7252-8771-6
eBook ISBN-13: 978-1-7252-8770-9
Publication date 9/2/2020
Previously published by Spurgeon's College, 2009

Contents

Foreword	ix
Introduction *David Coffey*	1
Contributors	5
Short tributes	7
Baptist 'Relating and Resourcing' in difficult times. A historical perspective *Raymond Brown*	11
New birth from water and Spirit *Alastair Campbell*	25
The coherence of freedom: can Church or state ever be truly free? *John Colwell*	39
Being a minister: spirituality and the pastor *Chris Ellis*	55
'The leadership of some...' Baptist ministers as leaders? *Rob Ellis*	71
Something will come of nothing: on *A Theology of the Dark Side* *Paul Fiddes*	87
Inclusive representation revisited *Paul Goodliff*	105
The radical ecclesiology of Nigel Wright *Steve Holmes*	117
Church planting, peace and the ecclesial minimum *Stuart Murray*	129

Part of a movement: Nigel Wright and Baptist life
Ian Randall   143

When Wright was right
Tom Smail   163

The Radical Evangelical. A critical appreciation
Derek Tidball   175

Crown rights of the Redeemer
Pat Took   191

Select bibliography of the writings of Dr Nigel G. Wright   205

Foreword

This is a book for Nigel Wright and it is a book for the Baptist churches, their leaders and would-be leaders. We think Nigel will like this because his aim has always been that theology should serve the churches.

Challenging to change: dialogues with a radical baptist theologian is first and foremost a present to Nigel to honour him for his sixtieth birthday and to make sure he will not soon forget it. Nigel, warm congratulations!

The contributors were invited to engage with an aspect of Nigel's life and work so far, in particular with his writings. The book does not contain a full biography but Coffey, Smail and especially Randall provide insights into the person Nigel Wright.[1] The contributors were not asked just to sing his praises but to engage in a critical dialogue. This foreword will not try to repeat or even summarise their words. I merely want to highlight one aspect of his work which does not receive much attention, basically because it is ongoing: Nigel is an excellent Principal of Spurgeon's and a great boss to work for and to work with - 'and so say all of us'. He is truly the right person for the job - which also enables him to continue a wider ministry of teaching, writing and leadership. We are glad that after a period of health problems he is back to full strength.

In the same way that Luke did not write for Theophilus alone, over and beyond Nigel this book is an endowment to the Church of Jesus Christ, in particular that part of it which calls itself Baptist or baptist.[2] As Nigel dedicates his life and his considerable energy to the well-being of the churches of Jesus Christ, so his Festschrift aims to make a modest contribution to their life and their theology. It does so by focusing largely on leaders, ministers and theologians. My hope and expectation is that people such as students training for baptist ministry will profit hugely from it - and from being encouraged to pick up Nigel's own books. One of the intentions of *Challenging to change: dialogues with a radical*

---

[1] Cf. his autobiographical notes in Tom Smail, Andrew Walker and Nigel Wright, *Charismatic Renewal: The Search for a Theology* (London: SPCK, 1993) 22-32.
[2] For the distinction see Nigel G. Wright, *Free Church, Free State: The Positive Baptist Vision* (Carlisle: Paternoster, 2005) xxiii; also pages 129, 137 and 154 in the present book, the subtitle of which is deliberately spelt accordingly.

baptist theologian is that its readers will indeed turn (again or for the first time) to Nigel's own publications.

I am grateful to Ian Randall for his help with the editorial process, to John Colwell for suggesting the title and to all contributors for their essays. Where their contributions touch on similar topics, I have added cross-references. Thanks be to God for his servant Nigel Goring Wright. May Nigel be given the time and energy to go on far beyond sixty, as an unremitting blessing to the Church of Jesus Christ on these shores and far beyond.

Pieter J. Lalleman
Academic Dean, Spurgeon's College
London, 13 May 2009

Introduction

David R. Coffey

I consider it a great privilege to represent the *tabula gratulatoria* of friends and colleagues of Nigel Goring Wright who wish to honour their highly esteemed and richly gifted friend. He has honoured so many others with his gracious magnanimity that it is a joy to celebrate his own considerable achievements and all of us, hopefully, can gain the greatest satisfaction in delivering this most wonderful of surprises for a man who likes to know everything that is happening around him!

I have known Nigel for 30 years since we first met as pastors through the Mainstream network which was founded in 1979. My memory of his early contributions to the burgeoning movement of 'Baptists for life and growth' was the warmth of his northern personality and his trenchant style of rigorous theological questioning of the traditional understanding of Baptist identity. Nigel loved making waves because he believed this was the legitimate role of a reform movement serious about making a radical contribution to the future of British Baptists, if indeed there was to be a future for Baptists. This was the period when deep concern was expressed publicly about the spiritual and numerical decline of the denomination. The despondency surrounding the future of the Baptist Union of Great Britain (BUGB) was part of the impulse behind the founding of Mainstream, and Nigel was in the forefront of the younger pastors who were questioning whether the BUGB was worth remaining in as a spiritually credible movement.

It was the first time I had encountered a radical Baptist theologian with evangelical, charismatic, restorationist and Anabaptist leanings who was also a paid up member of the Labour Party and wrote the occasional feature article for the left wing newspaper, *The Guardian*. I had a personal glimpse into Nigel's erstwhile political ambitions when, following a Mainstream gathering in the 1980s, we were walking late at night in the vicinity of The Palace of Westminster. Standing in the shadow of Big Ben, Nigel said wistfully that he would have loved to have served as a Labour Member of Parliament but he recognised clearly that God had placed a more significant calling on his life.

And what a considerable calling has emerged during the past 25 years, exemplified by the distinguished contributions in this volume of essays which display the breadth of Nigel's fertile friendships and the rich vein of interests which he can celebrate on his 60th birthday! One Festschrift does not permit an exploration of the full-orbed dimensions of Nigel's life and ministry so perhaps he is destined to follow in the steps of the German historian Joseph Vogt who was given a four-volume Festschrift to commemorate his 75th birthday in 1972. That has now grown to 89 volumes with several planned for over the coming years! Maybe succeeding Festschrifts can explore in greater depth the ministry of Nigel the Principal, a pastor-theologian who knows his students and cares for the fruitfulness of their future ministries. Students trust him because of his commitment to equip them for effective ministry as missionary pastors; they love him because he is an exemplar of passionate commitment to life-long learning for ministers of the Gospel.

Then there is Nigel the BUGB President, who self-confessedly enjoyed his presidential year more than he could have expected and in the course of the year revealed through his weekly columns in the *Baptist Times* a journalistic flair for pithy and humorous observations of Baptists at large. Those who have observed Nigel the internationalist know how he moves at ease in the multi-cultural world of global gatherings. Through his chairmanship of the Baptist World Alliance Ethics Commission he has learned the boundaries which mark the diverse cultures and traditions within the membership of the Alliance, but he is unafraid to test sensitively those boundaries in order to move people to a broader understanding of complex issues.

Nigel the leader is a fascinating character study. For all his pastoral skills, his proven track record as a team player and his spirit of joyful confidence in the Gospel, his default position for working with organisational life is probably benevolent dictator mixed with pessimism (his own self-description). He can be impatient with the procrastinations of the committee process and fears the institution will lose the plot on the long road to making a decision. But by a miracle of patience and faith, Nigel proved he can work with the frustrating processes of the institution when he chaired the influential group which formulated the report *Relating and Resourcing* which emerged out of the 1996 BUGB Denominational Consultation. The members of that group will know the brilliance of Nigel's creative leadership which steered the core vision of the report through the minefields of Committees and Councils to emerge as one of the major influences for shaping the new regional and national structures for the 21st century. This report on the renewal of association life popularised the theological vision that Nigel proposed in his 1991 book *Challenge to Change* and gave structural reality to the 'big idea' for Baptists, namely how the local church relates organically in Christ to the parts of the body which are nearest and where unity is most likely to be forged.

I conclude with a comment on Nigel the presence. Whenever he has been out of the College due to ill health or sabbatical leave, it is the common consent among Spurgeon's College tutors and other staff that Nigel's absence leaves a large space which cannot be filled. There are those who can deputise for him so that his duties are covered adequately, but however competent the deputy no one can replace Nigel the presence. Last year I observed this outstanding personal quality when Nigel returned to the College on the first day after his sabbatical. As we made our way to the College chapel for the service, he gathered people in as we walked the corridors; he greeted everyone by name; he made an enquiry of a student about a pastoral concern; there were some humorous asides; everyone was made to feel welcome. It is this huge capacity to exercise the hospitality of the heart and the home that is the mark of the man we honour with these tribute essays; and in the expression of this gift of hospitable friendship Nigel is accompanied so ably by his loving partner Judy.

I am proud to call Nigel my encouraging friend who has created for me so many openings to exercise my own gifts. He is a theologian of the first order who has provided substantial depth to the ongoing debates on what it means to be a Baptist and by his own pilgrimage has moved the debate from the open-ended question, 'Is this a denomination worth staying in?' to the more positive invitation: 'This is a Baptist Union worth joining!' He is a reliable mentor as a Christian disciple because he acknowledges there are many miles yet to travel on the road of spiritual formation. His friends honour him on this milestone birthday and dare to believe that the best wine is yet to be served.

Contributors

Dr Raymond Brown was a Baptist minister in three churches. He taught Church History at Spurgeon's College and was its Principal from 1973 to 1986.

Dr R. Alastair Campbell was a Baptist minister before joining Spurgeon's College as a research fellow and then as tutor of New Testament. He also worked in Nepal and Jamaica.

Dr David R. Coffey, a graduate of Spurgeon's College, pastored three churches before becoming Secretary for Evangelism and then General Secretary of the Baptist Union of Great Britain. He is currently President of the Baptist World Alliance and a Governor of Spurgeon's College.

Dr John E. Colwell, a graduate of Spurgeon's College, was pastor of two churches before joining Spurgeon's College as tutor in Christian Doctrine and Ethics.

Dr Christopher J. Ellis pastored four churches and is a former Principal of Bristol Baptist College. He is currently pastor of West Bridgford Baptist Church, Nottingham, and moderator of the Council of the Baptist Union of Great Britain.

Dr Robert A. Ellis is the Principal of Regent's Park College, Oxford. He previously served as minister in two churches and as tutor at both Bristol Baptist College and Regent's Park College.

Professor Paul S. Fiddes spent his career in theology at Regent's Park College where he was Principal from 1989 until 2007. He is currently Professorial Research Fellow.

Rev. Paul W. Goodliff pastored two churches before he became superintendent and then regional minister (team leader) in Central England. He is now head of the Ministry Department of the Baptist Union of Great Britain.

Dr Stephen R. Holmes is a graduate of Spurgeon's College where he was a research fellow from 1996 until 1999. He lectured at

King's College London before moving to the University of St Andrews.

Dr Stuart W. Murray Williams was a pioneer minister and then tutor for Church Planting and Evangelism at Spurgeon's College. He works as a trainer and consultant under the auspices of the Anabaptist Network, and is a consultant to Urban Expression.

Dr Ian M. Randall pastored two churches before he became tutor in Church History and Spirituality at Spurgeon's College. He also worked at the International Baptist Theological Seminary in Prague and is now Spurgeon's Director of Research.

Canon Thomas A. Smail was a Church of Scotland minister and later an Anglican priest. He taught theology at St John's College, Nottingham, and was Rector of All Saints, Sanderstead.

Dr Derek J. Tidball has been the minister of two churches, Secretary for Mission and Evangelism of the Baptist Union of Great Britain, and a tutor and Principal of London Bible College / London School of Theology. He is currently a visiting scholar at Spurgeon's College.

Dr Patricia M. Took, after a stint as pastor in a local church, is the regional minister (team leader) of the London Baptist Association and a Governor of Spurgeon's College.

Short tributes

Rev. Jonathan Edwards
General Secretary of the Baptist Union of Great Britain
It is a very great pleasure to offer words of appreciation for Nigel Wright's ministry on behalf of the Baptist Union of Great Britain within which he has served for 36 years. Nigel's ministry has been divided fairly equally between his local pastorates (Ansdell 1973-1986 and Altrincham 1995-2000) and his time at Spurgeon's College (1987-1995 and from 2000 to today). This twin commitment to local ministry and to careful theological reflection has characterized the whole of Nigel's ministry and this has been an immense gift to the denomination. Nigel can always be relied upon to offer incisive and challenging insights in a warm and gracious manner. His commitment to the denomination has been unwavering and his service as President of the Union and as a member of numerous committees has been a source of great encouragement to us all. We thank God for Nigel and his consistent commitment to the renewal of local church life and look forward to many more articles, books and stirring sermons.

Dr Stephen Finamore
Principal of Bristol Baptist College
One of the remarkable things about Nigel Wright is his capacity to combine in his character so many of the different attributes to which I aspire. Frankly, I'd settle for getting somewhere with any one of them, but Nigel seems to have collected the set. In particular I admire both his pastoral and his scholarly gifts. In the former area Nigel has an astonishing capacity for remembering people's names and always shows sensitivity to others and care for them. In the latter he has written a succession of truly wonderful, useful and readable books. I recommend them to my students and I myself go back to them again and again. Through his work and commitment Nigel has helped form a generation of ministers for the good of our Baptist denomination. I am very grateful to Nigel for his books, his scholarship, his example and his friendship.

Dr Timothy George
Founding Dean of Beeson Divinity School of Samford University and senior editor of *Christianity Today*
I am pleased to join with many other friends in honoring Dr. Nigel Wright on the occasion of his sixtieth birthday. His work as a pastor, scholar, and theological educator have made a lasting impact for good in the furtherance of the Gospel in our times and I pray that he will continue to go from strength to strength in the years to come. Dr. Wright embodies the best of both the evangelical and ecumenical impulses in the Baptist tradition and I am delighted that he is leading the theological school founded by one of my personal heroes of the faith, Charles Haddon Spurgeon. This celebration of Nigel's life and work is an occasion for all of us to learn from his wisdom and devotion to Christ.

Dr James Gordon
Principal of the Scottish Baptist College
Sensibly radical. Sounds like an oxymoron. But both words are needed to describe the way Nigel expresses his faith and ministry. Radical because his theology is rooted in Baptist origins, themselves traceable to New Testament convictions about Christ as the living centre, and the Church as community of believers covenanted together in the power of the Spirit. Sensible because new agendas need to be owned rather than imposed; sensible because any challenge to change must be persuasive and presented as practical planning in the service of vision.

There are of course other facets of the gift Nigel is to the Baptist community and beyond: capacity for pastoral friendship with colleagues; ability to make scholarship serve the interests of the people of God; unabashed but not uncritical holding to evangelical principle, as living movement rather than sacred tradition. My personal experience is of a supportive colleague and loved brother in Christ from whom I've learned much.

Dr Denton Lotz
Former General Secretary of the Baptist World Alliance
Dear Nigel, it gives me great joy on the occasion of your sixtieth birthday to send you our prayers and best wishes for this significant milestone! You represent the best of British Baptists, an academic not ashamed of the Gospel. When I first met you at a Baptist World Alliance meeting, like most people I was immediately impressed with your kindness, intellect and joy.

Your contribution to the BWA has been significant. Not only are you ecumenical and evangelical, but you are a convinced Baptist, with a big B and a small b! Thank you for presenting Baptist doctrines and causes brilliantly. I will never forget when we met at the Vatican. Cardinal Walter Kasper had just come from a boring meeting with the Orthodox but when he heard your paper he was enlivened and grateful for such a scholarly and excellent presentation. His comment was, 'I would rather be with you Baptists than a lot of liberal Protestants!'

May the Lord bless you and give you much joy and many years of service to Christ and His Kingdom! Baptists of the world are richer and better because of you. Thank you and may the Christ of all joy surround you!

Dr Michael Quicke
Professor of Preaching and Communications at Northern Baptist Theological Seminary and former Principal of Spurgeon's College
With joy and pride I pay tribute to my long-time friend Nigel Wright. Our stories have intertwined from early days as students, when we all knew his gifts of personality, mind and spirit would lead to great things. This book especially marks his flair for theological scholarship. I recall the Dean, Colin Brown, commenting, 'Nigel is so creative a theologian that if you asked him to come up with a theology of lawn-mowing, he would!' And what brilliant intellectual contributions have put us all in his debt.

But alongside the leadership, teaching and writing, those who know him best also revel in the fun of friendship with Nigel and Judy. Yes, I have often witnessed Nigel the theological Baptist giant at work, but watching 'West Wing' episodes with him, enjoying his beloved Lake District, eating his shepherd's pie, also fill me with immensely happy memories of the man we celebrate. Thank you, Nigel.

Dr John Weaver
Principal of South Wales Baptist College and President of the Baptist Union of Great Britain 2008-2009
Having known Nigel for nearly 30 years as a minister, tutor, and college principal, I am pleased to have this opportunity to reflect on the contribution he has made to our Baptist family. Nigel and I were members of the *Mainstream – Baptists for Life and Growth* executive (now *Word and Spirit Network*) for over ten years in the

1980s and 1990s, and since 2001 we have been fellow Baptist College Principals.

Nigel has served the Baptist family as a thoughtful, provocative and challenging theologian, writer and speaker, who has the gift of helping people to understand the challenge of theology for discipleship, the church's mission, and for pastoral ministry. Perhaps of more significance has been the ways in which Nigel has been a friend and support for so many – encouraging people to write, speak, and find God's call in the ministry and mission of Christ. I have personally benefitted from his encouragement and support as a valued partner in the Gospel of Christ.

Baptist 'Relating and resourcing' in difficult times. A historical perspective

Raymond Brown

A prominent aspect of the English Baptist story in the 1990's was the quest for more effective patterns of inter-church cooperation and enhanced forms of regional leadership. In his *Challenge to Change: A Radical Agenda for Baptists* (1991) Nigel Wright 'made a formative contribution to this debate'[1] and he was subsequently entrusted with the responsibility of coordinating a denominational task group to make radical suggestions about 'new ways of associating'. Convened in 1997, the group presented its findings to the Baptist Union Council in March 1998 in *Relating and Resourcing: The Report of the Task Group on Associating*.

Precedents

Happily for me, both Nigel's *Challenge* and the 1998 report quote significant historical precedents which recall that whilst Baptists treasured the autonomy of the local church, they also emphasised the importance of interdependence, giving practical expression to their ideal in the formation of 'associations'. They would have warmed to the view that, however competent, 'No local church is complete of itself and does well to seek for that of Christ which is expressed in the wider Body.'[2] Seventeenth century Baptists were committed to finding ways to express 'communion amongst themselves for their peace, increase of love, and mutual edification'.[3] Eager to assert that this ideal was more than a conventional acknowledgement of each other's existence, church representatives at the 1652 Abingdon Association expressed not

---

[1] Ian M. Randall, *The English Baptists of the Twentieth Century* (Didcot: Baptist Historical Society, 2005) 486; cf. Geoffrey G. Reynolds, *First among Equals ... Association and oversight among Baptist Churches* (Didcot: Berkshire, Southern, and Oxford and East Gloucestershire Baptist Associations, 1993).
[2] For this and later undocumented quotations, see *Relating and Resourcing* (Didcot: Baptist Union of Great Britain, 1998).
[3] *The Second London Confession,* 1677, republished 1689, XXVI, 14; cf. *The Confession of Faith of those Churches which are commonly (though falsly) called Anabaptists ... 1644,* XLVII: 'yet ... are they all ... to have the counsell and help one of another ... as members of one body'*,* in W.L. Lumpkin, *Baptist Confessions of Faith* (Chicago etc: Judson Press, 1959) 289, 168-169.

only their 'firme communion each with [the] other' but ventured to make a significant and, within the Independent tradition, even daring comparison. As 'proofe of their love to all saints', every church 'ought to manifest its care over other churches', recognising that 'there is the same relation' between these churches 'each towards [the] other as there is betwixt particular members of one church. For the churches of Christ doe all make up one body or church in generall'. Congregational autonomy was 'never appointed as a restraint of our love which should be manifest ... to all the churches'. Meaningful fellowship with other congregations could be used 'to quicken them when lukewarme, to help when in want, assist in counsell in doubtfull matters and prevent prejudices in each against [the] other.'[4] References to these historical precedents in Nigel's book and *Relating and Resourcing* encourage a Church historian to use this festschrift to pose a relevant question.

A mere eight years after the Abingdon representatives gave expression to their association ideals, England witnessed a dramatic political change. The exiled Charles II returned to reign, assuring Christians of different convictions of 'a liberty to tender consciences'.[5] But despite his genuine peace-loving ambitions, a series of parliamentary statutes over the next few years robbed Baptists (and all other dissenters) of their religious freedom. Gathering together for nonconformist worship became an illegal and costly activity.[6] Meeting in secrecy as a local congregation was itself hazardous, let alone publicly cooperating with other churches. Here is the question. Normally[7] prevented from exercising their previously vigorous association life, by what means did these churches encourage each other and implement their declared ideals about interdependency?

This article was written in a UK context of religious freedom, a liberty by no means undergirded with a perpetual guarantee, but with the awareness that millions of our fellow-

---

[4] B.R. White (ed.), *Association Records of the Particular Baptists of England, Wales and Ireland to 1660, Part 3: The Abingdon Association* (London: Baptist Historical Society, 1974) 126-127.
[5] Declaration of Breda, April 1660, in A. Browning (ed.), *English Historical Documents VI (1660-1714)* (London: Eyre & Spottiswoode, 1966) 57-58.
[6] For the persecution's effect on Baptists, see B.R. White, *English Baptists of the Seventeenth Century*, rev.ed. (London: Baptist Historical Society, 1983) 95-133.
[7] The qualification is important because, even during persecution, occasional association meetings were held among both Particular and General Baptists.

Christians suffer *now* for their faith. Religious intimidation with physical violence continues in this world. Should this book, or extracts from it, come their way, they might find encouragement in reading how fellow-Baptist congregations supported each other in an era of sustained repression. For almost thirty years in late seventeenth-century England, thousands had to pay crippling fines for not attending worship at their local parish church or for supporting an illegal dissenters' meeting held, often by night, in a large house, sympathetic farmer's barn, open fields or remote wood.[8] The many people who could not meet the exorbitant fines had their furniture and goods (including working tools) seized, and sold at give-away prices to cover the required payments. Hundreds of others endured years of imprisonment in appalling conditions;[9] many ended their lives there. Their story of inter-church cooperation in difficult times is shared here as a birthday tribute to a scholar who has always enjoyed and encouraged the study of Church History, in appreciation of his warm friendship and gifted leadership over the years.

Politics
First, in the precarious circumstances at the beginning of the new reign, Baptists cooperated in necessary political initiatives. Accustomed to joint confessional action,[10] General (Arminian) Baptist churches in Lincolnshire, for example, combined to issue in quick succession three publications that assured King and

---

[8] For example, one midweek 'Lecture Day' in 1682, the Bristol (Broadmead) church 'met in ye Rain, in a Lane, and Br. Jennings preacht to them in Peace'. Later, their pastor preached in a local wood, 'under a Tree, and endured ye Rain.' The next year, 'being a hard frost, and Snow on ye Ground, We met in ye Wood, and though we stood in ye Snow, ye Sun Shone upon us, and We were in peace'; Roger Hayden (ed.), *The Records of a Church of Christ in Bristol, 1640-1687* (Bristol: Bristol Record Society, 1974) [hereafter *Broadmead Records*] 241, 243, 257.

[9] It is said of London's Newgate Prison that 'the mingled stench of disease and faeces and the cacophonous din of wailing and screeching in the maze of unventilated wards was unutterably horrifying'. In 1662, one condemned prisoner anticipated execution with relief, saying, 'Hell itself in comparison, cannot be such a place.' In December that year, '289 Anabaptist and others' were in Newgate, 'taken at unlawful meetings'; Kelly Grovier, *The Gaol: the story of Newgate, London's most notorious prison* (London: John Murray, 2008) 94-95; *Calendar of State Papers Domestic, 1661-2,* 604-605.

[10] For example, *The Faith and Practice of Thirty Congregations,* 1651, signed by General Baptist leaders from eight Midland counties, in Lumpkin, *Baptist Confessions of Faith,* 171-188.

Parliament of their loyalty.[11] The first petition was handed to Charles II personally by Thomas Grantham, their county 'Messenger', then in his mid-twenties. Though sympathetically received, by the following year the young regional minister was in Lincoln gaol, and back there with a repeated sentence the year after, a mere two of his ten imprisonments. The quest for religious liberty was solely that they might worship God according to their understanding of biblical teaching and the dictates of conscience, and not, as frequently accused, as a cover for seditious purposes.

Their Particular Baptist (Calvinistic) contemporaries recognised the need for similar united action and already had the necessary mechanisms for inter-church cooperation.[12] They too declared their commitment to the returned monarch and his government, and expressed their hope of the promised religious freedom. In doing so, however, they crossed a major theological divide, giving expression to meaningful partnership by sharing in a statement signed by representative General Baptist leaders as well as their own.[13] Calvinists and Arminians had acted together on a significant cooperative venture.

As the persecution continued, and at times intensified, Baptists and other dissenters came to realise that little had been achieved by these assertions of political loyalty. They naturally looked for more immediate moral support in their localities by creating opportunities for congregations to meet together. It was a bold venture but the formation of 'clusters or networks' of churches gave them a sense of supportive solidarity and became an inspiration for many. In the Spring of 1670, the harsh 1664 Conventicle Act was renewed but with increased severity. That

---

[11] The Lincolnshire declarations were, first, *An Address to the King from Lincolnshire Baptists, 28th July, 1660,* then *A Humble Address of those ... called Anabaptist in ... the county of Lincoln,* 1660, and later (following Thomas Venner's 1661 London 'rising' with its suspicion of Baptist involvement), *The Third Address of ... Anabaptists in the County of Lincoln, 23rd February, 1661.* For similar initiatives on behalf of Kent's imprisoned General Baptist leaders, see *Sion's Groans for the Distressed* [1661], in E.B. Underhill (ed.), *Tracts on Liberty of Conscience and Persecution* (London: Hanserd Knollys Society, 1846) 345-382, cf. 297-308.

[12] For inter-congregational co-operation in the 1650's, cf. White, *Association Records, Parts 1-3.*

[13] *The Humble Apology of some commonly called Anabaptists,* 1660, with thirty signatories including London Particular Baptist leaders such as William Kiffin and Edward Harrison, and representative General Baptists like Henry Denne, in E.B. Underhill (ed.), *Confessions of Faith* (London: Hanserd Knollys Society, 1854) 343-352.

September about 1500 defiant dissenters met for outdoor worship in Brokerswood, North Bradley, near the Wiltshire-Somerset border, an area of considerable Baptist strength. Only a few days later, the numbers at this 'unlawfull Meeting and Conventicle' were nearer 2000.[14] These sizeable congregations gathered people from a wide area and drew together many local churches.

Relating and resourcing
In such threatening circumstances, many Baptist churches realised that the truths they treasured in common were infinitely greater than the issues that kept them apart. At the beginning of the new reign, brothers from the strictly closed-communion Pithay church in Bristol met with their friends in the Broadmead open-membership church to discuss the highly relevant but potentially divisive topic of oath-taking.[15] Later, on occasional Sunday afternoons, both congregations met for worship on the (safer) Somerset side of the River Frome. 'There were thought to be about 1500 people there.' Outdoor meetings with considerable numbers could not fail to attract attention, and did. 'And their adversaries lookt on, but being on ye other side' of the river were unable to molest them.[16]

They also realised that there were times when 'the church of Christ must inevitably reach beyond the boundaries of Baptist churches alone'. When the persecution was particularly fierce, local congregations of different denominational traditions believed it important 'to tap into the spiritual insights, wisdom and vitality of the wider Body'. Representatives from four Bristol churches (two Baptist, one Independent and one Presbyterian) formed a local 'cluster' to discuss the best strategy for dealing with immediate practical issues. As 'poore sheep driven together by Wolves', they had much to learn from each other, for example, about the persecution's legal complexities and how best 'to defend themselves by Law'. Two knowledgeable representatives were appointed from each church 'to advize, consider and manage' all

---

[14] Quarter Sessions Roll, 12 and 27 September, 1670, Wiltshire Record Office, Trowbridge. For this reference I am indebted to Richard D. Land, 'Doctrinal Controversies of the English Particular Baptists (1644-1691) as illustrated by the career and writings of Thomas Collier', Oxford D.Phil., 1980, 65.
[15] *Broadmead Records,* 115-116. Many 'scrupled' about the wording in the required 'Oaths of Allegiance and Supremacy' (which demanded submission to 'Whatsoever' was demanded of them), naturally fearing that such 'Extensiveness' might later challenge their Christian priorities.
[16] *Broadmead Records,* 240-241.

matters concerning 'their legall defence'. When three Bristol nonconformist ministers were in prison, some from each congregation met 'to Consult how to Carry on our meetings ... now our Pastours were gone.' Local partnership of this kind also enabled them to share news of the imaginative warning, delaying and escape mechanisms used in four different congregations, especially the provision each church made for the speedy and safe exit of their highly vulnerable preachers.[17]

In 1675, at a time when two convicted Bristol ministers and two of their members were being tried in London, members of these four congregations met to intercede for them one day from 7.00am to noon. This 'union, and joynt praying together, was Much liked of, by all parties thus being driven together by this universall trouble.'[18] It was suggested that the four churches might 'meet all together' on weekdays and 'turne our four Lectures into one', proposals which, though discussed in joint meetings and favoured by most, did not materialise due to difficulties raised by one of the participating churches, mercifully not Baptist. United quarterly days of prayer did continue, however, with additional 'dayes of Fasting and Prayer...as need shall require'.[19]

These united churches later formulated a joint code of practice for times when their meetings were disrupted, 'that none Stirr from ye Meeting when ye Informers or any officers come whatsoever (...) These were our Joynt conclusions for all ye Churches at that time.'[20] The four churches also discussed a suggestion from one congregation that changing their meeting times (to avoid clashing with parish churches) might ease local opposition but the majority decided not to pursue the idea. Conventicles were illegal, whatever their meeting time, so it was unlikely to deter their oppressors.[21] Pastors of these four nonconformist congregations each suffered periods of imprisonment, and two of them died in gaol.[22] People with such courageous leaders were not afraid to take risks.

---

[17] *Broadmead Records,* 147, 149, 150-152.
[18] *Broadmead Records,* 159.
[19] *Broadmead Records,* 159-163.
[20] *Broadmead Records,* 163.
[21] *Broadmead Records,* 179. The church that brought the rejected proposal changed its own meeting times but, as predicted, disruption continued.
[22] The Independent (Congregational) pastor, John Thompson, died in a Bristol dungeon in 1675, despite medical pleas to the bishop that, as a desperately sick man, he be moved 'out of that Stincking prisson' to more hygienic accommodation. Following nearly three years in Gloucester's gaol, the

Imprisonment removed ministers and members from their congregations but did little to hinder inter-church cooperation. Baptists were thrust into close proximity not only with Baptists from other churches but also found themselves alongside paedobaptist colleagues, sometimes for years on end. Imprisoned ministers were inspired by contact with other church leaders they might not otherwise have met, sharing biblical insights, pastoral and spiritual experience, as well as theological differences, all serving to widen their horizons

In 1683, Hercules Collins, a London Particular Baptist minister, was imprisoned in Newgate with the energetic General Baptist leader, John Griffith, and the erudite and prolific author, Francis Bampfield, a leading 'Seventh Day' Baptist, whose Sabbatarian views would not have appealed to either of his fellow-preachers. Respecting each other's convictions, Bampfield and Collins became close friends.[23] One of the many subjects on which all three prisoners had a common mind was that of 'associating'. Bampfield doubtless shared his frustration concerning the unresponsiveness of his 'Seventh Day' colleagues to his 1679 plea that they form an association of churches,[24] a disappointment that both Griffith and Collins would have understood, given their commitment to inter-congregational partnership.

Imprisonment became a time not only for closer relating but for effective resourcing. Thomas Hardcastle in Bristol, along with other nonconformists such as the Taunton Presbyterian, Joseph Alleine, and the Kettering Independent, John Maidwell, sent frequent messages of pastoral encouragement to their churches. These rich letters were read not only at the illegal Conventicle but

---

Broadmead Baptist pastor, George Fownes, died there in November 1685 (*Broadmead Records,* 150, 265-266).

[23] Bampfield died in the prison that year. Collins preached a joint funeral sermon for him and the Congregationalist, Jeremiah Marsden (alias Zachary Ralphson), another ejected minister who also died in Newgate at that time, cf. Collins, *Counsel for the Living occasioned from the Dead* (London: Printed by George Larkin for the author, 1684).

[24] For Bampfield's apologia for associating, see his autobiographical *A Name, an After-one ... An Historical Declaration* (London: Printed for John Lawrence, 1681) 24-25. Dr Bryan W. Ball is convinced that 'the Seventh-day movement was stifled and stunted by its own lack of response to a proposition which almost certainly would have ensured its stability and growth.' Cf. *The Seventh-Day Men, Sabbatarians and Sabbatarianism in England and Wales, 1600-1800,* (Oxford: Oxford University Press, 1994) 118, 316-318.

were passed on from one congregation to another.[25] Preachers were not silenced by their confinement[26] and sermons to prison congregations went far beyond the walls of a local gaol. Magistrates were sometimes incensed to discover that, far from breaking up a conventicle, they had merely changed the location and composition of its congregation.[27] During a nine-year confinement in Dorchester gaol, Francis Bampfield and others gathered a sizeable congregation. It included 'People of the Town who came to them, every day once, and on the Lord's Day twice' until, after some time, the jailer was disciplined for allowing local people into the prison to hear him.[28] John Bunyan preached to fellow-prisoners in Bedford even when he was feeling 'empty, spiritless, and barren'.[29] Despite the depression, he used the opportunity to produce his first sustained exposition of a biblical passage, a study of Revelation's closing chapters that moved speedily from spoken word to published book, thus resourcing a wider audience through its three editions within a few years. Other men were not idle in their incarceration either. In gaol, they prayed, preached[30] and produced inspiring resources for the churches. Sermons, letters, expositions, meditations, catechisms, evangelistic literature, books for children and collections of poems

---

[25] *Broadmead Records*, 172, 174, and cf. 252: In May, 1683 they 'had letters from Br. Fownes at Glouc[este]r [Prison], and those also at Ilchester Gaol.' For the Hardcastle letters, see E.B. Underhill (ed.), *The Records of a Church of Christ meeting in Broadmead, Bristol* (London: Hanserd Knollys Society, 1847) 257-354.
[26] During a 'long and teadious Prissonment', the Broadmead pastor, Thomas Ewins, preached through a high prison window to eager listeners outside, but 'so ... straining his voice ...that it hastened his dayes', *Broadmead Records,* 118. Hanserd Knollys and Andrew Gifford were among the many ministers who preached regularly to fellow-prisoners.
[27] *Broadmead Records*, 234-235: In the winter of 1681-1682, 'being above 20 of us in Prison, considered we would keep a Day of Fasting and Prayer ... and Br. Fownes our Pastour being also imprisoned, preacht about ye middle of ye day; and in the close, we sung, ye 46th psalm'. Entering the 'great Room' where they met, and seeing it 'pretty full' the local Sheriff 'was in a great Rage' saying 'we should not keep Conventicles there ... we should be lockt up in our Rooms'.
[28] Matthew Sylvester (ed.), *Reliquiae Baxterianae* (London: Matthew Sylvester, 1696) I, ii §423.
[29] *The Holy City, or the New Jerusalem,* in J. Sears McGee (ed.), *Miscellaneous Works of John Bunyan,* III (Oxford: Oxford University Press, 1987) 69, 'at that time I felt my self (it being my turn to speak) so empty ... that I thought I should not have been able to speak among them so much as five words of Truth, with Life and Evidence'.
[30] For a response to such preaching, in the conversion and baptism of an Ilchester prisoner, cf. *Broadmead Records,* 257.

were soon in print, inspiring hope and renewing confidence in readers who might not see the inside of a dungeon but were grateful for the resources that were prepared there.

Leadership and mobility

Exemplary leadership was of immense importance in hazardous times, and the Baptist commitment to interdependency meant that new appointments were judged worthy of a wider reference than the local church concerned. A newly established church must have the physical, prayerful and practical support of nearby congregations, always represented at its inauguration,[31] and its partners in other churches also shared in acts of ordination and induction to new responsibilities. Hanserd Knollys represented his London church and Edward Harrison the Petty France congregation when, in the year following the Plague and only weeks prior to the Great Fire, Thomas Patient was inducted as a colleague for William Kiffin at Devonshire Square. Patient died after only a month in office but Knollys joined others two years later for the ordination of his successor, Daniel Dyke.[32] Leaders valued each other's partnership in harrowing times. These were not formal occasions of conventional support but expressions of solidarity in a period of deprivation[33] and adversity, when quality leadership was a high priority. Knollys also attended the ordination of deacons at churches other than his own, persuaded that, ideally, if there was more than one congregation in any town or city they ought to regard themselves as 'one Church', meeting in different locations.[34]

The 'supportive trans-local ministries' of dedicated itinerants also played a considerable part in fostering healthy relationships between churches. Men like the young William Mitchel and his cousin David Crosley travelled hundreds of miles

---

[31] Hanserd Knollys, *The World that now is* (1681) Book I, 49-50. 'Ministers and Brethren of other Churches being also present, ought to own and acknowledge them to be a Sister Church, by giving them the Right hand of Fellowship; and so to commend them by Prayer unto God.'

[32] B.R. White, *Hanserd Knollys and Radical Dissent in the Seventeenth Century. Friends of the Dr. Williams's Library Annual Lecture* (London: Dr Williams's Trust, 1977) 19.

[33] Many members in those three inner London congregations will have suffered loss of property and work as a result of the Great Fire, to say nothing of family bereavements during the Plague.

[34] Knollys, *The World that now is,* Book I, 50.

on 'dark Nights, and over dismal Mountains',[35] preaching and encouraging about twenty churches in remote locations[36] and larger communities, in Lancashire and West Yorkshire, a ministry resulting in Mitchel's imprisonment in York Castle.[37] Thomas Collier was highly effective in encouraging inter-congregational activities in Somerset and Wiltshire towns and villages, and Andrew Gifford offered initial help and continuing encouragement to several young churches within striking distance of Bristol. Such devoted men gave scattered congregations first-hand accounts of what was happening in other churches, shared ideas for the enrichment of their corporate spiritual life, provided news of fellow-Baptists coping resourcefully with local harassment, and suggested imaginative ways in which they might support one another in hard times.

Inter-church relationships were also enhanced not only by the natural transfer of members and by occasional arrangements for temporary membership, but also by the mobility of businessmen whose work took them to different parts of the country. Samuel Buttall belonged to the 'Henry Jessey' open-membership church in London. Whenever his sugar trading business took him to either Bristol or Plymouth, he made a point of worshipping locally, whatever the hazards. On one occasion, whilst worshipping with the frequently disrupted Broadmead church, he was physically abused by a team of men who came to break up the meeting.[38] He would have dismissed it as nothing other than an unpleasant interlude. Ten days earlier, a very sick man, one of the same city's nonconformist ministers, had died in prison. Buttall would not have regarded a rough handling as suffering. There were immense compensations such as the Sunday morning when the church 'met in ye fields' and Buttall preached to 'near 1000 people'.[39]

---

[35] William Mitchel, *Jachin and Boaz* [1707], Preface by David Crosley, *Transactions of the Baptist Historical Society*, III (London: Baptist Union, 1912-1913) 68.

[36] For Mitchel's commitment to inter-congregational co-operation, see his *Jachin and Boaz, Transactions of the Baptist Historical Society*, III, 174-175 ('Concerning Discipline', 37-38).

[37] For previously unpublished letters exchanged between Mitchel and Crosley, see F. Overend, *History of the Ebenezer Baptist Church, Bacup* (London: Kingsgate, 1912) 7-58.

[38] *Broadmead Records*, 153-154.

[39] *Broadmead Records*, 240.

Another London businessman was Enoch Prosser, 'a Gifted Br[other]' who belonged to Benjamin Keach's church at Horsleydown Southwark. He too met with the Broadmead people when his work took him to the nation's second largest city. When he was preaching at one of their early Sunday morning meetings, the place was surrounded by about twenty officials and constables who, unable to gain immediate access, broke into the building. Several were arrested, including the preacher and another London tradesman, Samuel Crisp. Both men were in the city for its annual Fair. Goods were removed from their stalls and sold, well below value, in lieu of fines. Broadmead people did not forget their partnership in adversity: 'Thus they suffered for being at that Meeting.'[40]

Mediation
Leaders particularly needed one another in times of stress. Pastoral problems could arise that were not easily settled without external arbitration. The Porton church drew together a substantial congregation from villages around Salisbury. In the early 1680's it found itself in difficulties when Walter Pen, one of its two ministers, became embroiled in a difference of opinion with his people. They 'agreed to send' for leaders from a neighbouring congregation to help settle the issue but, possibly as part of the unhappy controversy, Pen and his colleague, John Rede, also became estranged and things were said on both sides which created tension between two dedicated men. Objective help from leaders in the wider constituency was used to heal the rift. Both ministers were firmly though compassionately reprimanded, one for 'not following the things that make for peace and brotherly love ... especially ... as a minister', the other for 'not ... giving such examples as a minister ought'.[41] These congregations admired and valued their pastors but recognised that church leaders were not exempt from life's temptations and, like themselves, were certainly not beyond correction. Appointed 'trouble-shooters' from another church could say necessary things in love which, however true, would probably exacerbate the situation if expressed by a well-meaning local.

---

[40] *Broadmead Records,* 236-237.
[41] *Porton Church Book* (Photocopy in the Angus Library, Regent's Park College, Oxford) 57-60.

Sensitive 'trouble-shooting' colleagues from neighbouring churches, offering 'counsell in doubtfull matters', were helpful not only when leaders were at variance but also when relationships between congregations became strained, often concerning debatable disciplinary procedures. Problems frequently arose when a disciplined church member requested transfer of membership to a neighbouring church, sharing grief at the manner in which an earlier perceived offence had been handled. Particular Baptist churches in the West of England enjoyed especially close relationships, enabling them to help each other in 1669 when the church at Crockerton became divided over the rejection of one of its members. Appointed representatives from seven churches in the area met together, having received a complaint not only from the aggrieved member but also from some of his fellow-members who were equally unhappy about their church's action. The Crockerton believers were urged to send messengers to a meeting of representative Baptists in the hope of restoring unity to their divided congregation as well as healing one of its wounded members.[42]

There were occasions when, in the quest for an objective judgment, both Particular and General Baptist leaders were asked to unite for arbitration in differences between two congregations. When the Old Gravel Lane (Wapping) church found itself at variance with the Keach congregation at Horsleydown, a sizeable group of London pastors from both traditions was asked to meet to settle the dispute. Names included Particular Baptist stalwarts such as William Kiffin, Daniel Dyke, and Henry Forty, along with General Baptist ministers, Jonathan Jennings and John Gosnold.[43]

There were occasions when Particular and General Baptist leaders united in theological disputation with paedobaptists,[44] for

---

[42] The West of England Messengers' letter is quoted verbatim in J.G. Fuller, *A Brief History of the Western Association* (Bristol, 1843) 11-12.

[43] Old Gravel Lane (Wapping) Particular Baptist Church Book, 3 [5 February 1678]. Once again, the problem concerned a disciplined church member.

[44] Influential Particular Baptist leaders such as Hanserd Knollys, Henry Forty and William Kiffin rallied to the support of Henry Danvers when his use of primary sources was challenged by Obediah Wills, see Hanserd Knollys et al., *The Baptists' Answer to Mr. Obed Wills, his Appeal against Mr. H. Danvers* (London: Printed for Francis Smith, 1675) and Joseph Ivimey, *History of the English Baptists,* 1811-30, II, 336-339.

example, and also with Quakers.[45] In 1674, when leading Friends appealed to Baptist leaders that their views had been misrepresented in the writings of Thomas Hicks, public debates and published accounts included both Particular and General Baptist contributors.[46]

These leaders and congregations recognised that inter-congregational partnership must also be expressed in active compassion and practical kindness. Before the Restoration, the Abingdon representatives claimed that associating meant offering meaningful 'help when in want'. Churches made regular provision not only for deprived members within their own ranks but also for people who belonged to partner congregations in other places. When Benjamin Keach was robbed in the winter of 1679-1680, General as well as Particular Baptist churches sent gifts to the respected leader.[47] Imprisoned preachers and members, and their deprived families, were given high priority. Amersham Baptists recalled with gratitude that John Griffith had represented the London General Baptist leadership at their church's formation and when he was in Newgate they sent monetary gifts to him and fellow-prisoners more than once.[48] Similarly, Andrew Gifford's Particular Baptist friends in Trowbridge had valued his ministry to them across the years and, when he was imprisoned in Gloucester Castle, sent one of his Wiltshire colleagues to deliver a substantial gift.[49]

Generous giving was relatively easy, but visiting nonconformist prisoners was a precarious exercise. When a

---

[45] For seventeenth century conflicts between Baptists and Quakers, see T.L. Underwood, *Primitivism, Radicalism and the Lamb's War: The Baptist-Quaker Conflict in Seventeenth Century England* (Oxford: Oxford University Press, 1997).
[46] Thomas Hicks, *A Dialogue between a Christian and a Quaker,* 1673, and [Thomas Hicks], *The Quaker's Appeal Answered,* 1674.
[47] Deptford General Baptist Church Book, 1674-1710, Dr. Williams's Library, London WC1H OAG, MS OD 15, 5 January, 1680, and Wapping Particular Baptist (Old Gravel Lane) Church Book, 8. For this detail, and other help in the study of this period, I am indebted to Timothy E. Dowley, 'The History of the English Baptists during the Great Persecution', 1660-1689', Manchester Ph.D., 1976. The generosity of *both* churches is impressive when one remembers that eight years earlier, Keach had left the General Baptist ministry for the Particulars, and that the Old Gravel Lane Church had earlier called for outside help over its strained relationships with Keach's congregation (see footnote 43).
[48] W.T. Whitley (ed.), *The Church Books of Ford or Cuddington and Amersham* (London: Kingsgate, 1912) 205-206, 223-224.
[49] For Gifford's letter of grateful acknowledgement, cf. Ivimey, *History of the English Baptists,* I, 414-415.

former conforming clergyman went to see his friend, the Broadmead minister, George Fownes, in Gloucester gaol, he was recognised by an informer, immediately charged with preaching at a Conventicle 'in ye fields' sometime during the previous two years, and imprisoned for eighteen months.[50]

Partnership was more than platitudes for these hardy believers, and could prove infinitely more costly than money. The Johannine exhortations were not lost on them. Christ 'laid down his life for us, and we ought to lay down our lives for the brethren (...) Let us not love in word, neither in tongue; but in deed and in truth' (1 John 3:16, 18).

---

[50] *Broadmead Records,* 251, 264.

New birth from water and Spirit

R. Alastair Campbell

Introduction
By any reckoning the story of the encounter of Jesus with Nicodemus in John 3 has been a foundation text for evangelical Christians. After centuries in which regeneration was more or less equated with baptism, the latter being the outward sign and effective means of the former, with the rise of Pietism in the seventeenth century, which gave birth to the Evangelical revival of the eighteenth century, voices are heard saying that baptism is not enough or not essential.[1] Regeneration, for which the preferred term became 'new birth', is defined as an experience of the Holy Spirit 'in the soul', without which baptism is of no account. From there it is a short step to saying that Christians are those who have been born again, whether or not they have been baptized.[2] 'You must be born again' becomes the war cry of evangelical Christians and John 3 their charter of salvation, but the mention of 'water' in that chapter becomes something of an embarrassment, so that even Baptist writers sometimes appear uncertain whether it refers to baptism at all!

This paper is written in the belief that under the pressure of contemporary debates we have left the original thrust of John 3 far behind, and that revisiting that story is necessary if we are to hear what it is really saying about new birth and baptism. It is respectfully dedicated to my good friend Nigel Wright, who has done so much to help us understand our identity as Baptists and Evangelicals, in the hope that he will find it both affirming and provoking.

Re-reading the story
1. Background
Ancient tradition and modern scholarship for the most part agree in believing that the Fourth Gospel, at least in its final form, dates from the closing years of the first century. It is also accepted that

---

[1] For a history of interpretation see Peter Toon, *Born Again: A Biblical and Theological Study of Regeneration* (Grand Rapids: Baker, 1987).
[2] The Lausanne Covenant, which has for a generation served as a benchmark of progressive evangelicalism, contains no reference to baptism at all.

the Gospel reflects the concerns and struggles of the Christians living at the time of its composition, so that for example when we read the vivid account of the healing of the man born blind and his subsequent interrogation by the Jewish authorities, we are hearing the arguments raging between the Church and the Synagogue in the years after the destruction of Jerusalem. When we read that the blind man's parents were afraid of being put out of the synagogue if they acknowledged that Jesus was the Christ, we are being made aware of the issue dividing the disciples of Jesus from other Jews in the late first century and the pressures commonly applied to them at that time.[3]

Scholars routinely refer to these disciples as 'the Johannine Community', as if they formed a religious movement distinct from the rest of the church. There is really no evidence for any such thing. There is of course a Johannine *mind*, that of the writer of the Gospel and Letters of John with his unique style and distinctive theological concerns, but there is nothing to suggest that his 'community' was anything other than the Christian churches of the province of Asia, where by common consent the Gospel was written. The province of Asia had a large and well established Jewish community and was also the area where the Christian movement was showing its fastest growth at this time, as evidenced over a period of fifty years by the letters of Paul, the Pastoral Epistles, the Book of Revelation and the letters of Ignatius.[4] Much of this growth was occurring among Jews attracted by the claims made for Jesus of Nazareth. The question tearing the Jewish community apart was whether Jesus was indeed the Christ and Son of God. It is against this background that the Fourth Gospel was written and it is this insight that,

---

[3] The term *aposynagōgos* ('put out of the synagogue'), like our word 'excommunication', appears to be a technical term describing formal steps taken by the Jewish authorities to define and protect Jewish identity. It occurs three times in John (9:22, 12:42, 16:2). J. Louis Martyn, *History and Theology in the Fourth Gospel* (New York: Harper & Row, 1968) may have been over-optimistic in thinking he could trace this word back to a decree of the Council of Jamnia, but his contention that it reflects a stage in Jewish-Christian relations later than the time of Jesus appears sound. [Editor: For a different view see Richard Bauckham, *The Testimony of the Beloved Disciple* (Grand Rapids: Baker, 2007) 116-117.]
[4] Paul Trebilco, *The Early Christians in Ephesus from Paul to Ignatius* (Grand Rapids: Eerdmans, 2007).

following the work of David Rensberger and Charles Cosgrove,[5] I propose to apply to the interpretation of the story of Nicodemus.

2. Nicodemus

We meet the figure of Nicodemus three times in the Gospel of John. On the first and most fully reported occasion (John 3:1-21) he comes to Jesus by night apparently to talk about the kingdom of God (see below). We next meet him at a meeting of the council where he demands a fair hearing for Jesus, but is promptly silenced (7:45-52). Finally, after the crucifixion, he appears together with Joseph of Arimathea to bury the body of Jesus. Nicodemus is a representative figure, speaking not just for himself but for others ('*we* know you are a teacher', 3:2). He is representative of the Jewish community, being a Pharisee and a member of the council, but for John representative also of those who were attracted to Jesus without being willing to go all the way in believing in him and who were besides unwilling to incur the displeasure of the Jewish authorities. John tells us that there were those who believed in Jesus when they saw the miraculous cures he was performing, but that Jesus himself did not trust them (2:23-24). Nicodemus is immediately introduced as just such a person. He is impressed by the miracles on the strength of which he is willing to allow that Jesus is a teacher come from God, but he falls short of declaring Jesus to be the Christ and Son of God, and famously he comes to Jesus by night, that is, secretly. Nicodemus's other appearances confirm the picture. His intervention at the council meeting is scarcely heroic, while in burying the body of Jesus he is associated with Joseph who is explicitly said to be 'a disciple of Jesus, but secretly because he feared the Jews' (19:38). The same description presumably applies to Nicodemus and places him in the company of those John tells us refused to confess their faith openly for fear of being put out of the synagogue (12:42). John knows plenty of people like that in the church situation for which he writes, and he is very critical of them.

---

[5] David Rensberger, *Overcoming the World: Politics and Faith in the Gospel of John* (London: SPCK, 1988); Charles H. Cosgrove, 'The Place Where Jesus Is: Allusions to Baptism and Eucharist in the Fourth Gospel', *New Testament Studies* 35 (1989) 522-539.

3. Kingdom

Nicodemus comes to Jesus to talk about the kingdom of God. This is evident from the way the topic is introduced. The Johannine Jesus does not otherwise speak of the kingdom of God, preferring to speak of eternal life. If he does so here, in a way that seems at first sight to suggest that he has not listened to a word Nicodemus has uttered, it must be because he knows that this is the Pharisee's real concern. Nicodemus pays Jesus the compliment of declaring him to be a teacher come from God on the evidence of the miracles he has performed, and Jesus replies that no one can see the kingdom of God unless he is born again. The reader is left to infer that this is an example of Jesus' ability to read the hearts of his interlocutors (2:25) so that in this instance he knows that what the Pharisee is really concerned about is the kingdom of God.

This should not surprise us. Many Jews were 'waiting expectantly for the kingdom of God', and interestingly one such is actually said by Luke to be Joseph of Arimathea, Nicodemus's partner in the task of burying Jesus (Luke 23:51), so it is entirely likely that Nicodemus shared this expectation. Jesus of course had much to say about the kingdom of God, including much that was new and shocking, but he did not invent the term. If people had not already been talking and dreaming about the kingdom of God, nobody would have known what Jesus was talking about. To declare that the kingdom of God is at hand only makes sense if your hearers already have some idea of that kingdom in the first place. Nowadays it is widely agreed that what faithful Jews were looking forward to was not a place (like the heaven of popular Christian belief), still less an organisation (like the Church as Roman Catholics used to believe), nor yet an ideal (such as love and brotherhood) but *an event*, the coming of God to put all to rights and to make his reign effective in a disordered world. As such it would include the deliverance of Israel from foreign domination and oppressive government, the overthrow of the dark powers that rule the world, and finally deliverance from sin and death. Central to this vision is the hope of resurrection![6]

As such the kingdom of God is essentially future, *God's* future. If in the light of Jesus' teaching and miracles, and still more of his death and resurrection, we want to say that the kingdom is present, then we have to add that it is present in a hidden and

---

[6] Tom Wright, *Surprised by Hope* (London: SPCK, 2007).

paradoxical way,[7] since the essential characteristics of the kingdom as just described are still not evident in our world. Believing as we do that Jesus has been raised from the dead we are able to assert that the kingdom has been inaugurated, because in Jesus the resurrection has begun; yet in other respects we are still, like Nicodemus and Joseph, 'looking for the kingdom of God'. This in fact is the understanding of the New Testament writers, who describe God's future in various different ways. Matthew has Jesus speak of 'the renewal of all things' (19:28). Luke has Peter speak of 'restoration of all things' (Acts 3:21). Paul sees the kingdom as something to be inherited in the future, speaking of it in terms of glory that will be revealed when the creation will set free from its bondage to decay and we shall experience a redemption not merely spiritual but bodily (Romans 8:17-25). Peter can speak of an inheritance ready to be revealed at the last day (1 Peter 1:5), while Revelation looks forward to a new heaven and a new earth. Jesus in John's Gospel similarly speaks of the believer being raised up on the last day (6:44).

All this - we may suppose - is common ground between Jesus and Nicodemus. Nicodemus is explicitly introduced as a Pharisee, and - as is well known - the Pharisees believed in the resurrection of the dead, what Paul was to call 'the hope of Israel' (Acts 23:8, 28:20). As such he would have reckoned not simply that God would establish his kingdom in this world but that he, Nicodemus, as a good Israelite, a Pharisee and a ruler of the Jews no less, would be accorded an honoured place in that kingdom, and it is of this that Jesus sets out to disabuse him.

4. New birth

Jesus tells Nicodemus that in order to see or enter the kingdom of God he must be born again. The Greek word translated 'again', *anōthen*, also means 'from above', and it is likely that both meanings are intended here. Nicodemus's puzzled reply shows that 'again' is the natural way to take the word, while Jesus' emphasis on the Spirit shows that 'from above' is the deeper meaning the reader is supposed to grasp. And both of course are true.[8] If a person is to be born again it can only be by the action of

---

[7] As the kingdom of Christ, perhaps, as opposed to the kingdom of God? See 1 Corinthians 15:24-25; Colossians 1:13.

[8] 'It is not necessary here to discuss whether *anōthen* here means "from above" or "over again". It is probable the evangelist was well aware of the ambiguity and

God and so must be from above; if one is to be born from above it can only be by a second birth.

But of what does this new birth consist? On this the commentators have surprisingly little to say. In the long history of interpretation new birth, or regeneration, has been invested with whatever interpreters or their tradition have understood by becoming a Christian. Most commonly it has been explained in terms of the restoration of the image of God lost through the Fall, or of a new heart as promised to Israel through Ezekiel (36:26), but of this John says nothing. If we want to know what 'born again / from above' meant to John, our only guide must be the Gospel he has written, and in its Prologue we read:

> But to all who received him, who believed in his name, he gave power to become children of God, who were born, not of blood or of the will of the flesh or of the will of man, but of God (1:12-13).

This suggests that the new birth of which Jesus speaks is a matter of becoming a child of God. In the ancient world the way a person became the child of another - other than by natural generation - was by adoption. A man would adopt another person, not necessarily a young child, and not to provide an orphan with a family, but as his heir, making him his son, so that born the son of one man in the course of nature (by blood) he became the son of another by that man's decision (or will), and was thereafter treated as a true son of his new father. It may be objected that birth and adoption are very different things, and so in our culture they are, but not in the ancient world. In Psalm 2 for example, a royal psalm, God says of the king: 'You are my son, today I have begotten you.' (v.7). At his coronation the king becomes a son of God by God's decree. We would describe this as adoption, but to the Hebrew mind he has been begotten, or born, again. An act of adoption is described in terms of new birth, but whatever language is used, whether that of birth or adoption, the result is the same: a person becomes a child of God. This says nothing in the first instance about a new nature, a new heart or a new character. It is a matter of a new identity and a new relationship, albeit one that can be expected to produce transformation over time.

---

intended both meanings.' C.H. Dodd, *The Interpretation of the Fourth Gospel* (Cambridge: Cambridge University Press, 1953) 303 note 2.

God has sent his Son so that many others may become his sons and daughters, and what Nicodemus needs to hear is that people do not become children of God by birth into a particular race or rank, nor simply by their own decision, but entirely by the grace of God. Birth as a member of the chosen race will not secure entry into the kingdom; new birth is necessary. That this is the issue is confirmed later in the Gospel, where Jesus is found debating with a group of Jewish people. They are described as 'the Jews who had believed in him' (8:31), but evidently their faith is of an unsatisfactory kind, like that of Nicodemus. They assert that they are Abraham's children (8:39) and children of God (8:41), but their actions show them to be children of the devil (8:44). It is not enough to be Abraham's children by physical descent; by implication they need to be born 'of God'.

5. Spirit

If we ask with Nicodemus how a person can become a child of God in this sense, the answer must be by the action of God alone. No one can cause him or herself to be adopted and no one can arrange his or her own birth. In this passage Jesus ascribes this birth to the mysterious action of the Spirit, which like the wind blows where it wills. Although there is a call here to seek or submit to new birth, it is not something people can affect for themselves. As John says in his prologue, it is not a matter of human decision; God's children are born of 'of God'. So there is no knowing whom God will draw into this family, for, as Jesus says later in the Gospel, 'No one can come to me unless the Father who sent me draws him.' (6:44)

So what is the role of the Spirit in this? The best commentary on the new birth described in this passage is provided by John in his First Letter. Here believers are addressed as 'dear children' (1 John 2:18), 'children of God' (3:1-2), and are said to be 'born of God' (2:29; 3:9; 4:7; 5:1, 18), the same language and imagery that is used in the Fourth Gospel (1:13; 3:3). From this we may conclude that the Spirit draws people to God, a work he shares with both the Father (John 6:44) and the Son (12:32). He enlightens the mind and opens eyes long blind, causing people to know the truth, as we see in the story of the healing of the man born blind (9:1-41, cf. 1 John 2:20). Then he assures people that they are indeed beloved children of God (1 John 3:1-2), revealing God to them as Father and enabling them to address him as 'Abba' (cf. Galatians 4:6). Third, he enables people to live as children of God, confessing Jesus as Messiah and Son of God (1 John 5:1), living upright and obedient lives (2:29, 3:9-10), and loving other members of the community of faith (4:7-8), so that 'We know that we have passed from death to life, because we love our brothers' (3:14). These are the marks of those who have been 'born of God', and the emphasis on love reminds us that the new birth is a social thing. One is born anew into a new family, a new community, and this in turn will explain how it is that a person must be born not only 'of the Spirit' but also 'of water' (3:5).

6. Water

Only God by his Spirit can bring about new birth, but this does not mean that the human recipients of this remain completely passive, as if there were nothing they can or need to do. We have seen that the most probable meaning of 'born from above' is supplied by the statement in John 1:12-13: to be born from above is to receive 'the right to become children of God', but this gift is given 'to all who received him, to those who believed in his name'. No doubt this receiving and believing are themselves brought about by the Spirit, but they are inescapably something that believers *do* and not simply something that happens to them. John makes plain that this believing cannot be a secret or private matter. It means coming out and joining the community of Jesus' disciples, and this in turn means being baptized. It is to this baptism, understood as an initiation rite and boundary marker, that 'water' refers in this passage.

This has of course been questioned. Some suggest that water here refers to natural human birth, water being understood as a reference to the breaking of the waters in childbirth,[9] but this is very unlikely. There is no evidence for this being a normal way to refer to childbirth at this time, and the phrase 'water and spirit' most naturally refers to one event, albeit one with two sides to it. Others take 'water and spirit' to be two ways of saying the same thing, so that water is simply a symbol of the spirit, as in Ezekiel 36:25-27, and conclude that baptism is not in view, either because they want to avoid the suggestion of baptismal regeneration (which doesn't of course bother Roman Catholic commentators!) or because they wish to avoid the anachronism (as they see it) of

---

[9] For example Gail O'Day, 'The Gospel of John: Introduction, Commentary and Reflections', *New Interpreter's Bible*, Vol. IX (Nashville: Abingdon, 1995) 550.

having Jesus speak about Christian baptism.[10] However, if as we believe John is telling the story of Jesus in such a way as to address the needs of the church at the end of the first century, this should not be a problem. The conversation with Nicodemus is closely followed by an account of Jesus' own baptizing ministry and John probably intends thereby to explain the meaning of 'water' in 3:5 and the origin of Christian baptism.[11] The early Church was in no doubt that the water of which Jesus speaks refers to baptism. Justin, writing perhaps fifty years after John, is quite clear. Describing the process of Christian initiation and quoting this very passage he says, 'Then they are brought by us where there is water, and are born again in the same manner in which we ourselves were born again.'[12]

Water then refers to baptism, but to baptism not so much as the 'outward and visible sign of an inward and spiritual grace', but as the outward and visible sign of personal faith and commitment. Nicodemus as a secret believer in Jesus needs to come out into the open and confess Jesus to be the Christ and Son of God and so join the family of God as a newborn child of God. Only so will he enter the kingdom of God. In making this challenge to his contemporaries, to Jewish Christian believers who believe that they will have a place in the kingdom in virtue of their being born Israelites, John is not being untrue to the original meaning of baptism. For had not John the Baptizer told people that it was not enough to be physically descended from Abraham (Matthew 3:9), and dramatized this by requiring people to go through the waters of Jordan all over again if they were to be God's true people?

Much of our difficulty with this passage comes, I believe, from our trying to make it answer questions it was never designed to address. We label baptism as a 'sacrament' and then ask how it 'works', how the Spirit is given in or through baptism. Of this John says nothing. But Rensberger is right to see that John's interest in baptism is in the way it functions as a boundary marker for the community of Jesus. He writes:

> Baptism is thus viewed in John in the same light as public confession, as an acknowledgement of adherence both to

---

[10] D.A. Carson, *The Gospel according to John* (Leicester: IVP, 1991) 191-196.
[11] C.H. Dodd, *Historical Tradition in the Fourth Gospel* (Cambridge: Cambridge University Press, 1963) 286.
[12] Justin, *Apology* I, 61.

> Jesus as the divine Son of God and to the community whose testimony to him is thereby accepted. It forms a boundary between those inside the believing community and those outside it, and to be baptized is to cross that boundary in an openly recognized way. To be born from above is to undergo a change of communal affiliation and is therefore a social as well as a spiritual event.[13]

Similarly Cosgrove writes:

> Jesus tells Nicodemus that no one can enter the kingdom without being born 'of water and the Spirit' (v.5). One would think the Spirit should suffice, which is what Jesus goes on to say in v.6. But birth by the Spirit, however inexplicable and mysterious, is not a matter simply of the individual heart. It is tied up with 'water', which means entry into the community through baptism.[14]

Terry Griffith brings the same insight to bear on the interpretation of the difficult passage about 'the Spirit, the water and the blood' in 1 John 5:6-8. He writes:

> Together the gift of the Spirit (cf. 3:24, 4:13), the water of baptism, and the cleansing blood of Jesus (which provides forgiveness and is presumably witnessed to in the eucharist) form the identity markers that distinguish the Johannine community from its Jewish milieu; they provide the symbols and shared experiences that strengthen their separate identity as believers in Messiah Jesus. These symbols are the sociological analogue of their christological beliefs.[15]

Crossing the boundary and identifying oneself with the Jesus community will be a costly step, as Jesus himself makes plain to his disciples. 'They will excommunicate you from the synagogue. Indeed the hour is coming when everyone who kills you will think he is offering service to God' (16:2). For the first readers of John's Gospel that hour is now, and Nicodemus is put on notice that secret discipleship is not an option. Cosgrove again:

---

[13] Rensberger, Overcoming, 69.
[14] Cosgrove, 'Where Jesus is', 531.
[15] Terry Griffith, 'A Non-polemical Reading of 1 John', *Tyndale Bulletin* 49 (1998) 272.

Public confession of Jesus in such an historical setting would have incurred a form of social death (excommunication) together with the risk of physical death (martyrdom).[16]

7. Summary

Nicodemus is representative of members of the Jewish community who were sympathetic to the disciples of Jesus but were unwilling to be publicly identified with them for fear of incurring the anger of the synagogue leaders (of whom Nicodemus was himself one). Like Joseph of Arimathea, he is looking for the kingdom of God, perhaps even intrigued by the claim of Jesus that the kingdom was near, but he erroneously supposes that as an Israelite and a Pharisee he is guaranteed a place in it when it comes. Jesus tells him that his birth as an Israelite is not enough. He needs to be born again, become a child of God in a new way, a member of the new family of God that is coming into being and an inheritor of the coming kingdom. Such new birth can only be 'from above'. Only God through his Spirit can draw people to himself, open their eyes and enable them to live as his children. Nicodemus needs to be born 'of the Spirit'. He also needs to be born 'of water', where water alludes to the baptism by which believers in Jesus express openly their faith in him even at the cost of severing their connections with the wider Jewish community into which they were born.

Conclusions

What conclusions might we draw from this reading of John 3? I suggest three: one about new birth, one about baptism and one about Church and state.

To be born again or from above is not about receiving a new nature. It is about receiving a new identity as a member of a new community. It is about becoming a child of God in his new family. We should beware of pressing the metaphor too far, as if everything we know about human birth is true also of the new birth. Doing so has often led to extravagant claims for newness and

---

[16] Cosgrove, 'Where Jesus is', 532. This was Paul's view too and the meaning of being 'baptized into his death' as I have argued elsewhere: Alastair Campbell, 'Dying with Christ: The Origin of a Metaphor?' in Stanley E. Porter and Anthony R. Cross (eds.), *Baptism, the New Testament and the Church, Historical and Contemporary Studies in Honour of R.E.O. White* (Sheffield: Academic Press, 1999).

transformation that have not been borne out in experience. New birth is not to be equated with instant sanctification (or gradual sanctification for that matter), but refers rather to our adoption by God as his sons and daughters, from which of course it is to be hoped that a life of holiness will follow (1 John 3:2-3). God gives his Spirit to those whom he declares to be his children (cf. Luke 3:21-22, Galatians 4:6), but 'new birth' refers not to the sanctifying work of the Spirit but to our new identity as children of God. This helps to explain why sincere believers can claim to be born again despite often manifesting the same insecurities, prejudices, compulsions, life-style and politics as they did before!

During the last half century Baptist theologians, especially in Britain, have laboured to persuade us that baptism is not merely a sign, but an effective sign conveying God's grace to the repentant believer and not merely declaring it, while Baptist congregations (and their ministers in many cases) have continued to see baptism as an act of obedient witness. As Nigel Wright puts it:

> In the desire to avoid any sense of a magical rite which we control and to preserve the priority of faith, there is an instinct to reduce baptism to an act of bare witness with little expectation that anything would happen in the baptismal act which has not already happened in the regeneration of the heart.[17]

To which he replies on the next page:

> When baptism is the means by which people offer their lives to God in repentance and confess their faith then the Spirit of God is pleased to use the moment and the action to work in people's hearts those things of which baptism speaks. Baptism is a symbol, but not a *mere* symbol since symbols enable participation in the realities of which they speak.

If we are correct to see 'water' in John 3 as a reference to Christian baptism understood as a boundary marker for the community of Jesus, both positions receive some support. On the one hand baptism is undoubtedly an act of obedient witness (such as Nicodemus was unwilling to make). On the other hand it is a

---

[17] Nigel G. Wright, *Free Church, Free State: The Positive Baptist Vision* (Milton Keynes: Paternoster, 2005) 97.

sign of the grace of God and not a mere symbol. Baptism effects what it declares, namely membership of the family of God. It is as James McClendon argues a *performative* sign.[18] Just as the words and actions of a wedding service do not merely witness to a relationship but actually effect one (You enter the church single and leave it married, though not in any other respect changed!), so the words and actions of baptism effect what they declare: you become by God's grace a member of God's family. Such membership carries with it the promise of the Holy Spirit, yet we suggest the water of which Jesus speaks in John 3 is not a symbol of that invisible and individual grace but of a public and social belonging.

Finally, it will readily be seen that this reading of the Nicodemus story fully supports Nigel Wright's advocacy of the separation of Church and state. He writes:

> In its origins the Christian faith was a movement of both political and religious dissent. It dissented religiously within the established religion of its point of origin, Judaism, because of its belief that the Messiah had come in Jesus. It dissented politically within the Roman Empire because of its belief that Caesar was not Lord, since only Christ could be Lord.[19]

Nicodemus was being challenged to renounce the privilege of his first birth, and by publicly declaring his faith in Jesus as Messiah and Lord enter the new family of God. In so doing, John makes plain, he could expect to lose the good opinion of significant members of his community and even to be put out of the synagogue (John 12:42). Significantly, the step by which this separation would become visible and irrevocable was baptism, as it still is in many parts of the world today. Yet 'water' is only regenerating in the sense put forward here if it is the water of believer's baptism. Applied to infants it becomes not so much the means of dissent as that of conformity, 'the means by which the sacral order was maintained and enforced'. David F. Wright (no relation) has written, 'Universal infant baptism was one of the constitutive elements of the unitary world of church-state

---

[18] James W. McClendon, 'Baptist as a Performative Sign', *Theology Today* 23 (1966) 403-416; also McClendon, *Systematic Theology: Doctrine* (Nashville: Abingdon, 1994) 388.
[19] Wright, *Free Church, Free State*, 214.

Christianity, which is what Christendom commonly denotes.'[20] It is to be hoped that this reading of the story of Nicodemus will be grist to the mill of an honoured friend who has shown us that authentic Christianity will always mean 'disavowing Constantine'.[21]

---

[20] David F. Wright, *What has Infant Baptism done to Baptism?* (Milton Keynes: Paternoster, 2005) 9.
[21] From the title of his book, *Disavowing Constantine: Mission, Church and the Social Order in the Theologies of John Howard Yoder and Jürgen Moltmann* (Carlisle: Paternoster, 2000).

The coherence of freedom: can Church or state ever be truly free?

John E. Colwell

'...if the Son sets you free, you will be free indeed' (John 8:36)

Given that, according to the narrative from which this quotation is taken, those in conversation with Jesus were those who had believed in him, their affronted reaction to this promise of freedom is extraordinary. As their anger illustrates, freedom is immeasurably precious to us and we are liable to take offence if it is suggested that, in fact, we are less than truly free. We rightly (if belatedly) repudiate slavery; in every respect we promote civil freedoms (or liberties), whether it be freedom of conscience, freedom of speech, freedom of religion, or any manner of personal freedom; freedom is perceived as a political and religious virtue – though too readily it is reduced to a political or religious slogan – and to proclaim oneself as against freedom, or even to question whether such freedom is possible or coherent, would seem politically and religiously reprehensible.

Defining freedom

Yet freedom is a notoriously elusive notion to define or to identify.[1] What factors (or better, the absence of what factors) would constitute true freedom? Are we ever entirely free from some form of external constraint; can we so simply extricate ourselves from our context, from the pressures to conform, from the expectations of others? And even if we can free ourselves from all external constraint, can we free ourselves from ourselves, from that inevitable internal constraint that renders us consistent and coherent as persons; can we ever be free from habit, custom, temperament or prejudice? The difficulty is compounded by the assumption that freedom tends to be conceived and expressed as an absolute; it is irreducible; by definition it is beyond qualification and unlimited. As with the now ubiquitous claim to 'rights', the claim to freedom permits no discussion or mitigation; it is an

---

[1] For a relatively recent discussion of freedom in general, albeit chiefly in the form of historical survey, see J. Andrew Kirk, *The Meaning of Freedom: A Study of Secular, Muslim and Christian Views* (Carlisle: Paternoster, 1998).

absolute claim. But whereas the claim to 'rights' can be translated into corresponding obligations and thereby rendered negotiable (and consequently, meaningful and perhaps even attainable), the claim to freedom permits no similar negotiation or translation. One is either free or unfree. To be free is to be entirely and absolutely free. Liberty is unqualified. Moreover, to limit or to challenge this claim to freedom, as the conversation in John's Gospel illustrates, threatens the very essence of our self-perception as persons. But, as Jesus' response to his critics in this narrative suggests, this self-perceived personal freedom may prove delusional.

Perhaps most famously this claim to personal freedom was challenged theologically and philosophically by Jonathan Edwards, the eighteenth-century preacher, theologian, and philosopher.[2] While we may be free to do that which we choose or will to do, we are not free to choose or to determine our own will underlying that choice; or maybe better, we are not free to choose or determine our own nature as the persons doing the willing or the choosing. We are free to do as we choose but we are not free to determine our own nature in making those choices – and to believe that we are free to determine our own nature, to will our own will, is delusion. The point being made here is essentially the same as that made previously and somewhat more abrasively by Martin Luther.[3] One does not necessarily have to subscribe to specific understandings of predestination and divine providence to concede this very human and apparently negative point: by experience alone we are compelled to concede the difficulty – or rather the sheer human impossibility – of changing our own nature or personality. Whatever external constraints may or may not confront us, we are inevitably constrained by who we are as persons; we can do as we choose but we cannot change the 'we' doing the choosing; in this personal sense true freedom appears delusory.

Nor should this internal limitation upon personal freedom be viewed merely negatively. The positive way of expressing this apparently negative constraint is that we are free to be ourselves. Without this internal constraint of self-consistency, we would lack the positive freedom to be the persons that we are. Arguing for

---

[2] Jonathan Edwards, *Freedom of the Will* in *Works of Jonathan Edwards*, general ed. Perry Miller, vol. 1, ed. Paul Ramsey (New Haven & London: Yale University Press, 1957).

[3] Martin Luther, *The Bondage of the Will* in *Luther's Works*, gen. ed. (vols. 31-55) Helmut T. Lehmann, vol. 33, 15-295 (Philadelphia: Muhlenberg Press, 1972).

what appears to be an absolute notion of personal freedom, Richard Swinburne concludes that '... men having moral beliefs, are morally responsible for their actions if and only if they have free will in the traditional sense that their intentional actions are not causally necessitated in all their detail by prior causes'.[4] But, as I have argued elsewhere,[5] such a notion of cause-less action is not just incoherent, it is horrific; it seems to suggest a quite monstrous notion of self-alienation as the pre-requisite for responsible action. I am responsible for an action if that action is mine, if such action is 'willed' action. But for an action to be mine, deriving from my will, it cannot be cause-less, its cause lies in my nature, itself formed through my history and context. An action that was wholly unpredictable, wholly uncaused by my previously shaped nature, would not merely be incoherent, it would be indicative of madness. A wholly arbitrary freedom, a freedom of caprice, could not (by definition) be a truly personal freedom. A freedom that is truly personal cannot, by reason of its being truly personal, be absolutely free. As Stanley Hauerwas has put it,

> ... the very aspects of our experience that seem to support the idea of self-agency, freedom, and responsibility are paradoxically impossible if man is an indeterminate cause. The indeterminist must deny that a man's action can be explained wholly in terms of his will, motives, desires, or character, for to do so would imply that man is not entirely a free agent. But if acts are completely spontaneous (having no sufficient condition), then how are we to attribute responsibility to anyone? ... not only does free will not contradict determinism, it is inconceivable without it.[6]

A free state or a free Church?

Sustained reflection upon the phenomenon of personal freedom, then, renders the notion of absolute freedom incoherent: if freedom is truly personal it cannot be absolutely free. But these introductory observations raise consequent questions of the nature of freedom when such is ascribed to the Church or the state: can it be any

---

[4] Richard Swinburne, *Responsibility and Atonement* (Oxford: Clarendon, 1989) 63.
[5] John E. Colwell, *Living the Christian Story: The Distinctiveness of Christian Ethics* (Edinburgh & New York: T & T Clark, 2001) 175ff.
[6] Stanley Hauerwas, *Character and the Christian Life: A Study in Theological Ethics* (Notre Dame & London: University of Notre Dame Press, 1994); originally published San Antonio: Trinity University Press, 1975) 19f.

more coherent to speak of a free Church or a free state than it is to speak of a free person? If not, what (beyond hyperbole) is intended by speaking of a free Church and a free state? Or, to be more precise, can the Church ever be wholly free without denying its integrity as the Church and can a state ever be wholly free without denying its integrity as a state anymore than a person can be wholly free without denying their integrity as a person?

As is the case with personal freedom, for a state to act capriciously, without respect to its corporate identity as rendered by its history and traditions, would be monstrous; a wholly arbitrary state would act with the unpredictability of tyranny; an absolutely free state, therefore, would be incapable of acting justly. Here again, absolute freedom is incoherent: it would issue in chaos and random abuse. And, of course, an absolutely free state is similarly incoherent in the sense of being inconceivable: a society together with its political structures is formed (and thereby inevitably determined) by its history and traditions. I intend, consequently, to argue that a just state has a moral responsibility to act consistently and coherently in the light of its history and traditions. In other words, a just state has a moral responsibility to repudiate caprice, to repudiate the supposed freedom to act other than coherently and consistently. I will return to this theme at the conclusion of this brief essay.

In similar manner (and in some tension with a tradition of Independency), for any church to be validly identified as 'Church' it cannot be wholly free from a connectedness and consequent coherence with the Church's history and traditions across the centuries. The Church is one, is catholic, is apostolic, by definition; its authentic holiness cannot be separated from its essential unity. If a local church 'has liberty, under the guidance of the Holy Spirit, to interpret and administer [Christ's] Laws' (as the Baptist Union's Declaration of Principle has it) then that guidance of the Holy Spirit must at least partly be mediated through that local church's catholic connectedness and coherent consistency. As Nigel Wright reminds us, those who came to be called the 'Free Churches' were previously called Dissenters and their dissent focused chiefly on an Act of Uniformity.[7] A commitment to Independency is primarily a rejection of the establishment of the Church by law, a rejection of any coercion by state or by supposed external ecclesial power. It is

---

[7] Nigel G. Wright, *Free Church, Free State: The Positive Baptist Vision* (Milton Keynes: Paternoster, 2005) 205ff.

historically and theologically misconstrued as a rejection of a proper catholicity and coherent connectedness (and that it so frequently has been so misconstrued does not validate the error).[8] The freedom of the Church then, like personal freedom and the freedom of the state, cannot be an absolute or capricious freedom if it is to have coherence as specifically the Church's freedom.

The more focused question raised by Nigel Wright's discussion in *Free Church, Free State*, however, relates to the correlation of the freedom of the Church and the freedom of the state: Wright maintains that the assertion of the one freedom should lead to the assertion of the corresponding freedom.[9] It is the coherence of this assertion of consequence and complementarity, or better an exploration of the manner in which these twin freedoms may be mutually limiting, that will be the concern of the remainder of this discussion.

Similar voices
Wright, of course, is representing and reappraising a Free Church tradition with its roots in the seventeenth century but, in contemporary context, he enjoys unexpected allies: perhaps surprisingly (though arguably reflecting Papal pronouncements earlier in the twentieth century), one of the major documents of Vatican II, *Dignitatis Humanae*,[10] similarly affirms both religious freedom and the freedom of the state:

> The Vatican Council declares that the human person has a right to religious freedom. Freedom of this kind means that all men should be immune from coercion on the part of individuals, social groups and every human power so that, within due limits, nobody is forced to act against his

---

[8] [Editor: See the essay by Brown in this volume.]
[9] Wright, *Free Church, Free State*, 228: 'A constant assertion of this book has been that what is believed about the church has implications for what is to be believed about the social order and the state. The counterpart of a free church is a free state.'
[10] *Dignitatis Humanae* or *Declaration on Religious Liberty* (Vatican II, 7th December 1965), trans. Laurence Ryan, ch. 1, s. 2, in *Vatican Council II: The Conciliar and Post Conciliar Documents*, ed. Austin Flannery (Dublin: Dominican Publications, 1975) 799-812 – hereafter referred to as *DH*. For sharp criticism of the document see Stanley Hauerwas, 'Not Late Enough: The divided mind of *Dignitatis Humanae Personae*' in *A Better Hope: Resources for a Church confronting Capitalism, Democracy, and Postmodernity* (Grand Rapids: Brazos, 2000) 109-116.

convictions in religious matters in private or in public, alone or in associations with others.[11]

All depends here, of course, on what is intended (that is to say, what is intended as included and excluded) by the phrase 'within due limits'. But by whatever limitation, the 'right' and 'freedom' endorsed here is no absolute; in the context of the document as a whole, it is qualified by revelation, by tradition and by reason.[12]

Nigel Wright's discussion of the relationship between the Church and the state is impressively careful and nuanced. He even concludes by advocating a 'non-Constantinian Christendom' as a means of affirming both the public and private truth of Christ and, following Gerald Schlabach,[13] recognises that this same affirmation identifies the consistency of Stanley Hauerwas' advocacy of the Church as *polis* (a Christian society) while rejecting Constantinianism (any worldly attempt to establish this godly society).[14] A comparison between Hauerwas and Wright is, perhaps, instructive: Stanley Hauerwas notoriously repudiates both Constantinianism and political and philosophical liberalism; Nigel Wright certainly repudiates Constantinianism but seems to remain committed to a chastened form of political liberalism in his advocacy of religious liberty and toleration[15] and herein, perhaps, lies the persistent and nagging difficulty in his otherwise compelling vision.

As Wright acknowledges, the degree to which English Baptists were influenced by an earlier Anabaptist tradition is disputed[16] - 'the formal line of descent is most demonstrably from separatist Puritanism'.[17] But what is not in dispute is that the seventeenth century which witnessed the flowering of British Puritanism also witnessed the birth of the Enlightenment with its

---

[11] *DH* 2 (800).

[12] *DH* 9 (806): 'The Declaration of this Vatican Council on man's right to religious freedom is based on the dignity of the person, the demands of which have become more fully known to human reason through centuries of experience. Furthermore, this doctrine of freedom is rooted in divine revelation, and for this reason Christians are bound to respect it all the more conscientiously.'

[13] Gerald W. Schlabach as cited (without reference) in Stanley Hauerwas, *After Christendom? How the Church is to Behave if Freedom, Justice, and a Christian Nation are Bad Ideas* (Nashville: Abingdon Press, 1991^2) 7-8; quoted in Wright, *Free Church, Free State*, 276.

[14] Wright, *Free Church, Free State*, 276ff.

[15] Wright, *Free Church, Free State*, 215ff.

[16] Wright, *Free Church, Free State*, 37.

[17] Wright, *Free Church, Free State*, 38.

own and parallel notions of liberty and voluntarism.[18] Wright again acknowledges this and recognises, following David Fergusson, that 'modern conceptions of tolerance owe more to the liberalism of John Stuart Mill than the free church tradition'.[19] In this context Wright notes the predilection of secular liberalism to privatise religion, but what remains largely unacknowledged is the corresponding supposition that belief can be divorced from practice – perhaps tellingly, the only practical tension between Church and state that Wright explicitly discusses is the use of lethal force.[20] In any discussion of freedom a corresponding discussion of legitimate and illegitimate force is inevitable but a religious commitment to non-violence is by no means the sole religious commitment in tension with secular commitments.

Practice
The difficulty of so much discussion of religious liberty is that it remains abstracted from religious practices – or, more precisely, that it appears to capitulate to the Enlightenment assumption that belief and practice can be distinguished and separated. It is this radically dualistic assumption, of course, that undergirds liberalism's marginalisation of religion as a merely private affair and, consequently, permits the supposed promotion of religious liberty. But if belief and practice cannot be so simply separated – indeed, if religious belief is itself a commitment to religious practice and incoherent without such – then religion cannot be so conveniently marginalised as a private affair and liberalism's trumpeted commitment to religious liberty is rendered problematic and ultimately unsustainable.[21]

It is, of course, not at all difficult to identify such problematic religious practices. As I am writing this essay, at least a year before publication, a ranch in Texas run by the Fundamentalist Church of Jesus Christ of the Latter Day Saints has been raided and over four hundred children have been held in 'protection' following allegations of abuse, enforced child marriage and under-age sex. The defence mounted by distraught parents, forcibly

---

[18] cf. Wright, *Free Church, Free State*, 215ff.
[19] Wright, *Free Church, Free State*, 217.
[20] Wright, *Free Church, Free State*, 246ff.
[21] Hauerwas discusses this in several places; see e.g. (and in particular) Stanley Hauerwas with Michael Baxter, 'The Kingship of Christ: Why Freedom of "Belief" is not enough' in Stanley Hauerwas, *In Good Company: The Church as Polis* (Notre Dame and London: University of Notre Dame Press, 1995) 199-216.

separated from their children, rests on the claim that their religious liberties have been infringed. In comfortable British suburbia a case like this appears both extreme and remote – though not as remote as human sacrifice or the practice of Suttee – though there are and have been many polygamous cultures and many cultures in which those whom we would consider to be children have been deemed to be of marriageable age. But far more immediately, would we not defend judicial intervention if parents belonging to the Jehovah's Witnesses sect attempted to deny their child a potentially life-saving blood transfusion? And are we not supportive of legislation prohibiting the enforced circumcision of young girls? Maybe in practice – or when it comes to practice – religious liberty is not so compelling or persuasive.

Nor is it sufficient to make distinctions on the basis of true and false religion since, in a context that promotes plurality and multiculturalism, who is to determine that which is true or false; by what criteria are such judgements to be made; are not such judgements rendered meaningless precisely by a commitment to plurality? That contemporary British society accepts, or at least tolerates, the circumcision of young boys while forbidding the circumcision of young girls is due at least partly to the continuing predominant influence of a Judaeo-Christian tradition and betrays the fact that, in practice and in tension with a professed commitment to plurality and multiculturalism, a decision concerning proper and improper religious practice has been assumed. Medically, sexually and socially the consequences of female circumcision and male circumcision differ significantly but it would be difficult to argue that both do not constitute non-voluntary mutilation and that the assessment of sexual, social and even medical outcomes is not itself religiously and culturally determined. It is difficult, therefore, to avoid the conclusion that the Enlightenment's proclaimed promotion of religious liberty rests on an entirely erroneous assumption of a division of belief from practice and, once that erroneous assumption has been repudiated, the ideal of absolute religious liberty is exposed as unattainable and probably undesirable.

Attempts to respond to this practical impasse generally perpetuate the assumed distinction of belief and practice, of the private and the public, which gave rise to the impasse in the first place. Liberalism appears incapable of acknowledging that a belief commitment is itself an ethical commitment; that religion is necessarily and inevitably social, political and cultural; that the private informs and shapes the public – or am I alone in growing weary of hearing partisan politicians and broadcasters castigating bishops for their meddling in politics?

Perhaps more promising, at least initially, are attempts to distinguish between restraint and constraint. There are religious practices and religious beliefs which must be restrained for the sake of the well-being and security of society but no person should be constrained, against conscience, to particular religious belief or practice.[22] As Nigel Wright observes, it is entirely coherent to be intolerant of intolerance,[23] to restrain coercively that which threatens the well-being and security of society by its proclaimed dogmas and encouraged practices. *Dignitatis Humanae* similarly asserts the appropriateness of coercion as a defence against coercion:

> ... since civil society has the right to protect itself against possible abuses committed in the name of religious freedom the responsibility of providing such protection rests especially with the civil authority. However, this must not be done in an arbitrary manner or by the unfair practice of favoritism but in accordance with legal principles which are in conformity with the objective moral order.[24]

The difficulty with this assertion, however, rests with the adjective 'objective'. Although it is not explicitly acknowledged, it is reasonable to suppose that reference to an 'objective moral order' is rooted here in a Catholic tradition of natural law – but it is precisely the objectivity of any moral order, or the coherence of notions of objectivity, that is in question. Central to the Enlightenment project, and central at least to some forms of Catholic response, was the hopeful conviction that an objective foundation for morality could be discerned by pure reason, without reference to religious tradition or dogma. Yet even at its inception this humanistic assumption was challenged by David Hume and others and post-modernism is defined by an abandoning of the

---

[22] Jonathan Schell distinguishes between positive freedom and negative freedom, the freedom to speak and act and the freedom from coercion in these respects: Jonathan Schell, *The Unconquerable World: Power, Nonviolence, and the Will of the People – why peaceful protest is stronger than war* (Harmondsworth: Penguin, 2005) 238-239. I am grateful to James Henley, one of my students, for this reference.
[23] Wright, *Free Church, Free State*, 217.
[24] *DH* 7 (805).

quest for purely objective and rationally discernable moral foundations.

But notwithstanding all that has been said concerning the correspondence and identity of belief and practice, the restraint of belief alone is problematic: the state can legislate against various forms of discrimination and intolerance. By doing so it may promote a social context where habits of tolerance are encouraged and nurtured, but prejudice proves persistent and resilient to such encouragements and prohibitions. Moreover, if such restraint is accepted – and surely for the security and well-being of any society it must be – has not this liberal ideal of religious freedom already been fatally compromised? Prejudice and intolerance do not occur in a cultural vacuum – nor, for that matter does the repudiation of prejudice and intolerance.

But rather more problematically, the repudiation of coercive constraint, though commendable in theory, appears similarly elusive in practice. Alongside liberalism's delusory distinction between belief and practice, the private and the public, lies its other characteristic delusion of detached neutrality – or rather, the delusion noted previously of a purely rational foundation from which (and in comparison with which) religious commitments may be assessed. The fallacy of liberal foundationalism is not so much that it assumes a rational foundation as the basis for coherent and consistent judgement as that it is either oblivious or in denial concerning the particular historical, cultural and religious parameters within which this supposed purely rational foundation has been formed. Reason takes for granted its own parameters: if I were to add the figure 1001 to the figure 1101 the result would be two thousand one hundred and two – unless the original figures were binary numbers, in which case the result would be twenty-two (or 10110 as a binary number). Both results are 'rational' given their assumed parameters but, unless I am aware of those assumed parameters, unless I am aware that a figure is expressed in terms of base two or base ten (or base three or base sixteen for that matter), I will not recognise the rationality of the result. I can only do the sum successfully if I know the form in which it has been expressed – or rather, I am constrained by that which is presumed by the sum.[25] There can be no detached neutrality. The

---

[25] For a standard and now classic exposure of the fallacy of foundationalism see Alasdair MacIntyre, *Whose Justice? Which Rationality?* (London: Duckworth, 1988).

coherence and consistency in which a just state seeks to legislate, to restrain and to constrain presumes a particular understanding of justice, itself formed through a particular history and cultural context. More problematically expressed, a state is inevitably religiously and culturally constraining; it cannot but assume and promote its own religious and cultural presuppositions.

The USA and the UK

Conflicts resulting from a commitment to a supposedly free Church and a supposedly free state are commonplace in the United States of America with its constitutional (and therefore intensely problematic) commitment to freedom of religion.[26] The constitutional 'right' to practise polygamy, to teach creationism and to marginalise the teaching of evolution (as if such were opposed to a doctrine of creation), to perpetuate forms of racial segregation or to demonstrate against abortion clinics have been perceived as religious freedoms and governmental attempts to oppose such are denounced as non-constitutional constraint. Notwithstanding current constitutional controversy concerning the inclusion of the phrase 'one nation under God' in the pledge of allegiance, the 'founding fathers' almost certainly assumed a religious consensus that was almost immediately constitutionally undermined and has been demonstrated historically to be delusory.

The Establishment of the Church of England by law at least nominally renders the United Kingdom a very different religious context. Historically, at least, there has been no pretence here to religious neutrality. Rather constraint, or at least encouragement to conformity, has been commonplace. Nor did nineteenth-century moves towards religious toleration nullify constraint: perhaps ironically with hindsight, the local authority funding of Church of England and Roman Catholic schools at the beginning of the twentieth century was resolutely opposed by the Free Churches precisely because such financial underwriting was perceived as a

---

[26] The first amendment of the Constitution states that 'Congress shall make no law respecting an establishment of religion, or prohibiting the free exercise thereof; or abridging the freedom of speech, or of the press; or the right of the people peaceably to assemble, and to petition the Government for a redress of grievances'. For a previous discussion of this see my article 'In defence of Christendom: the claim of Christ and the confidence of the Church' in *Baptist Ministers' Journal* 298 (April 2007) 21-29.

continuation of religious constraint.[27] The incident is instructive: in the name of religious liberty a religious group was opposing the promotion of particular religious interests and expressions. As the twentieth century unfolded, and largely without prejudice to the continued (though now barely more than decorative) Establishment of the Church of England, governmental drift towards a supposed religious neutrality proved inexorable: 'We don't do God' a Downing Street Press Secretary famously objected yet antidiscrimination legislation of the late twentieth and early twenty-first century betrays a distinctly religious disposition.

The maintenance of religious exemption with respect to some elements of antidiscrimination legislation (though this not without controversy) preserves at least the appearance of non-coercion but in many respects constraint towards a distinctively liberal agenda is overt and inescapable. While at present churches cannot be charged with sexual discrimination for refusing to accept or even to consider a female priest or minister or an openly homosexual priest or minister, pressure to view priests and ministers as employees rather than as office holders may yet prove an intimation of the removal of such dispensation. This promotion of equal liberties through anti-discrimination legislation is perceived by churches (not to mention Islam) as intolerable (and intolerant) religious (or anti-religious) constraint. And this contemporary and controversial example may also (and finally) prove instructive.

As already noted, it is characteristic of so-called post-modernity to be anti-foundational, to be unconvinced by the claim to religious or cultural neutrality and to repudiate the quest for such. Contemporary British society may be post-Christian but by virtue of such it is not and cannot be religiously or culturally neutral: it is post-*Christian* rather than post-*Hindu* or post-*Buddhist* or post-*Moslem* or post-*Sikh* or post-*pagan*. Its laudable commitment to religious and cultural toleration (or perhaps better, hospitality[28]) derives not from some inconceivable and unattainable neutrality but precisely from that Judeo-Christian

---

[27] For an account of this Free Church opposition see Ian M. Randall, *The English Baptists of the Twentieth Century* (Didcot: Baptist Historical Society, 2005) 36ff.
[28] For a discussion of hospitality as a preferred concept to that of toleration see Luke Bretherton, *Hospitality as Holiness: Christian witness amid moral diversity* (Aldershot: Ashgate, 2006); cf. Alan Bartlett, *Humane Christianity: arguing with the classic spiritual disciplines in the light of Jesus of Nazareth* (London: Darton, Longman & Todd, 2004).

heritage from which it supposedly seeks to distance itself. Consequently, such toleration cannot coherently be absolute; religious freedom is inevitably limited; the promotion of toleration is itself religiously and culturally constraining. This of course raises the uncomfortable question of whether antidiscrimination legislation with respect to sex and sexual orientation – so repudiated by fundamentalisms – might not similarly derive from a Judeo-Christian heritage rather than from the repudiation of such.

Personal and eschatological
In the Gospel passage which introduces this paper Jesus juxtaposes truth and freedom. This juxtaposition itself ought not to be evaded or overlooked: no authentic pursuit of freedom can be without prejudice to truth and, correspondingly, no authentic assertion of truth can be prejudicial to freedom;[29] any claim to truth that militates against freedom is fallacious; any claim to freedom that is disregarding of truth issues in bondage.[30] But with equal pertinence, in the Fourth Gospel truth is both personal – identified with Jesus himself – and (at least arguably) eschatological. That truth is eschatological - presently provisional and thereby presently unattainable in any absolute and objective sense - may be a positive way of affirming that which post-modernism affirms merely negatively: truth, by definition, is absolute but its fullness and completion lies ahead of us and is not perceivable in the present other than in anticipation. And maybe in the light of this Gospel juxtaposition we should affirm that freedom is similarly eschatological (and similarly personal). That freedom, like truth, is eschatological may deliver us from the paralysis of absolutism noted at the beginning of this essay: freedom, like truth, is

---

[29] This juxtaposition of truth and freedom is assumed throughout the text of *Dignitatis Humanae*: '... both impelled by their nature and bound by a moral obligation to seek the truth, especially religious truth. They are also bound to adhere to the truth once they come to know it and direct their whole loves in accordance with the demands of truth.' *DH* 2 (801).
[30] Commenting on this Gospel passage in the encyclical *Veritatis Splendor* (87), Pope John Paul II opines that 'Christ reveals, first and foremost, that the frank and open acceptance of truth is the condition for authentic freedom. (...) Jesus ... is the living, personal summation of perfect freedom in total obedience to the will of God. His crucified flesh fully reveals the unbreakable bond between freedom and truth, just as his Resurrection from the dead is the supreme exaltation of the fruitfulness and saving power of a freedom lived out in truth.'
http://www.vatican.va/holy_father/john_paul_ii/encyclicals/documents/hf_jp-ii_enc_06081993_veritatis-splendor_en.html [accessed 16th June 2008].

irreducible but here and now we can only humbly and hesitantly anticipate its fulfilment. Approximations to truth and freedom are the best to which we can aspire; the present assertion of absolute freedom is as delusory as the supposed certainties of fundamentalism. But if freedom, like truth, is ultimately personal – that is, Christological – then, as this narrative suggests, it is ultimately to be sought and found in Christ and not elsewhere or independently. Moreover, since Christ himself is ultimate truth and the bestower of ultimate freedom, any authentic anticipation of truth and freedom, inasmuch as it is authentic, is (consciously or otherwise) an anticipation of Christ and, consequently, an intimation of his Spirit.[31]

When a state, therefore, in promotion of freedom, opposes any discrimination on the basis of race, sex or sexual orientation, liberalises the law with respect to abortion or grants limited licence for embryo experimentation, it is reasonable and appropriate for the Church to challenge the state regarding the truthfulness of any or all of these supposed freedoms. Moreover, if (as is the case) that state has been shaped historically through a Judaeo-Christian tradition, it is reasonable and appropriate for the Church to urge the state to act and legislate in coherence with that tradition if it is to avoid the tyranny that is consequent on incoherence and inconsistency. However, in challenging the state in this manner – which is the proper prophetic outworking of Dissent rather than Establishment – the Church itself must be humbly open to the possibility that, since its own comprehension of the truth of the gospel is provisional, the coercive legislation it opposes may yet prove to be a closer approximation to truth and freedom than that which the Church presently espouses. Even in its conscious forsaking of the gospel, the state is never God-forsaken and more than once in the past the Holy Spirit has spoken to God's people through a seemingly pagan state since God's people had become moribund in their presumptions of truth.

Authentic truth and authentic freedom are to be identified in Christ and, as such, lie always ahead of us in that eschatological future that is his final coming. Though truth and freedom, thus identified, are irreducible, here and now our comprehension of truth is provisional (if not flawed). Consequently, no claim to freedom can be absolute; some measure of coercion is both inevitable and appropriate while apprehensions of truth are partial.

---

[31] [Editor: Cf. the essay by Took in this volume.]

It is the obligation of a truly free Church (a Church that is not established by law) to challenge a truly free state (a state making no claims to theocracy) concerning issues of truth and freedom. But, in that challenge, that truly free Church must expect itself to be challenged by the Spirit concerning its own grasp of truth and freedom, albeit even through an overtly pagan state, lest it find itself inadvertently in the company of those 'believers' in this Johannine narrative whose presumption of truth and freedom proved fallacious.

> May God, the Father of all, grant that the human family by carefully observing the principle of religious liberty in society may be brought by the grace of Christ and the power of the Holy Spirit to that 'glorious freedom of the children of God' (Romans 8:21) which is sublime and everlasting.[32]

---

[32] *DH* 15 (812).

Being a minister: spirituality and the pastor

Christopher J. Ellis

'In their understanding of ministry, British Baptists appear to have moved from a position of relative clarity to one of some confusion', Nigel Wright declared in the opening of his adventurous attempt to clear the air in 2001. His article 'Inclusive Representation: Towards a Doctrine of Christian Ministry'[1] reviewed and critiqued a number of issues which he identified as 'dualities' and 'sticking points', before offering a Baptist understanding of Christian ministry as 'inclusive representation'.

It is not my plan here to review the article as a whole[2] but rather, from the perspective of Christian spirituality, to explore one particular theme, namely the idea that ministers are called to 'a way of being'. I will do this from the perspective of pastoral ministry, though much will be of relevance to other representative ministries within the Church.

The 1995 discussion document produced by the Doctrine and Worship Committee of the Baptist Union of Great Britain, entitled *Forms of Ministry among Baptists: Towards an Understanding of Spiritual Leadership*, argued:

> The call to be a minister is not only the call to exercise various functions, but to 'a way of being' or 'order of life'. Doing cannot be separated from being, as the functions of ministry shape what a person is, as well as being grounded in a personality which has been 'formed' in the process of ministerial training. (...) a way of life is more than a mere job description...[3]

The report was quick to observe that there are 'many ways of being for Christian disciples; it is not something confined to a Christian minister', and that such a ministerial 'way of being' does not imply *per se* an 'indelible' order of ministry but one which needs to remain open to the call of Christ.

---

[1] Nigel G. Wright, 'Inclusive Representation: Towards a Doctrine of Christian Ministry', *The Baptist Quarterly* 39.4 (October 2001) 159-174.
[2] [Editor: In the present volume Paul Goodliff and Robert Ellis also interact with this article.]
[3] *Forms of Ministry*, 31.

Nigel commented that the phrase 'way of being' provoked some controversy at the time 'but that it is not really controversial' and argued that, following ordination, we ought,

> to look for a significant change in the sense that persons as an act of response to their call and ordination orientate themselves radically toward God for the fulfilment of that call and ordination. This cannot be 'indelible' since a person might choose to retract it and no longer live in this way, but a 'way of being' it surely is.[4]

Way of being

It is interesting that the contentious phrase is 'way of being' not 'way of doing', that the identity of the minister might be seen as more problematic than the minister's actions or responsibilities. So in what sense does the phrase 'way of being' inform as well as explain pastoral ministry?

Two recent theological themes may help us. The first is the exploration of 'virtue ethics' in which attention is drawn away from ethics as primarily decision-making towards an understanding of Christian character from which good, or Christian actions, flow.[5] Such an ethical perspective encourages us to understand Christian behaviour as not simply a series of free-standing actions but as a consequence of Christian character and calling. In warning against false prophets, Jesus said,

> You will know them by their fruits. Are grapes gathered from thorns, or figs from thistles? In the same way, every good tree bears good fruit, but the bad tree bears bad fruit. A good tree cannot bear bad fruit, nor can a bad tree bear good fruit. Every tree that does not bear good fruit is cut down and thrown into the fire. Thus you will know them by their fruits (Matthew 7:16-20).

Here is an approach to the phrase 'way of being' which recognises that the actions of Christian ministry flow from who the minister is. The value of the words of someone who claims to be a servant or

---

[4] Wright, 'Inclusive Representation', 169.
[5] See James W. McClendon, Jr., *Systematic Theology: Ethics vol. 1* (Nashville: Abingdon Press, 1986) especially 104-109; Stanley Hauerwas, *The Peaceable Kingdom: A Primer in Christian Ethics* (Notre Dame: University of Notre Dame Press, 1983) especially 35-49; and Alasdair MacIntyre, *After Virtue* (London: Duckworth, 1984).

representative of God is discerned through the evidence of their deeds – not because deeds are what matter most but because who a person is and what a person does cannot be separated. Furthermore, the question of character cannot be separated from questions of how that character is formed and shaped, either by its location in the Christian community or by its commitment to practices which will direct and nourish it.

Formation
This observation leads us to the second theme which offers an approach to understanding 'way of being' without the distraction of ontological language. This is the recent tendency to speak the language of 'formation', both as a way of understanding Christian nurture and development and, more particularly, the preparing and shaping of women and men for Christian ministry. Further, the language of ministerial formation can refer to the process of life-long learning and 'professional development', not simply to the initial preparation prior to ordination.

Recent use of 'ministerial formation' language implies a culture shift away from seeing 'ministerial training' as primarily the acquisition of knowledge and skills to a more holistic view in which character and calling are important perspectives. While this interpretation may not be contentious, the implication that ministerial training has been primarily about knowledge and skills might be. If we take the 'long' historical view we might want to say that it has always been an expectation of ministers and, by implication, their preparation for ministry, that they combine learning and spiritual zeal. Towards the end of the eighteenth century, the intentions of Hugh Evans as Principal of the Bristol Academy were summed up by his son and successor Caleb:

> ... as not merely to form substantial scholars but as far as in him lay he was desirous of being made an instrument in God's hand of forming them, able, evangelical, lively, zealous ministers of the Gospel.[6]

Yet we should acknowledge that Caleb Evans may well have been responding in part to a suspicion which has persisted: namely, that ministerial training colleges have unduly concentrated on book

---

[6] Caleb Evans, 'Elisha's Exclamation: A Sermon Occasioned by the Death of Rev. Hugh Evans, preached at Broadmead, Bristol, April 8, 1781' (Bristol, 1781) 31.

learning and may even have had a detrimental effect on the spiritual well-being of the trainee.

We should also note that while the 'long view' might justify an integrated understanding of ministerial formation, recent years have seen an increased emphasis on training and the acquisition of skills. In the last third of the twentieth century a number of factors have led to the widespread development of pastoral studies as a distinct discipline within ministerial training and, more widely, in certain university departments.[7] Alongside the influence of the clinical practice movement there was an increased awareness of the need for listening skills as well as a general appreciation of psychological and sociological insights. If we add to these the emergence of leadership studies and a tendency to professionalise ministerial identity, then the wind is set fair for a task-focused approach to ministerial training. Ian Stackhouse claims,

> Within the seminary there has been a discernable shift from the *theology* of ministry towards the *praxis* of ministry, to the extent that the practice of ministry has become the theology of ministry. (...) This absence of a theology of ministry is precisely why the evangelical-charismatic church has been prey to the various techniques and strategies emanating from the world of management.[8]

It is response to such developments that the language of ministerial formation has been coined, treating the minister as an integrated person who develops as a single entity rather than as a collector of skills and information.

Of course, we should not play formation language off against the language of training or the language of learning. Indeed, we ought to see each of these three areas as part of an integrated whole and such an integrated model of ministerial identity has in recent years been used by colleges and others involved in the preparing and supporting of women and men for Christian ministry.

---

[7] For a survey of these developments, see James Woodward and Stephen Pattison, *The Blackwell Reader in Pastoral and Practical Theology* (Oxford: Blackwell, 2000) especially 1-70.

[8] Ian Stackhouse, *The Gospel-Driven Church: Retrieving Classical Ministries for Contemporary Revivalism* (Milton Keynes: Paternoster, 2004) 225. Arguably, the very recent concentration on 'core competencies' might also be understood as a part of this functional trajectory, though denominational lists of competencies have tended to include more integrated understandings of ministry.

We might present each of these areas as overlapping spheres of concern, both in the exercising of ministry and in preparation for it. There are things which it is reasonable to expect a minister to *know*, there are things it is reasonable to expect a minister to be able to *do* and there are certainly expectations about how a minister should *behave*. So knowledge requires a commitment to learning, the development of skills requires an investment in the practising of those skills and character requires a personal integrity without which the ministry, however learned or accomplished, would be undermined.

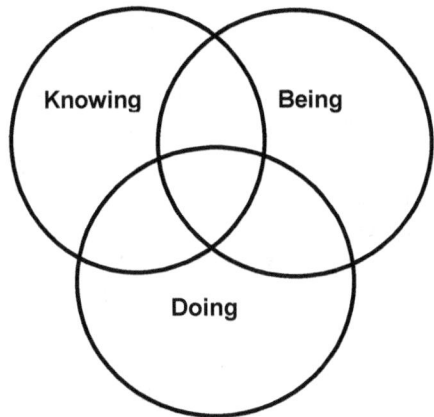

The commonly used diagrammatic model presents these three spheres of 'knowing', 'doing' and 'being' as an integrated and interactive model of ministry. This model has very real strengths but it is not without its shortcomings. In particular, it does not adequately present the central and all-encompassing position of the *person* of the minister. In other words, the being of the minister, their character and spirituality, is not simply a *part* of the whole, however interactive, it is a vital way of *viewing* the whole.

I want to propose a small adjustment to this model which I believe will contribute constructively to our refection on the notion of a ministerial 'way of being'. The modification I am proposing is based on a definition of Christian spirituality proposed by Philip Sheldrake:

> Spirituality is understood to include not merely the techniques of prayer but, more broadly, a conscious

relationship with God, in Jesus Christ, through the indwelling of the Spirit and in the context of the community of believers. Spirituality is, therefore, concerned with the conjunction of theology, prayer and practical Christianity.[9]

As can be seen, Sheldrake argues for a broad definition of spirituality which is wider than the life of prayer or any system of devotional practices. It is an integration of a person's life from the perspective of their relationship with God, what the New Testament calls 'life in the Spirit'.[10] It is the 'conjunction', a bringing together, of what a person does with what a person believes and how a person prays.

This understanding of spirituality has a number of characteristics which are relevant to our discussion. First, it is an embodied reality in which belief and prayer take form in action. Secondly, it is an integrative reality in which the various parts and concerns of a person's life are brought into a unity. Thirdly, it is an expression of identity because it embraces how they act and are known in the world, what they know and what they believe and how they relate to the ultimate reality of God. We might apply this holistic view of spirituality to the model of ministerial identity by making two modifications. First, the circle labelled 'being' or 'character' is replaced with a narrower definition of spirituality, namely, 'devotional practices'. Secondly, the whole of the three circles is encompassed by a circle entitled 'ministerial way of being'. This is the holistic spirituality of Sheldrake's definition which encompasses all that the minister is or does in their life before God.

It might be argued at this point that 'way of being' refers primarily to a ministerial lifestyle rather than to the personhood of a particular minister. However, the nature of Christian vocation as the calling of a person, rather than the allocation of a task, ought to encourage us not to make too large a distinction between lifestyle and personhood.

---

[9] Philip Sheldrake, *Spirituality and History: Questions of Interpretation and Method* (London: SPCK, 1995) 60.
[10] See Gordon D. Fee, *Listening to the Spirit in the Text* (Grand Rapids / Cambridge and Vancouver: Eerdmans and Regent College Publishing, 2000) especially 33-47.

Ordained ministry as promise-keeping
Something of this integration of Christian and ministerial identity is expressed in the promises asked of those being ordained as pastors in *Gathering for Worship*, the worship book of the Baptist Union of Great Britain:

> Will you serve and pastor the people of God
> with gentle nurture and faithful teaching?
> Will you set before them the whole counsel of God
> as you proclaim Christ, the living Word?
> Will you be faithful in worship and prayer,
> and, through word and sacrament,
> will you celebrate the grace of God,
> seeking to pattern yourself and those you serve
> after the likeness of Jesus Christ?

> **As a disciple of Jesus Christ,
> I will minister in his way.**

Other responses include:

> **Abiding in the love of God,
> and relying on his grace, I will.**

and:

> **As a disciple of Jesus Christ
> and with the help of God's Spirit, I will.**

After the final promises, the presiding minister concludes:

> May the God of grace
> keep you steadfast
> in the vows you have made,
> living and serving
> in the power of the Holy Spirit
> as a faithful disciple of Jesus Christ.[11]

Early in the service it has been made clear that,

> All are called to be disciples.
> All are called to be servants of God in Christ Jesus
> through the power of the Holy Spirit.[12]

However, the way in which this discipleship is worked out for a pastor is *as* a pastor and, as such, the minister is called to be faithful to the promises made at ordination. In an essay on ordination, Eugene Peterson uses an image taken from the story of Ulysses where the hero commands his sailors to lash him to the mast of their ship so that he isn't beguiled by the siren voices luring them onto the rocks. However much he begs or demands them, they are not to release him from the mast. Peterson suggests that the ordination promises made by minister and church are a lashing to the mast of the pastoral calling:

> Be our pastor, a minister of Word and sacrament in the middle of this world's life. (...) This isn't the only task in the life of faith, but it is your task. (...) One more thing: We are going to ordain you to this ministry, and we want your vow

---

[11] Christopher J. Ellis and Myra Blyth (eds.), *Gathering for Worship: Patterns and Prayers for the Community of Disciples* (Norwich: Canterbury Press, 2005) 125-126.
[12] Ellis and Blyth, *Gathering for Worship*, 121.

that you will stick to it. (...) With these vows of ordination we are lashing you fast to the mast of Word and sacrament so you will be unable to respond to the siren voices.[13]

The image is a powerful one and vividly represents Peterson's view that many contemporary ministers have forsaken their historic calling and gone 'whoring after other gods' such as 'relevance' and 'success'.[14] The implication for our understanding of 'way of being' is significant. It presents 'faithfulness' as a fundamental aspect of being a minister and an intentional concern to guard the way in which that ministry is undertaken.

This is not so much about what a minister does as what a minister is called to be: a servant of Word and sacrament, one who invites the people of God back to God's embodiment in Christ and their calling to follow Christ, one who points to grace in Word and bread and wine and who embodies grace in a grace-filled ministry of servant care. Yes, this involves faithful actions – the studying and expounding of Scripture, the faithful leading of worship and proclaiming of the gospel, pastoral care and spiritual direction – but each of these actions flows from who the pastor is in relation to God and the community.

These faithful actions, together with the standards of conduct expected of a minister as a representative of the gospel, will become an intolerable burden if seen primarily as the *tasks* of ministry. They can only be celebrated as life-giving and life-affirming actions of ministry if they flow from a life lived in grace before God. This is what it means to be a *Christian* minister. Beyond professionalism, beyond ecclesiastical function, beyond competence, there is a calling to be a minister as the way in which this particular person is called to be a Christian.

Being and becoming
'How can this be?', as Mary said to the angel. We need to acknowledge that while we have used the phrase 'way of being' it might be more accurate and more theologically adequate to speak of a ministerial 'way of becoming'. It would be a mistake to think that keeping ordination promises is somehow about maintaining an

---

[13] Eugene H. Peterson, *The Contemplative Pastor: Returning to the Art of Spiritual Direction* (Grand Rapids: Christianity Today and Eerdmans, 1989) 138-139.
[14] Eugene H. Peterson, *Working the Angles: The Shape of Pastoral Integrity* (Grand Rapids: Eerdmans, 1987) 1.

original enthusiasm, as though a life of ministry were one of holding the line against adverse pressures. It may feel like that sometimes, and there is some sense of that in Peterson's presentation of ordination vows, but the way of ministerial being is more about a journey of exploration than it is the defence of a battlement.

In any spiritual or theological explanation of Christian ministry the theme of calling will be central - not simply central to the experience of the minister or minister-to-be, but central to how we understand a human being might in any way step up to the challenge of such a role. However, it would be a mistake to only see vocation as an explanation of origins; we should also see it as a way of understanding the relationship of the minister to the God who continues to call. The form or context of a ministry may change, not because siren voices pull us off course, but because the living God invites us to step out in faith in a life of dynamic openness, trust and obedience.

Good practices and gracious disciplines

Just as we might identify a number of examples of good professional practice to improve the competence of pastors, so we should look to examples of good devotional practice as a means of enabling this growth in grace. Here we might list some of the spiritual disciplines and some of the Christian practices[15] which have long marked the serious disciple but which we might see as having particular relevance for an intentional approach to a ministerial way of becoming. The list is illustrative and not intended to be comprehensive:

1. Worship

Perhaps the foundational spiritual discipline for the pastor is faithfulness in worship. In local churches the pastor will be essential to the good order of the community's liturgical life, whether as a leader or as the one exercising oversight amongst those who lead. But the pastor's engagement with worship will be of a different order from that of the other members of the local church community. The pastor will want to plan for a balanced diet

---

[15] For the spiritual disciplines see Richard J. Foster, *Celebration of Discipline* (London: Hodder and Stoughton, 1980, repr. 1999); for Christian practices see Dorothy C. Bass, *Practicing our Faith: A Way of Life for a Searching People* (San Francisco: Jossey-Bass, 1997).

of worship and engagement with Scripture, will be concerned with identifying and using people's gifts and will seek to enable the church to worship in Spirit and in truth. While the pastor will need to seek opportunities to be led in worship, often outside the local church, it will often be in the very leading of the community in worship that the pastor will in turn be nourished. In the breaking of bread and in the opening and proclaiming of the Word, the pastor will meet with God as well as serve the community.

2. Waiting on God

A central theme of Baptist spirituality has been openness to the Holy Spirit in worship. This has often been expressed in terms of extempore prayer but it needs to be understood more fundamentally as a waiting upon God, even as prepared material is being used for the building up of the body of Christ. Giving attention to God is at the heart of Christian devotion; it needs to be built into the very exercising of the central responsibilities of ministry and not simply be seen as an attitude for a personal quiet time. The church is a community whose well-being and faithfulness is the special responsibility of the pastor. Worship is the central arena for the encounter between pastor and congregation as well as between the congregation and God.

3. Sabbath keeping

This may not seem an obvious discipline for the pastor to exemplify as they will usually be working when others are experiencing the sabbath or the Lord's day. That is precisely why the pastor needs to approach the matter of sabbath – or time away from ministerial duties – with serious and consistent intent. Eugene Peterson has hard words to say of the busy pastor:

> The adjective *busy* set as a modifier to *pastor* should sound to our ears like *adulterous* to characterize a *wife* or *embezzling* to describe a banker. It is an outrageous scandal, a blasphemous affront.[16]

He locates this busyness in vanity and laziness but I would want to add that often the overcrowded diary and lack of time off are a result of professional insecurity and an inability to take seriously the gospel of grace, so easily preached to others. It is only when my value as a child of God takes precedence over my need to be

---

[16] Peterson, *Contemplative Pastor*, 17.

affirmed as a successful minister, that I will be set free to enjoy the sabbath God has providentially placed in the structures of creation. Drivenness does not exemplify grace but rather its absence, and the ability to rest and play should be welcomed as an anticipation of the coming kingdom (Hebrews 4:9-11).

4. Reading Scripture

It might be stating the obvious to exhort pastors to read the Bible. After all, they are entrusted with preaching regularly and much of their training has traditionally been in the study of Scripture. However, the reading of Scripture should be genuine study – a struggling to understand and to hear God's Word addressed to the minister's and the congregation's situation. Giving attention to God through the reading of Scripture is not just about writing a sermon but being open to God and the guidance of the Holy Spirit. This takes time and persistent faithfulness.

The practice of *lectio divina* or spiritual reading may be an important way forward for many pastors as they engage with God's Word. While traditional historical critical methods will offer some illumination, as well as a safety check that Scripture is not being misused, they do not in themselves answer the question, 'What is God saying here?' *Lectio divina* offers one model for how that question might be asked and does so in a way which presents the living voice of Scripture through the practice of prayer. Pastors need to beware the opportunism of using Scripture as a peg for their own strategic interests and 'visions', however sincere, and the discipline of *lectio divina* can encourage and enable a reading of Scripture within the context of their relationship with God rather than their role as pastor. This distinction might seem to suggest the opposite of what I have been proposing in this paper where I have argued for the conjunction of the person with the ministerial role. In reality, the opposite is the case. I want to propose that the way of being of a minister should not be separated from that minister's relationship with God and should in fact be influenced by it. Vocation is the calling of persons to serve and it is the renewal of the person which offers most hope for their ministry. The flow should be from discipleship to ministry, or rather the minister can only minister *Christianly* as a disciple.

5. Prayer

It would be a platitude to say that ministers should pray more, but the reality is that the pressures of busy diaries and the anxieties and stresses of church leadership often leave pastors without the time or mental space to pray as much as they should. The debate about time, discipline, diaries and desires is for another occasion. Here I wish simply to state that prayer is a vital part of the calling of the pastor because it is a vital part of being a disciple.

However, I believe that particular ways of praying can offer much to the pastor both as a disciple and as a pastor.[17] Three historic ways of praying may be mentioned here. First, there is the Ignatian method of imaginatively entering into a Scripture story so that the one praying becomes a participant or close observer of the action. As the pastor constantly needs to make connections between the world of Scripture and the world in which the church exists and witnesses, the hermeneutic which could arise from inhabiting Scripture in this way has real potential to see the world and the minister's calling differently.

Secondly, the practice of *examen*, or review of the day, could provide a grace-filled release to many pastors bowed low by unfinished tasks and messy and consuming church work. To review the day in the presence of God enables the acknowledgement of failures, omissions, misjudgements and clangers; but to do so from the perspective of grace and with the continuing promise of forgiveness has similarities with various tools which pastors and others are now encouraged to use as a way of working, such as reflection on practice, theological reflection and journaling. What *examen* offers is a way of engaging in these important activities as a method which locates the minister's understanding and response where they belong – in the gospel.

Thirdly, the practice of contemplative prayer may only appeal to some. However, its promise is the nurturing of a relationship with God which goes deep both in self-understanding and in awareness of God. Whether we see this way of praying as a discipline or a longing, its strength lies in its search for God and its resting in God. What other Christian activity promises so much?

6. Spiritual direction

This is a discipline which is growing in use and influence among Christians from many denominations. Sometimes its proponents

---

[17] Two good and practical books on different ways of praying are Sue Mayfield, *Exploring Prayer* (Oxford: Lion, 2007) and Richard J. Foster, *Prayer: Finding the Heart's True Home* (London: Hodder and Stoughton, 1992).

shy away from the word 'direction' as to modern ears it can imply a relationship which is authoritarian in structure rather than pastoral in intent. This is far from the case and much recent writing on spiritual direction has emphasised the role of listening for the Spirit amidst the circumstances and reflections of a directee's life.[18]

While we should not confuse spiritual direction with either pastoral counselling or professional supervision, there are similarities. For many ministers, the help of another in the search for self-awareness, the reflecting on practice, attempts at accountability before God and the constant listening for the Spirit's voice will not only be welcome but a literal 'Godsend' and a lifeline in ministry.

7. Giving attention to the grace of God

I am not sure whether this can be described as an historic spiritual discipline, but the theme is central to the Christian gospel and is too often ignored by Christian ministers. In particular, those who are called to be ministers of grace often do not take the grace of God seriously enough in terms of understanding their own lives or ministerial 'performance'. How can mature pastoral care take place without the self-awareness which grace makes possible? How can reconciliation occur when the minister has not daily received God's forgiveness and been set free from self-justification? How can grace be proclaimed and practiced when it is not appropriated and celebrated?

How grace might be taken seriously will vary from one situation and person to another. But each minister should seek to plan times when they are regularly exposed to the liberating and life-affirming power of the grace of God for them as disciples who follow Jesus Christ as ministers of the gospel.[19] Spiritual disciplines and practices as intentional and planned opportunities to be open to God will be vital in this.

---

[18] See e.g. Kenneth Leech, *Soul Friend: Spiritual Direction in the Modern World* (London: Darton, Longman & Todd, 1994); David Lonsdale, *Dance to the Music of the Spirit: The Art of Discernment* (Notre Dame: Ave Maria Press, 1992); Margaret Guenther, *Holy Listening: The Art of Spiritual Direction* (London: Darton, Longman & Todd, 1992) and Gordon H. Jeff, *Spiritual Direction for Every Christian* (London: SPCK, 1987, repr. 2007).

[19] See Christopher J. Ellis, 'Spirituality in Mission: Gathering and Grace', in Paul S. Fiddes (ed.), *Under the Rule of Christ: Dimensions of Baptist Spirituality* (Oxford and Macon: Regent's Park College with Smith & Helwys, 2008) 169-187.

A way of being as a rule of life

In conclusion, I believe that much of what has been explored above can be brought into focus by understanding the notion of a ministerial 'way of being' as a 'rule of life', using the term in its historic sense of a pattern of living. While its origins are to be found in monasticism, the most famous and influential example being the rule of St Benedict,[20] the concept of a rule of life has increasingly been seen as a cluster of practices embraced with the intention of seeking faithful Christian living. In Latin *regula* simply means 'rule, pattern, model, example'. Bishop Harold Miller writes:

> By embracing Rule, we make for ourselves a standard to which we would like to attain, through the power of the Spirit, and we are enabled from time to time to do some appropriate assessment of where we have got to.[21]

In its monastic origins, a rule is a document which sets out 'the particular ethos and purpose of religious communities and their way of life'. Philip Sheldrake suggests that these documents are not primarily legislative but are examples of wisdom writings for the building up of communal Christian living.[22] Inherited wisdom may be a good way of understanding historic spiritual disciplines and Christian communal practices. Our embracing them today involves both learning from the experience of the past and acknowledging the need of such wisdom for our own living in the present.

I have here focussed on what might be termed 'devotional practices' and not attempted to produce a comprehensive list of disciplines and practices which might constitute a rule of life, or way of being, for a Christian minister. That is work for another day

---

[20] The first extant rule for communal monastic living was written by Pachomius (d 346) but the most widely known and influential rule is that of St Benedict (c 480 - c 547). See Patrick Barry, *Saint Benedict's Rule: A New Translation for Today* (York: Ampleforth Abbey & Gracewing, 1997), also reprinted in Anthony Marett-Crosby, *The Benedictine Handbook* (Norwich: Canterbury Press, 2003). For an introduction to Benedictine spirituality for all Christians, see Esther de Waal, *Seeking God: The Way of St Benedict* (London: Fount, 1984), Esther de Waal, *A Life-Giving Way: A Commentary on the Rule of St Benedict* (Collegeville: The Liturgical Press, 1995) and Brian C. Taylor, *Spirituality for Everyday Living: An Adaptation of the Rule of St Benedict* (Collegeville: The Order of St Benedict, 1989).
[21] Harold Miller, *Finding a Personal Rule of Life* (Bramcote: Grove Books, 1984) 4.
[22] Philip Sheldrake, 'Religious Rules', in *The New SCM Dictionary of Christian Spirituality* (London: SCM, 2005) 549.

and perhaps other people. However, I would observe that just as the *Rule of St Benedict* does not restrict itself to so-called spiritual matters, but deals with the very practical details of communal life, so a rule of life for ministers should be a combination of spiritual disciplines with practical examples of good ministerial practice and behaviour, good practices which might relate to the other two spheres of 'doing' and 'knowing'. For the Baptist Union of Great Britain this might perhaps be a project for its Ministry Department in partnership with the Baptist Retreat Group and the Baptist Ministers' Fellowship. However it is arranged, the development of such a rule would have many benefits both for those undergoing ministerial formation and for ministers seeking continuing formation under God.

Pattern is a feature of daily life for most people. Some kind of routine enables us to do the things we want to do, and a rule of life provides the elements of a regular pattern to address the concern for developing and maintaining a Christian identity. Similarly, ministerial identity, as ministerial discipleship lived before God, can be nurtured and strengthened by embracing a similar, intentionally developed, ministerially focussed pattern of disciplines and practices. This is what we may mean when we speak of a ministerial 'way of being' and I suggest that such a way of being a minister would be for the protection and nourishment of those who embrace it and a blessing for the churches they serve.

'The leadership of some...'[1]
Baptist ministers as leaders?

Robert A. Ellis

In the last decade or two a subtle change has occurred in the way in which Baptist ministry is spoken of. We have in fact often stopped talking of 'ministry' and started to speak instead of 'leadership'. For many Baptists and others leadership has become what Nigel Wright calls the 'dominant paradigm' for ministry.[2] How and why did this happen, and what difference does it make? Does the expression 'servant leader' deal with any difficulties the change might bring in its wake? Is *Baptist* leadership' distinctive? In this essay I will interact with some of Nigel Wright's writing on ministry, adding further theological resources - including the Baptist Union's Declaration of Principle, a cautionary Old Testament passage, and some recent work by an Anglican theologian - in attempting to make a balanced assessment of this contemporary trend.

When did we start talking less about 'ministers' and more about 'leaders'? Wright himself identifies two important factors impacting on ministry:[3] the charismatic movement with its emphasis on the gifting and participation of all, and a social and political drift towards a less deferential culture, more informal, better educated, more egalitarian, less hierarchical. Wright suggests that these two factors may not be unconnected, and that is surely correct. Other writers chart these and similar social changes.[4] When these changes are combined with traditional Baptist reflexes – like a certain distrust of hierarchies,[5] especially

---

[1] 'The Leadership of Some and the Ministry of All' is a section heading in the chapter 'Ministers and Members: Ordination and Enabling,' in Nigel G. Wright, *Free Church, Free State: The Positive Baptist Vision* (Milton Keynes: Paternoster, 2005) 160.
[2] Nigel G. Wright, 'Inclusive Representation,' *Baptist Quarterly* 39.4 (October 2001) 165. Here Wright denies that leadership *should* be the dominant paradigm, but implicitly suggests that it has become so for many. [Editor: In the present volume Christopher Ellis and Paul Goodliff also interact with this article.]
[3] Wright, 'Inclusive Representation', 162.
[4] See e.g. Steven J.L. Croft, *Ministry in Three Dimensions: Ordination and Leadership in the Local Church* (London: Darton, Longman and Todd, 2nd ed. 2008) 5ff.
[5] See Wright, 'Inclusive Representation', 167. Cf. Jürgen Moltmann, *The Church in the Power of the Spirit* (London: SCM, 1977) 300.

priestly ones - we find it easier to explain this change in language. As Wright suggests, for some Baptists the term 'minister' when applied to individuals suggests a separation from and an undermining of the 'ministry of the many'.[6] As such, 'leader' might be seen as a more inclusive term than 'minister', including those not ordained to ministry but exercising leadership: a 'leaders' conference' might seem a more inclusive affair than a 'ministers' conference', though it has to be said that exclusion still operates, for not everyone can be a leader either.

In addition to these general cultural changes a body of research suggests that evangelicalism has a peculiar relationship to contemporary culture.[7] While on the one hand using a rhetoric that sounds quite *separated* from culture, in many ways its practices and language *reflect* that culture quite closely. The language of leadership is one example. Steven Croft underlines the extent to which Anglican evangelicals have been more amenable to leadership theory and language than other parts of the church. Baptists are clearly in the evangelical camp here, even if our proclivity for such theory and language has a different basis.[8]

Openness to our culture's language and theories is certainly not straightforwardly problematic, though given much evangelical rhetoric it is certainly interesting. Christians always – to a greater or lesser extent – appropriate aspects of their contemporary culture and, even when this may not be an entirely good thing, God indulges us and works with us. This, I think, is one way of reading 1 Samuel 8. Despite the clear statement that the only king is God the Lord, all around Israel there were nations with kings. That seemed to be the way to do things, if you wanted to be a 'proper nation'.

A church where I was once pastor was built in the 1860s. There are a number of Baptist churches around the country built in a similar style – a cruciform shape, stained glass, central table. This design reflects a theology of church but it also reflects a social aspiration: to be a 'proper church'. The people in 1 Samuel 8 want to be like other nations, to be a proper nation: they want a leader, a king.

---

[6] Wright, *Free Church, Free State,* 180.
[7] E.g. Pete Ward, *Selling Worship: How What we Sing Has Changed the Church* (Paternoster: Milton Keynes, 2005). [Editor: See also the essay by Tidball in this volume.]
[8] Croft, *Ministry,* 22-23.

The very first Baptists themselves appropriated aspects of their contemporary culture in the way they understood themselves to have 'recovered' the marks of the authentic New Testament church. It is no coincidence that the understanding of church marked by the members coming together to discern the mind of Christ developed at precisely the time that early notions of political democracy were circulating among the population. This is not to say that these ideas of participation, equality and so on are not present in the New Testament, just that these particular aspects of the New Testament were what struck the first Baptists as significant, novel, important. All reforming groups have seen slightly different elements of Scripture and pursued different emphases. In doing this they are often influenced by their own cultural context. There is nothing wrong about this, it is inevitable. It is wrong only when we are completely unaware that we are doing it. We have to see as clearly as we can how and where we are being influenced by various cultural factors and build that awareness into our enthusiasms and concerns.

1 Samuel 8 and Lord Acton
Leader language reflects our culture. As the world changes more rapidly than ever, the turn to leaders represents both a positive and a negative: a positive sense of looking to suitably gifted people to take command; a more negative sense of insecurity indicating that we need someone to protect us through change. Leader language also fills a human need. It is not too fanciful to compare our need for leaders with 1 Samuel 8: 'Give us a king like the other nations.' But in that passage we also see some of the problems with leaders, especially those who lead in particular ways. Note the repeated 'takings' of the king: 'He will take your sons ... your daughters ... the best of your fields and vineyards and olive orchards ... one-tenth of your grain and of your vineyards ... your male and female slaves, and the best of your cattle and donkeys ... one-tenth of your flocks, and you shall be his slaves. And in that day you will cry out because of your king ...' (verses 11-18).

Samuel warns the people about the dangers of leadership and it as well to recognise these head on. According to Lord Acton, 'Power tends to corrupt, and absolute power corrupts absolutely.' Acton was a devout Roman Catholic who wrote these words in a letter to an ecclesiastical historian, later an Anglican Bishop, in 1887. He was not referring to the power politics of the state but to ecclesiastical power, to church leadership. The promulgation of papal infallibility in 1870 exercised Acton. Papal infallibility had been informally assumed on previous occasions, but not formally defined until this moment when faith felt under siege from a number of 'modernist' pressures. In protestant circles this same era saw the emergence of fundamentalism: Catholics and Protestants defined their particular kinds of infallibility in the same period.

Acton was troubled by what he saw as an attempt to quash independent thinking and enquiry. Mandell Creighton had urged him to accept papal infallibility because the Pope, like kings, should be judged by different standards to other human beings. Appointed by God, it was believed they would exercise their powers correctly. The parallel to ministers of religion, who believe that they are called by and accountable only to God, is not difficult to see. Acton demurred:

> I cannot accept your canon that we are to judge Pope and King unlike other men with a favourable presumption that they did no wrong. If there is any presumption, it is the other way, against the holders of power, increasing as the power increases. (...) Power tends to corrupt, and absolute power corrupts absolutely. Great men are almost always bad men, even when they exercise influence and not authority: still more when you superadd the tendency or certainty of corruption by authority. There is no worse heresy than that the office sanctifies the holder of it.[9]

These words represent an interesting footnote to 1 Samuel 8. It is as if God through Samuel says, 'power will corrupt your kings – you will be sorry.' Ministers do themselves and their congregations a disservice when they underrate even their meagre power. It can corrupt *them* just as it can corrupt anyone else, and there is more than one way of exercising power inappropriately. Malcolm Grundy, for instance, identifies several problematic styles of leadership: the Narcissist who thrives on the buzz of leading but is insecure and authoritarian when challenged; the Empty Suit who lacks a sense of inner authority and copies others or buys 'off the peg solutions'. They are deeply threatened by shared leadership because people who get too close will see through them.[10] Anyone

---

[9] The text of Acton's letter can be found in John E.E. Dalberg Acton, *Essays on Freedom and Power* (London: Thames and Hudson, 1956) 335-336.
[10] Malcolm Grundy, *What's New in Church Leadership?* (Norwich: Canterbury Press, 2007) 121-122.

who has been in ministry for a while will recognise his figures, and being honest, may even see elements of these patterns in themselves. As with the culture issue, the key is to see what is happening and to work with it rather than to deny it.

The Baptist Union Declaration of Principle is a resource rarely considered in this debate, yet it might provide some Baptist insights on the issues. It affirms that Jesus Christ is the 'sole and absolute' authority in all things relating to faith and practice. Jesus Christ is the leader and the Holy Spirit guides God's people. True leadership, then, comes from God, who alone is the True Leader. Acton highlighted some of the dangers of leadership - what we might call the '1 Samuel 8 factor'. How do we lead in such a way as to try to ensure that God leads, true to the warning behind 1 Samuel 8 and the rest of Scripture, and to our Declaration of Principle? There are several dimensions to a satisfactory answer.

1. Baptist ministers must be authentically themselves before God

A key task for ministerial spirituality is the practicing of openness to God's purposes for us as individuals and for our churches. Ministers ought to be people of prayer, but they must each be so in their own way, as they each seek their own ministerial shape or leadership style. Brian McLaren talks about leadership *models* echoing Grundy's 'Empty Suit' style:

> The word *model* itself is interesting enough in this light (...) Follow the instructions, imitate the picture on the front of the box, and you will be 'successful'. I can smell the glue even as I write. Not that I'm against success. The fact is, I care a lot about it, probably too much. But my biggest complaint with the 'success' models is that we are almost certain not to succeed by obediently (but mindlessly) imitating them.[11]

McLaren argues that some of the most 'successful' evangelical leaders in recent times, Bill Hybels and Rick Warren for instance, became successful through bold innovation and creative synthesis. We can imitate them – but their successful styles earned success by risk-taking and learning from mistakes, not by reproducing a template. For McLaren, personal authenticity is vital. If preaching is

---

[11] Brain McLaren, *The Church on the Other Side* (Grand Rapids: Zondervan, 2000) 111.

truth through personality, leadership works in a similar way. God calls individuals to a particular place to do a particular job – the person and the situation are unique. While others' success may offer clues, mindless imitation risks failing to value what God wants from us – our very selves. Authentic ministry is not like being an Elvis impersonator. Only Elvis can be Elvis, only Warren can be Warren. We might learn a great deal from them, but in the end *we* are who God calls *us* to be.

2. Baptist ministers model their leadership on Jesus

That said, there is one example we should and must follow, one whose word we should and must make flesh: Jesus Christ. Jesus' use of power is in marked contrast to that predicted in 1 Samuel 8. Here is not a power which corrupts but a power which liberates. Wright affirms that Jesus Christ has subverted human patterns of leadership and power: 'Jesus makes it clear that in his community leadership was to be done differently.'[12] Just as Jesus Christ is the true leader, he is also the model for all who would lead in the church. I am sceptical about attempts to distil surprisingly modern leadership patterns and tips from the gospel accounts: they seem hermeneutically naive. But it does seem to me to be possible to identify key themes for leadership from Jesus' ministry. Looming large in any sketch of Jesus' ministry for this purpose will be Mark 10:42-45 ('whoever wishes to become great among you must be your servant') and John 13:3-17 ('I have set you an example'). We become true leaders when we are fully ourselves, shaped by the ministry of Jesus and when we become the leaders God calls us to be in the particular places where we are.

3. Baptist ministers model their leadership on the Trinity

By placing the doctrine of the Trinity right at its centre, the Declaration of Principle points us to another way of focusing on the true leaders, Christ and the Holy Spirit. Paul Fiddes reminds us that 'what we think God is like, and the way we understand *divine* power, will determine all our understandings of power and authority in relationships between pastor and people.'[13] He sees in the Scriptural witness not a divine absolute monarch who demands obedience (perhaps along the lines of the divine right of kings that

---

[12] Wright, *Free Church, Free State*, 159; cf. Moltmann, *Church*, 292.
[13] Paul S. Fiddes, *Tracks and Traces: Baptist Identity in Church and Theology* (Carlisle: Paternoster, 2003) 83-84.

Mandell Creighton assumed) but a God who desires partnership and friendship.[14] The True Leader leads not by domination but in partnership. Whereas Wright works largely from a breadth of New Testament passages, Fiddes works from the doctrine of God as much as from the ministry of Jesus in identifying the nature of true leadership. He suggests that in our participation in the life of the Triune God we are caught up in a constant movement of 'giving and receiving in love, a self-giving of Father, Son and Holy Spirit, each to the other and beyond each other to the world.'[15] Whether we use the language of participation or imitation, what we see is a true leader who invites human leaders into a generous and self-giving love that moves out beyond itself in passionate concern for the other.

Baptist leadership is leadership for mission (again, implied in the Declaration of Principle) because it is a leadership modelled on, or participating in, the leadership of the Triune God. Conversely, we can argue with Moltmann that a 'monotheistic' (as opposed to Trinitarian) notion of God legitimates patterns of domination and hierarchy, resulting in what he calls 'clerical monotheism':[16]

> It is only when the doctrine of the Trinity vanquishes the monotheistic notion of the great universal monarch in heaven, and his divine patriarchs in the world, that earthly rulers, dictators and tyrants cease to find any justifying religious archetypes anymore.[17]

Imitation is the sincerest form of flattery, the saying goes, and it is not surprising that the idea of God in our minds when we worship shapes our own aspirations and behaviours. The similar arguments of Moltmann and Fiddes are that the correct picture of the Triune God is not one of domineering power but of loving self-giving, intimate relationship and outward-moving mission. This is our True Leader.

---

[14] Fiddes, *Tracks*, 96.
[15] Fiddes, *Tracks*, 100.
[16] Jürgen Moltmann, *The Trinity and the Kingdom of God: the Doctrine of God* (London: SCM, 1981) 200ff.
[17] Moltmann, *Trinity*, 197.

4. Baptist ministers never lead alone

The Declaration of Principle speaks of the Spirit's guidance not of individuals but of churches. God's leadership is discerned *collectively*.

> The most substantial change for the minister, and the one which is the most difficult to make, is the necessity to work collaboratively and involve others in the tasks of pastoral care, nurture and mission.[18]

In Baptist congregations shared leadership means a number of overlapping things: one or more ministers, elders, deacons, church meetings, other individuals and groups. At its best, it describes the work of a church members' meeting: prayerfully, carefully, boldly, discerning the mind of Christ, following God's lead at a given moment in a given place. Of course, that does not mean that the church meeting can fulfil this function without itself being led, stimulated, shaped and offered structured prayerful discussion that allows it to take a lead – which is where the leadership of individuals comes in. It needs ministers and others who prepare for meetings and contribute in them, who communicate a vision, or help the congregation articulate a shared vision which is then taken up by individuals and groups to work on. As Fiddes says, the pastor and other leaders are among the resources God gives the church meeting to help it discern the mind of Christ.[19] For that to make any sense those individuals and groups also need to exercise leadership *away* from the meetings.

The pastor will lead as a shepherd – taking the flock to new pastures, nourishing and nurturing, protecting - but the shepherd image, which still has a great deal going for it in our predominantly urban culture, is sometimes a little solitary in feel. The 'leadership of one' can be lonely, isolated and isolating, exposed, vulnerable in the wrong kind of way. Shared leadership pools gifts and skills, expands networks of relationships, releases synergies. It will be informal and formal. Formal when established in proper teams or groups, with proper lines of accountability and appointment so that people can see where power lies and how it is exercised, and by what authority. But individuals can offer informal, Spirit-filled, wise leadership, independent of any office, and so can loose groups of individuals, combining to offer leadership in churches. The group

---

[18] Croft, *Ministry*, 8.
[19] Fiddes, *Tracks*, 86.

who come together to pray and who end up planning a new group for young people; the parents who talk as they wait for their youngsters to finish at Friday night club who end up organising a new sports ministry or a sponsored event to raise money for the local homeless shelter. Baptists are familiar with this tension between 'leadership through office' and the Spirit's unstructured leadership initiatives, and ministers need to be aware of, encourage and enable the leading of others whether it arises formally or informally.

But it is to more formal shared leadership that we need to turn our denominational attention more systematically. Croft cites sketchy evidence that the more familiar Baptist pattern of leadership of one stipendiary minister in each congregation often produces growth.[20] But he also convincingly shows how culturally this model has problems. Its weaknesses must be mitigated even as its strengths are exploited.[21] Baptist ministers have too often functioned as individuals – sometimes using the rhetoric of teams as a kind of fig leaf, but with little reality on the ground to match the high-flown talk. Ministers need to be formed as team players, as individuals secure enough in their own gifting to identify, welcome, nurture and release the gifts of others. College courses are changing to recognise this.

5. Baptist ministers, in leading with others, must know themselves

No one can function properly in a team and work well with others unless they have a sufficient degree of self-awareness. Just as in being true leaders we must be true to ourselves, so to work well with others we must know ourselves. We become more self-aware, strangely, by being with others and reflecting on why that is sometimes difficult and sometimes exciting. Self-awareness grows from other-awareness.[22] I never feel more Baptist than when in an ecumenical context - despite being an enthusiastic ecumenist! This is true of church leadership too. Ministers need to be secure enough not to envy others their gifts or simply to want to copy them; and they need to be secure enough in their own contribution to allow it sometimes to be overlooked.

---

[20] Croft, *Ministry*, 222.
[21] Croft, *Ministry*, chapter 1.
[22] Fiddes, *Tracks*, 100.

6. Baptist ministers must not adopt the language of leadership uncritically

The switch from 'minister' to 'leader' is not a neutral one. There is rarely a direct equivalence of words across languages. Talking about leaders rather than ministers has some advantages, but something is also lost in translation. Leadership language, as we use it with reference to ministry now, is largely influenced by a body of literature and a way of thinking that derives from management theory. The Church and its ministers have much to learn from such theory but theological reflection upon it is also vital. It is not the absorption of our culture's ideas that creates problems – it is the uncritical absorption of those ideas. This might be the point to note that one word that does not appear in the New Testament is the Greek word *archōn*, the word for a leader, in fact, in business politics or industry![23] Wright also expresses reservations about leadership language and the management theory that comes with it:

> I suspect the choice of the term 'leader' unintentionally skews expectation in a 'managerial' direction. (...) Managerial skills are to be valued and prized... However, ministers are not primarily managers of organizations, or if they are they should not be. (...) While acknowledging the crucial skills of leadership the language of 'ministry' remains more appropriate as the dominant paradigm for the task.[24]

A trenchant critic of management ideas in the church is Stephen Pattison and a number of his sharpest essays on the subject have recently been gathered.[25] He explores, for instance, the undeclared assumptions and 'creeds' of managers, leaders and those who write on the subjects. Are these undeclared beliefs Christian? He warns of the dangers of accepting management assumptions uncritically and of blunting the church's prophetic voice. Management ideology, he argues, is concerned to eliminate risk (something which the church may not always applaud) and gives the misleading impression that everything can be controlled.

---

[23] Croft, *Ministry*, 26; John Finney, *Understanding Leadership* (London: Daybreak, 1989) 59.
[24] Wright, 'Inclusive Representation', 165; cf. Eugene Peterson, *Working the Angles* (Grand Rapids: Eerdmans, 1993) 1ff.
[25] See the section 'On Organisation and Management' in Stephen Pattison, *The Challenge of Practical Theology* (London: Jessica Kingsley, 2007).

He has cautionary words for churches who have adopted 'mission statements' and similar management tools. These, he suggests, reflect the process of McDonaldization and its tendencies to efficiency, calculability, predictability and control. None of this is to say that management theory and leadership theory do not have much to offer – as Pattison himself admits. It is, however, to urge greater caution than is sometimes in evidence in churches and in ministers.[26] Is there a theological tool which will help us to receive these leadership ideas critically?

7. If Baptist ministers are leaders, they are 'servant leaders'

It is often suggested that the problems which follow from seeing 'ministers' as 'leaders' can be adequately addressed by the prefixing of 'servant' ('servant leader'). Does the prefix 'servant' put the 'minister' back into leadership? It does, and it does not.

One mark of leadership we can infer from the Declaration of Principle is that leaders will be forgiven and forgiving people who bear the mark of humility: the church is made up of those who have been baptised, and those who are baptised have shown repentance. Good leaders know themselves as imperfect people who make mistakes. At our best we learn from them, and the parable of the Unforgiving Steward (Matthew 18:21-35) should never be far from our minds. We are people who make mistakes and we work with people who make mistakes. When they do so we do not give up on them or stop trusting them or delegating to them. This is the way God deals with us too.

If we model ministry on the ministry of Jesus, the one who came 'not to be served but to serve' (Mark 10:45), the shape of ministry is likely to be servant-shaped. This much is actually assumed in our historic vocabulary. The word 'minister' derives from a Latin word from which we get the term 'servant'. Speaking of service immediately suggests humility. There is a difficult balance to be observed here for the *language* of servanthood can easily be adopted without its substance being evident. As Wright says:

> Those who exercise power over others often clothe themselves with ideology and present themselves in a

---

[26] See also Martyn Percy, *The Salt of the Earth: Religious Resilience in a Secular Age* (London: Sheffield Academic Press, 2001) 341ff.

benevolent light; but the inner reality remains the exercise of domination.[27]

Stephen Sykes makes a similar point indicating that 'there is ... some danger in an authority cloaking itself with the ideology of service, and still, by skilful manipulation, silencing critics and setting them on the margins.'[28] Because one fears that some ministers may lead by domination or manipulation while mouthing platitudes about servanthood, these are stern but necessary warnings: use of the language of servant leadership proves nothing; only the reality counts. The need for self-awareness, for an adequate spirituality, is again evident.

But equally uncomfortably we have to recognise the equal and opposite error. Sykes is an Anglican Bishop and one might expect him to say this, but he complains that some are too squeamish in their assessment of power, its language and its exercise. Bishops, of course, need sometimes to make tough calls. They are part of a system which Moltmann labels 'clerical monotheism' – one God, one bishop, and so on, in a chain of command from the 'top' down. But in the real world, Sykes tells us, tough calls have sometimes to be made by people appointed to make them and to live with their decisions. Talk of servant leadership cannot be used as a way of escaping responsibility for the difficult decisions that must be made by ministers – though there are very few indeed that cannot in some way be shared decisions.

The significant contribution here in terms of leadership ideas is, of course, Robert Greenleaf's work on servant leadership. Greenleaf formulated these ideas while working in a major American corporation and published his groundbreaking essay in 1970. It seems difficult to believe that his ideas were not influenced in some way by Christian ones. For Greenleaf, the leader is first of all a servant: leadership is one way of being a servant; servant is the proper way of being a leader. The servant has a number of leadership tasks, according to Greenleaf. One he tests with these questions:

> Do those being served grow as persons; do they, while being served, become healthier, wise, freer, more autonomous, more likely themselves to become servants?

---

[27] Wright, *Free Church, Free State*, 159-160; cf. Moltmann, *Church*, 300.
[28] Stephen Sykes, *Power and Christian Theology* (London: Continuum, 2006) 73.

> And what is the effect on the least privileged in society; will she or he benefit, or, at least, not be further deprived?[29]

The 'least privileged' might mean, in a church context, those in danger of being pushed to the margins, unheard and unvalued. He pushes these ideas further still:

> No one will knowingly be hurt by the action, directly or indirectly ... the servant will reject the 'utilitarian' position, which accepts a very large gain ... at the cost of a small but real hurt to some. ... would reject the rapid accomplishment of any desirable ... goal by coercion in favour of the slower process of persuasion – even when no identifiable person was hurt by the coercion. (...) Hurting people, only a few, is not accepted as legitimate cost of doing business.[30]

This is challenging for leaders who talk about the inevitable casualties of change.

Greenleaf's concern about the use of power leads us back to 1 Samuel 8 and towards Lord Acton. He distinguishes carefully between coercive and persuasive power, and manipulation. Power is always to be accompanied by accountability: 'No one, absolutely no one', he says, 'is to be entrusted with the operational use of power without the close oversight of [fully functioning trustees].'[31] Our Baptist patterns ought to exemplify these strengths: the accountability of church meetings; the need to persuade church meetings to adopt significant change. This is, we recall, Fiddes' point about the way of God with the world, and how this divine way of working must also be ours.

But the servant has at least one other significant function in Greenleaf's writings, which again connects with the Declaration of Principle. Greenleaf asks, what is an organisation *for*, what is its mission? The church's mission is really God's mission: the *missio Dei*. But how that is to be worked out in each local church requires some work in prayer and discernment. It cannot be read off some national template or from the latest best-seller. Given that 'it is the duty of every disciple to bear personal witness to the Gospel of Jesus Christ, and to take part in the evangelisation of the world', leadership among Baptists is *leadership for mission*.

---

[29] Robert K. Greenleaf, *The Power of Servant Leadership* (San Francisco: Berrett-Koehler, 1988) 43.
[30] Greenleaf, *Servant*, 43-45.
[31] Greenleaf, *Servant*, 48.

Leadership and vision are often, and rightly, mentioned together. Leaders should offer insights to the congregation as they seek together to discern their part in God's mission in the world. But leaders should rarely communicate a full vision, complete in every part. That would bring problems of ownership, and almost certainly involve marginalisation or plagiarism in the process! A key role of leaders is to be servants in the process of discernment. They give the congregation the opportunity, the vocabulary and other resources with which, together, a vision can be discerned. Servant leaders help the people articulate the vision God is giving them. Perhaps they offer key pieces which hold it together and integrate the parts, but the vision for the community comes up from within the community at the leading of the Spirit. In language that we don't often use in church, the servant leader is the servant of the organisation's learning process.[32]

This vision cannot be bought in from outside simply off the peg – churches, like individual leaders, have to be *themselves*. Baptist churches are autonomous communities. We protect our autonomy fiercely when someone tells us what to do; we give it away cheaply when we simply buy off the peg solutions to complex missiological questions. Because we are *interdependent* communities as well as *independent* ones, we will learn from one another and from the wider Church in authentic ways, and be open to the respected leadership of some from beyond the local congregation in our associating.

Baptist ministers are servant leaders in three dimensions

Nigel Wright has not been alone in helpfully discussing matters of 'office' and 'order' in relation to ministry.[33] While the New Testament's terminology is fluid and should not be pressed to yield one order that holds for every time and situation,[34] it is generally agreed that three different terms are used for patterns of ministry: deacon (*diakonos* – in pastoral care and service), presbyter, priest or elder (*presbuteros* – in teaching and preaching and care for the local congregation) and bishop or overseer (*episkopos* – in

---

[32] See Thomas Hawkins, *The Learning Congregation* (Louisville: Westminster John Knox, 1997) - an interesting application of another piece of management theory to the life of the church!
[33] E.g. Wright, 'Inclusive Representation', 162ff; Wright, *Free Church, Free State*, 160ff; Fiddes, *Tracks*, 88ff; Paul S. Fiddes, *A Leading Question* (London: Baptist Publications, no year [1983]).
[34] Moltmann, *Church*, 306.

oversight; see e.g. 1 Timothy 3:8; 5:17; 3:1). In Episcopalian traditions these have become three distinct, even hierarchical, orders of ordained ministry. Historically Baptists have been very much aware of these offices. Typically, with a distinct wariness of a separated order of *episkopoi*, we have collapsed the second and third order into one another,[35] as in the Second London Confession of 1677 which states that 'the Officers appointed by Christ to be chosen and set apart by the Church ... to be continued to the end of the World, are Bishops or Elders and Deacons'.[36] Here the overseer and the presbyter become one - what we would normally now call 'pastor'. In part this is a recognition that in Baptist understanding the oversight of the church is shared at least between pastor and church meeting, and also through our various patterns of associating. But as Fiddes notes, the more recent development of elders to share oversight with the (ordained) minister suggests that for Baptists 'there is no absolute boundary'[37] between these various forms of ministry.

Steven Croft charts the various leadership themes, practices and motifs through the Old Testament and suggests that in the ministry of Jesus and the gift of the Spirit to his disciples these various elements might be said to pass through a prism, emerging in the life of the early church in charismatic ministries which then settle into the pattern of *diakonos, presbuteros* and *episkopos*.[38] He then varies the traditional Anglican position by suggesting that these three patterns are all embodied in the ministry of a parish priest – that the local vicar is deacon, presbyter and overseer simultaneously. This he calls 'ministry in three dimensions'. It may be useful to recall that Anglican priests are ordained deacon before they are ordained priest; a bishop carries these two ordinations with him into his ministry. In summary, Croft suggests that the pastor is a *deacon* in simple acts of service, care for the wider community and competent administration; is a *presbyter* in preaching, teaching, administering the sacraments and praying for the sick; is an *overseer* in formulating vision, dealing with conflict, working with whole communities and in handling safeguards and legal matters. It is important to note that 'oversight' includes clear elements of leadership, though these are

---

[35] Fiddes, *Tracks*, 90-91.
[36] Quoted from William L. Lumpkin, *Baptist Confessions of Faith* (Chicago: Judson, 1959) 287.
[37] Fiddes, *Tracks*, 92-93.
[38] Croft, *Ministry*, 39.

also present at the presbyteral level. Croft has much more to say, but the drift ought to be clear. All three dimensions of ministry are present in the pastor, and this is a helpful way of speaking about Baptist ministry too. It allows us to place 'service' and 'leadership' in a constructive theological model for ministry, holding all elements in creative tension.

The initial pattern, the diaconal, is present in and through all the others – rather like Russian dolls nesting inside larger dolls, perhaps. Everything the minister does should bear the mark of *diakonia*, service – whether ferrying someone to a hospital appointment, teaching in a house group, monitoring child protection or articulating the vision of the congregation. All are opportunities for servant leadership, a ministry in three dimensions. This model enables us to adapt critically management and other theories, and to ground our ministerial practice in Scripture and the story of the Church. Baptist ministers are leaders in that they are diaconal, presbyteral overseers.

Much of the negative reaction to talk of leadership in the denomination can be explained by a perception that alien ideas are being uncritically adopted, and the suspicion that Scripture and the story of the Church are being marginalised. In this essay I have worked from the Declaration of Principle and a biblical passage not often used in discussions of leadership. I have suggested that the language of leadership is taken primarily from our cultural context but that critically done this can have benefits. All true ministerial leadership is modelled on the True Leader and will be shared leadership in various ways. Servant leadership is most helpfully understood by using Croft's discourse of ministry in three dimensions so that Biblical *diakonia* can be held in tension with other necessary elements, and so that all aspects of ministry can be seen to be shot through with the most basic, diaconal service.

Something will come of nothing: on *A Theology of the Dark Side*

Paul S. Fiddes

Nothingness and its connections

'Nothing will come of nothing: speak again...', says Lear to Cordelia in Shakespeare's tragedy, just before he disinherits her for refusing to flatter him as he wanted.[1] His dismissive statement repeats a truism of Greek philosophy, but many of Shakespeare's audience would have known that this tag denies the Christian doctrine of creation from nothing (*creatio ex nihilo*), and that it is one more false conception to be credited to Lear's heavy account. Unlike the Platonic and Aristotelian assumption of the eternity of matter and the eternity of mind, Christian faith has affirmed that God created the material universe from nothing alongside God's own self. Something did indeed come from nothing. Similarly, the Christian intellectual tradition, following Augustine, has regarded evil as strictly 'nothing', having no ontological standing of its own. Indeed, this concept has been connected with creation from nothing, as we shall shortly see. Just as God made something from nothing in creation, it has been the good news of Christianity that God can make even the 'nothing' of evil into God's servant, and can still bring something beneficial out of evil events that God has not planned or intended: 'in everything God works together for good with those who love him' (Romans 8:28). Something can come even of the nothingness that is evil.

Now, Nigel Wright, whom we are justly honouring in this volume, has long been fascinated by the theme of the 'nothingness' of evil. His unpublished MTh thesis at Glasgow University was on the subject of evil as *Das Nichtige* (nothingness) in the thought of Karl Barth,[2] and further reflection on this idea has emerged in his published writings since then, especially in his book *A Theology of the Dark Side* (2002). This itself was a revised version of his earlier book *The Fair Face of Evil* (1989), published not long after the completion of his MTh thesis, and incorporating

---

[1] Shakespeare, *King Lear*, I.1.90.
[2] Nigel G. Wright, *Karl Barth and Evangelicalism: A study of the relationship between Karl Barth and the evangelical tradition with particular reference to the concept of 'nothingness'* (Unpublished MTh Thesis, University of Glasgow, 1987).

some of its ideas in a popular form. My intention here is not to explore the thesis itself, but to reflect on the two versions of the book, along with a number of associated books and articles, focusing on the theme of evil as 'nothingness'.

Such a study, esoteric as it may seem at first, is in fact connected with the wider range of Nigel Wright's thought as surveyed in this volume. Theological convictions about the nature of evil and its overcoming by God in Christ are at the heart of his work on the relation between Church and state, with its consideration of the nature of 'principalities and powers'. They are also highly relevant to his sympathetic critique of aspects of the charismatic renewal movement, with its concern for freeing people from the oppression of evil powers. It is a mistake to regard *A Theology of the Dark Side* simply as a 'survey of views on evil', as does one reviewer.[3] It is a remarkable instance of the way that good systematic theology can connect Christian doctrines not only with each other but also with the concerns of the surrounding culture, which in this case is often both fascinated by co-called 'demonic' phenomena and quick to express a sense of protest about suffering in the world. It is no mean achievement to write a theological work which connects the problem of suffering, an assessment of the reality of the demonic, and the place of church in politics, and to do so in a way that is 'popular theology' in the best sense, both critical and accessible. It is the concept of evil as nothingness, I suggest, that links these topics, as well as Wright's theological reflection on creation, atonement in Christ and the mission of the Church today.

While expressing appreciation for Nigel Wright's creative thinking in this area, he will not be surprised to find that I am taking the opportunity in analysing his work to make my own suggestions about developing the theme that 'something can come of nothing'. We have already engaged twice in public conversation about 'a theology of the dark side', and I am delighted now to continue this debate in print, in order to celebrate his distinguished ministry in church and college over many years.

---

[3] Review by Joseph L. Castleberry, *Religious Studies Review* 32 (2006) 177.

Nothingness and the Satan

Nigel Wright's basic conviction about evil is that it is strictly 'nothing'.[4] It is neither a created thing nor an eternal force, and has no 'ontological' reality – that is, it has no place of its own in the order of being. As Augustine taught, its metaphysical status is merely that of *privatio boni*, the absence of the good, the darkness that comes from turning away from the light. It is 'nothing' (*mē ōn*), not because it is powerless, but because its power is entirely parasitic, fastening on to those things that do have being, and drawing life and energy from them.[5] In particular, while having no 'ontological' reality of its own, it occupies an ontological ground in the freedom of created beings. It is their mis-use of freedom, turning away from God, which gives evil the opportunity to take hold and exist in its own way. Barth's concept of evil as *Das Nichtige* continues this ancient theme. *Das Nichtige* ('nothingness') is a power that sets itself in opposition to God but is entirely negative, without any right to exist and without any validity. Its very existence is a perversion, utterly unlike the existence of either God or created beings. Nothing positive can be said or thought about it. It is real, but has no right to be.[6]

Now, the next step in Wright's thought is to transfer all this talk about nothingness from evil itself to the figure of Satan, as the quintessence of evil. Satan too is real but is strictly 'nothing'. Satan must not be given the dignity of a place in the order of being that God grants to creation. Wright moves easily from the language of evil as 'nothing' to Satan:

> The point is that the *devil* has no legitimacy. He does not have a place assigned to him by God. If he exists he exists in violation of all that is right, true and legitimate. *Evil* cannot be assigned an acceptable place of dignity within God's universe – it has no such place, it has no right to exist. It is total and complete aberration. (...) For this reason the *devil* is not something or someone to be believed in.[7]

We cannot then believe in an 'ontological devil'. This is a deeply significant move on Wright's part, and nearly everything else about

---

[4] Nigel G. Wright, *A Theology of the Dark Side. Putting the Power of Evil in its Place* (Carlisle: Paternoster, 2002) 26-32, 37-42.
[5] Augustine, *De Civitate Dei* 11.9; *Enchiridion* 4.13-14.
[6] Karl Barth, *Church Dogmatics* III.3 (Edinburgh: T. & T. Clark, 1960) 289-313.
[7] Wright, *Theology of the Dark Side*, 31.

the confrontation of human beings with the dark powers stems from it. Partly, no doubt, Wright has followed Barth here, who sees a real Satan and real demons as the 'form' that *Das Nichtige* takes. In the cross of Jesus, nothingness is exposed as the 'adversary' and as 'the evil one which is also the destructive factor of evil and death, that stands in sinister conflict against the creature and its creator, not merely as an idea ...'[8] But Wright's stress that Satan is strictly 'nothing' also reflects his practical, pastoral concern to 'take the power of darkness seriously without taking it too seriously'. The whole point of his book, he explains, is to reflect on the theme that 'It is wrong to reject the existence of the powers of darkness but it is equally wrong to believe in them in the wrong way'.[9] We must 'disbelieve in the devil' or 'believe against the devil'; that is, we cannot place the same belief in Satan as we place in God, which is a belief with overtones of faith. The intention of the book is to offer a way of thinking about the devil that 'might deprive the devil of the subliminal respect from Christians and give the glory to God'.[10] Wright obviously has a target in the kind of sloppy thinking that says, 'if you don't believe in Satan then you can't believe in God either', where God and Satan are characters in a class of supernatural beings. This, he judges, is 'close to blasphemy'.[11]

Satan, then, cannot be a person, Wright stresses, because persons exist in relationship and make others personal. God, by contrast, is supremely personal. Nor can Satan be easily classified as an individual, since individuals have boundaries and strict limits, and Satan is a pervasive power which is co-existent with all humanity. We have already seen, further, that Satan has no place in the realm of being. For this reason Wright prefers the designation 'power of darkness'. Yet he admits that, due to the inadequacy of human words, it also seems necessary to use personal language about Satan as 'a tentative and limited analogy', in order to express the intelligence and the agency of evil.[12]

---

[8] Barth, *Church Dogmatics* III.3, 312.
[9] Wright, *Theology of the Dark Side*, 15.
[10] Wright, *Theology of the Dark Side*, 16.
[11] Wright, *Theology of the Dark Side*, 31.
[12] Wright, *Theology of the Dark Side*, 28-30. However, on page 73 Wright (following Tom Noble) also suggests that Satan might be an individual without being a person.

Satan is both the personification of evil and also an objective reality. It is clear that, for Wright, Satan is like evil in existing as 'nothing'. How then does this Satan (and also the lesser powers of demons) arise? Here Wright offers two possibilities. First, the devil and demons might be understood according to the Christian tradition of fallen angels. Wright suggests that 'nothingness' expresses well what an angelic power might *become* if it departed from obedience to God. If angelic powers were to commit an act of aberration out of their own free will, it 'would deprive [them] of their true existence and would cause them to exist only in a negative and chaotic form, feeding parasitically on the good and ordered creation.'[13] Effectively, they would become nothing by falling victim to the nothingness of evil. They were once created beings, but have now forfeited this status. Wright acknowledges that Scripture supplies very little evidence for the idea of fallen angels, and observes that Barth denies the idea in his own treatment of *Das Nichtige*. However, in *The Fair Face of Evil* Wright inclines to this explanation as the best on offer.[14] In *A Theology of the Dark Side* he inclines against it, in favour of another explanation. He now prefers the idea that the Satan is a projection out of human fallenness; the fall of humanity into disobedience was the point when evil as the power of death and darkness increased its strength by feeding on estranged human life, and so was 'the moment when the devil as a powerful adversary begins to be constructed.'[15] Satan is a 'mythic personification of collective human evil', though Wright stresses that it is the language and not the reality that is mythical.[16]

For this insight, Wright credits an article by Tom Noble,[17] published in a volume in which he himself had contributed a paper on 'Charismatic Interpretations of the Demonic'. However, Noble's account is essentially that of Walter Wink, while combining it with a stress on the objective reality of Satan in a more unambiguous way than Wink does himself. Wright draws extensively on the work of Wink, citing his verdict that:

---

[13] Wright, *Theology of the Dark Side*, 64.
[14] Nigel G. Wright, *The Fair Face of Evil. Putting the Power of Darkness in its Place* (London: Marshall Pickering, 1989) 62-65, 68.
[15] Wright, *Theology of the Dark Side*, 158, cf. 70-73.
[16] Wright, *Theology of the Dark Side*, 71.
[17] Tom Noble, 'The Spirit World: A Theological Approach' in A.N.S. Lane (ed.), *The Unseen World: Christian Reflections on Angels, Demons and the Heavenly Realm* (Carlisle: Paternoster, 1996) 214-220.

> Satan thus becomes the symbol of the spirit of an entire society alienated from God, the great system of mutual support in evil, the spirit of persistent self-deification blown wide. (...) Satan is the real interiority of a society that idolatrously pursues its own enhancement as the highest good.[18]

Wink's interpretation of the dark powers is that they are interior to human structures, whether these be social, economic, religious or political. Spiritual powers are the 'innermost essence' of earthly realities and have no separate existence from their manifestation in them.[19] Evil draws its negative strength and energy by preying on the energy of sin to be found in human life and its corporate structures. There is some ambiguity about how much objective reality Wink himself attributes to this 'interiority', but Noble and Wright are clear that Satan is 'a supreme power of evil' which, while drawing its strength and perverse vitality from human wickedness, is projected as a *hypostasis* ('distinct reality') out of it.[20] The same can be said, to a lesser extent, of the powers called 'demons'. Spiritual powers cannot be simply *reduced* to human structures, or even to their essence, but the two exist in symbiotic relation with each other.

We shall return later to this duality between structures and spiritual powers, but for the moment we may observe that this second explanation of the origin of the Satan is more congruent with the Satan's character as 'nothingness' than the first. Wright explains that 'Without a created ontology, [Satan] is none the less real, but in the same way that a vacuum or black hole or death are real.'[21] If Satan is a fallen angel then he *was* at some point a created being, and – as Wright points out – should therefore be open to being redeemed along with other creatures. Neither of these aspects fits 'nothingness'. By the time of writing *A Theology of the Dark Side* Wright has come to a decision about the origin of Satan. He is now more consistent with his highly creative move to apply the logic of evil as 'nothing' to the devil and demons. However, I suggest that the reader may find the explanation of the

---

[18] Walter Wink, *Unmasking the Powers. The Invisible Forces that Determine Human Existence* (Philadelphia: Fortress Press, 1986) 70.
[19] Walter Wink, *Naming the Powers. The Language of Power in the New Testament* (London: Marshall Pickering, 1984) 104-108.
[20] Wright, *Theology of the Dark Side*, 72.
[21] Wright, *Theology of the Dark Side*, 70.

first edition of this work still exerting both a strong presence and an influence in the second, and we shall later have to ask how much it has actually been 'exorcised' from the text.

Nothingness and necessity

If the origin of Satan lies in being a construct, albeit a real one, of fallen human society, can we say more about the origin of evil itself as nothing? In this account evil must, after all, precede the rise of Satan, taking its opportunity in human freedom. Wright comments on two attempts to account for the origin of 'nothingness', those of Karl Barth and Jürgen Moltmann.

Barth's explanation is that the 'Nothingness' does not exist by the positive will of God, but as a result of God's *not* willing it. In saying 'yes' to creation, God uttered an implied 'no' to what would destroy creation, and since even the 'no' is a potent word of God it gives rise to the realm of nothingness. It is God's action on his left hand rather than the right, but 'On this basis it really "is".'[22] Moltmann's explanation relies on the Jewish mystical idea of the *zimsum*, or the 'contraction' of God in the act of creation. The idea goes that since nothing exists outside God, God must withdraw from God's self in order to produce a space of 'nothingness' from which to create *ex nihilo*. The result is a space which is 'God-forsaken', and so a hostile 'nothingness' comes into being which negates God, and which persists in creation until Christ enters the God-forsaken place in the cross and overcomes it.[23]

Wright suggests that we can learn from both accounts that God's act of creation has necessary consequences that *involve* evil, but he criticises them for implying that evil itself is a direct and necessary outcome. It seems difficult to maintain the goodness of God if evil is a necessary accompaniment to creation. He maintains, rightly in my view, that the necessary result of creation is not evil itself but the *possibility* of evil, and so a *threat* to creation.[24] Here he refers aptly to the description of human existence given by Reinhold Niebuhr, in which created beings live in a state of tension between their freedom and their finite limits (such as time and death), and so become anxious.[25] They are put

---

[22] Barth, *Church Dogmatics* III.3, 351-352.
[23] Jürgen Moltmann, *God in Creation: An Ecological Doctrine of Creation* (London: SCM, 1985) 85-91.
[24] Wright, *Theology of the Dark Side*, 50, 66.
[25] Reinhold Niebuhr, *The Nature and Destiny of Man* (London: Nisbet, 1943) Vol. 1, 191-198.

in a 'testing environment' in which evil is possible: there is the temptation to resolve their anxiety in some other way than trust in God – for example by putting their security in themselves or in things that are less than God. We can read the story of Adam and Eve in the primeval garden in this way, rather than as living in the perfect environment envisaged by Augustine. Sin, concludes Niebuhr, 'posits itself' in this testing situation.

Strangely, Wright does not go on to refer to Niebuhr's comment that sin is 'inevitable, but not in such a way as to fit into the category of natural necessity.'[26] It is, we might say, *practically inevitable* but not *logically necessary*. This statement is realistic about the kind of pressure that is put on a free personality living under tension; given human weakness it seems not just possible but highly likely that anxiety will lead to fallenness. In this practical inevitability there is a very fine difference between possibility and necessity, and to maintain it requires an element of paradox. But, since evil is strictly 'nothing', we can never produce a rational account of its origin; some paradox will always be present. Paul Tillich likewise avers that existence is bound to be estranged, but that this is simply the 'original fact – that it has the character of a leap and not of structural necessity'.[27] These considerations underline the responsibility God has for making the kind of creation in which evil is such a real possibility, and we will return to this in thinking about theodicy.

In line with the idea of creation as a 'testing environment', Wright is attracted (in the second edition of his book) by yet another explanation of the origin of evil as 'nothing'. He refers to the proposal by Robert Cook, again in the volume entitled *The Unseen World*, that creation is under a constant threat of collapsing back into chaos. Creation has been brought out of chaos by God, but an element of chaos persists, like a 'black noise' from the moment of the beginning of the universe.[28] Wright stresses that collapse, which is evil, is not necessary but is always a possibility. In fact this proposal by Cook has a long tradition in Christian theology, which neither Cook nor Wright appears to notice. Augustine had proposed that, just because the world has

---

[26] Niebuhr, *Nature and Destiny of Man*, Vol. 1, 279.
[27] Paul Tillich, *Systematic Theology* (Combined volume; Welwyn: Nisbet, 1968) Vol. 2, 50.
[28] Robert Cook, 'Devils and Manticores: Plundering Jung for a Plausible Demonology', in Lane (ed.), *The Unseen World*, 180-182. See Wright, *Theology of the Dark Side*, 68-69.

been raised by God from nothing, created beings only have to turn away from God to slip back towards nothing. This slipping back is a hostile kind of nothingness – *mē ōn* – as distinct from the absolute nothing – *ouk ōn* – from which they have been created.[29] The nothing of creation *ex nihilo* is not evil, but the nothingness of turning from God certainly is. We might observe here that Moltmann's proposal about the 'God-forsaken space' confuses one kind of nothingness with another.

Now, Wright finds this threat of a collapse to chaos (or Augustine's fall to nothingness) to be an explanation for the kind of evil which is attributable to human free decision, often called 'moral evil'. The threat of a return to chaos characterises an environment in which human beings freely turn from God and so give evil a chance to 'posit itself'.[30] The question is *why* human persons should use their freedom in this way, a question which baffled Augustine entirely, since he envisaged Adam as created in a state of bliss and perfection with no good reason to slip away from the Good towards nothingness. He was able to fall, but why should he bother? We begin to see an answer if human beings are created not perfect but immature, intended for a process of growth and development, as Irenaeus proposes, as evolution implies, and as Wright accepts. However, to make sense of this argument, we need some such paradoxical statement as that of Niebuhr's 'inevitability', stressing the unbearable nature of the pressure back towards chaos. Perhaps, in insisting on mere 'possibility', Wright is anxious to lighten the weight of blame that might lie on the Creator, though he does recognise once that 'God is not without responsibility'.[31]

Nothingness and the problem of evil

So far we have been tracing, with the help of Wright, the preconditions for the emergence of evil in human decisions, or 'moral evil'. Here he adopts the so-called 'free-will defence' of the existence of evil,[32] whose argument runs as follows. God's purpose in creating the universe was to make a world of personal beings with whom he could enter into a relationship. For them to be real persons they must have been created free to do either

---

[29] Augustine, *De Civitate Dei* 12.7-8; *De Libero Arbitrio* 3.1.2.
[30] Wright, *Theology of the Dark Side*, 68-69.
[31] Wright, *Theology of the Dark Side*, 66.
[32] Wright, *Theology of the Dark Side*, 83-86.

good or evil; the only other option was a world of puppets and robots. If doing right is to have any meaning, there must be the alternative of doing wrong (evil), with all the suffering this entails.

With Wright, I consider this to be the most adequate – or least inadequate – kind of *intellectual* theodicy. It has, however, a limited reach into the problem of evil, as he admits and as we shall see. There is, for instance, one notable deficiency with this theory: there appears to have been evil in creation before humanity develops. The science of evolution shows us a natural world in which there is death, decay, waste and animal pain – nature 'red in tooth and claw' – before human beings even appear on the scene. This is often called 'natural evil', and it seems to persist in human life as causes of suffering that are nothing to do with human moral choices – for example in earthquakes, floods and harmful bacteria.

At this point Wright insists that we need to distinguish between evil and what Barth calls the 'shadow-side' of creation. There is a difference between the 'nothingness' which is hostile to God, and a 'negative side' of a good creation which is given by God. According to Barth, the shadow includes dark hours, failure, tears, age, loss, decay and death.[33] The shadow does not jeopardise the goodness of creation, but is intended by God to prompt human beings to depend on him and to provide a context in which they can grow and develop as persons. The idea of the 'shadow' is akin to the philosophical concept of 'instrumental evil', but it is limited to events that only appear harmful and difficult on first sight, which are ultimately beneficial, and which are misnamed as evil. Even death, as God originally intended it, argues Barth (and Wright with him), is part of the God-given shadow. But there is also evil which is not of this character, which is *really* destructive ('nothingness') and which may hide itself behind the shadow (the 'negative'). Now, to return to so-called 'natural evil' which preceded human moral evil and still persists in the world, Wright judges that 'the majority' of this is in fact the shadow-side of creation and not evil at all.[34]

Indeed, in a jointly-written essay on 'Suffering' in 1997, Wright implies that *all* so-called natural evil, and so *all* disturbance, 'ugliness' and pain in nature before the human fall, is of the

---

[33] Barth, *Church Dogmatics* III.3, 296-302. See Wright, *Theology of the Dark Side*, 92-97.
[34] Wright, *Theology of the Dark Side*, 93.

shadow kind, and is not to be confused with evil itself.[35] Moreover, he roots the origin of the shadow in the freedom given by God to the natural world to 'engage in creative interaction with God', to 'make itself' and to 'bring forth new possibilities'. This freedom of nature is characterised by such aspects as randomness, chance, unpredictability and spontaneity.[36] By the time of *Theology of the Dark Side*, however, Wright evidently thinks that it is too simple to identify all pre-human conflict and disturbance as the God-given 'shadow'. He now suggests, tentatively, that the freedom of nature is also a tendency to collapse back into chaos, and that this is the occasion for 'deviation', 'wrong turns' and 'aberration' – i.e. real evil:

> It might be possible to argue that a process of deviation leading to suffering was already at work in nature prior to human beings. If nature has its own kind of freedom to explore its God-given potential by means of development and evolutionary processes, this opens up the possibility of wrong turns and wrong developments as part of this freedom. If creation itself is pressured by the possibility of collapse back into the chaos then this could have an effect upon creation.[37]

This is, in my view, a key perception and deserves a great deal more expansion, especially reflection on what might be the character of 'freedom' in nature. If this is only the randomness and unpredictability of natural processes, then it looks as if the collapse back into nothingness in the case of nature (as distinct from the collapse in human life) will be a matter of sheer necessity and not just possibility or even probability. Wrong turns are bound to happen. We have lost the idea that evil as nothingness takes its opportunity in the freedom of creatures as they *turn away* from the purpose of God. I suggest then that the origin of natural evil lies in the fact that the whole of creation has drifted (or 'fallen') from the divine purpose and does not function exactly as God intends. This only makes sense if nature has the capacity, at every level and in its own way, to respond to the creative lure of God, who calls out a response from it.

---

[35] Nigel Wright and Sheila Smith, 'Suffering' in Ernest Lucas (ed.), *Christian Healing. What Can We Believe?* (London: Lynx, 1997) 123, 125-126, 132-133.
[36] Wright and Smith, 'Suffering', 124-125.
[37] Wright, *Theology of the Dark Side*, 93.

If the world is an organic community, then all its members work together, affecting each other. If human beings are able to respond to God, then it is not unreasonable to think that there must be something at least akin to response to God at all levels of creation, some 'family-likeness' within the cosmos. There is more freedom than can be accounted for as 'randomness' or 'unpredictability'. Even if we cannot describe exactly how this relationship between God and the natural world works, we do have various kinds of language to point to the mystery. Process theology offers one kind of language, in which all entities in the world have the capacity for feeling enjoyment, and all can reach after satisfaction through 'prehending' each other and God.[38] While thorough-going adherents of process theology take this picture of the world as a scientific description, I suggest that it may be better to regard it as metaphor, pointing to an inexpressible underlying reality. The vision of the whole environment being in some way alive and responsive strikes some chords with the biblical understanding of God's relationship to the natural world. According to the Old Testament, God makes covenant not only with human beings but with 'every living creature - the birds, the cattle, the beasts of the earth' (Genesis 9:8). Not only human beings but the world of nature sings praise to Yahweh; the waves roar before him, the heavens pour forth speech, the trees of the fields clap their hands as he comes to his world, and God plays with the sea-monsters in the deep (Psalms 19:1-4; 29:5-6; 96:12-13; 98:7-9; 104:26). In the New Testament, according to Romans 8:19-22 the whole universe is 'groaning as in childbirth', waiting for God to set it free, with its destiny deeply bound up with the redemption of God's human children. This is certainly poetic language, but it offers testimony to some kind of response which the natural world can make, or fail to make, to the purposes of God; it also hints that this response is implicated in some way in the human response.

I suggest that there are implications here not just for the way evil takes hold in nature, but for the emergence of the 'Satan'. If we accept that the whole natural world has the capacity to drift away from the purpose of God, then the Satan can also be projected out of *that* fallenness, and not just out of the human psyche. The freedom of the whole of creation is the seedbed for

---

[38] E.g. John Cobb, *A Christian Natural Theology* (London: Lutterworth Press, 1965) 30-35, 87-88, 152-156.

the emergence of hostile nothingness. This may partly account for the objectivity of evil, our experience of its being 'over against us', and the serpent who appears in Genesis 3 may well be a symbol of this construct out of fallen nature.

The passibility of God
I propose, then, that we make the free-will defence more convincing by extending it into the whole of creation. This seems to me to be entirely compatible with the account that Wright is sketching out.[39] Further, he maintains that the defence is inadequate on its own and that its rather intellectual approach needs to be supplemented by something more practical and consoling – the belief that God is with us in our suffering and suffers with us. Only this will meet the demand for meaning of those who are suffering pain and desolation. He properly and movingly asserts the truth that in the cross of Jesus God has embraced our sufferings, writing:

> God knows what it is to be rejected and to suffer. We can assert that God is with us even when, perhaps most especially when, we experience pain and sorrow and do not understand why.[40]

However, I want to add that belief in the passibility of God is not just a supplement to the argument from free-will, but an integral part of it. The reasonable case is not reasonable without it. Belief in a suffering God not only strengthens the argument. It is essential for it to have any explanatory power at all. Among several reasons for this I want to mention two.

First, we return to the notion of evil as a hostile 'nothingness'. When God limits God's self in humble love to allow freedom to creation, this humility allows something strange and altogether alien to God to emerge from God's own creation. There is something that God has not planned, something to be confronted, something therefore to be suffered by God. If evil issues from the created universe through the free-will of the creatures, it is something that *happens* to God; it *befalls* God. The Creator does not make it, and so has to endure it.[41] God takes the

---

[39] Indeed, he hints at 'response' once in 'Suffering', 125, without building anything on it.
[40] Wright, *Theology of the Dark Side*, 98.
[41] For extensive argument, see Paul S. Fiddes, *The Creative Suffering of God* (Oxford: Oxford University Press, 1988) 210-229.

risk in creation that 'nothingness' will emerge, and suffers its impact. Philosophical theories that present God as eternally overcoming 'non-being' in God's own life present a rather harmless view of non-being as another side of being itself, and are consistent with the impassibility of God. But if 'nothingness' befalls God as something strange from the world, God is truly vulnerable.

A second point follows on from this. The emergence of 'nothingness' raises the matter of divine *responsibility* for a broken world. God took a considerable risk that this would happen, and we can only go on having trust in the goodness of this risk-taker if God also shares the consequences with us. The suffering of God is necessary to make a free-will defence credible. A free-will defence also requires that the God who gives freedom should do everything possible to overcome evil. The Christian message is that God has indeed taken responsibility and conquered evil in the cross of Christ. As Wright urges, we call evil 'nothing', not only because it has no place in being, but because it has been negated or *brought to nothing* by the redemptive act of God.[42] We view evil only in the light of God's revelation of love in Christ. Nor, I suggest, is there any need to propose a satisfying of the wrath and justice of God as a pre-condition for the defeat of evil and the Satan, as Wright seems to suggest at one point.[43] When Christ refuses to submit to the powers of darkness, rejecting the temptation to calm anxiety by putting his security in something other than trust in his Father, he exposes the powers for the tyrants and frauds that they are, and enables his followers to share in breaking free from them.[44] When Christ experiences the very depths of nothingness in entering the God-forsaken space of the cross, he enables those who trust in him to rise with him out of the realm of nothing into a new world of life and fellowship with God. The suffering of God in Christ is actually the means of overcoming evil. Suffering love is the power than makes something come from nothing.

Nothingness, 'possession' and structures

From considering the metaphysics of evil, Wright turns to two practical areas: the interest by the charismatic movement in 'deliverance' of individuals from demonic powers, and the place of 'principalities and powers' in the structures of the state. With

---

[42] Wright, *Theology of the Dark Side*, 151-152.
[43] Wright, *Theology of the Dark Side*, 153, 155.
[44] Wright, *Theology of the Dark Side*, 160.

regard to the first, Wright is cautious and balanced in his approach, opining that while 'demonization', or 'oppression' by demons, is a real phenomenon, it is rare. The situation can be confused with the exercise of psychic energies, which are disturbing but morally neutral – good nor bad in themselves. Or buried archetypes can be released by the mind, or somebody can be held captive by a habitual sin. He stresses that there is the constant danger of living in a fantasy realm or in a state of paranoia where demons lurk behind every corner and are to be blamed for every setback.[45] Yet for all this, there are occasions, Wright thinks, where deliverance from demonic oppression is needed, and he gives careful and sensible guidelines in this situation, mainly centring on proclaiming the victory of Christ rather than getting involved in any kind of magical warfare. 'As in the ministry of Jesus', he writes, 'the demonic factor and its remedy should not be given any more than incidental attention.'[46]

Our interest here is not so much in the details of 'deliverance' but in asking how the identifying of evil, the Satan and demons as strictly 'nothing' bears on Wright's view of a 'deliverance ministry'. Wright's discussion is informed by his preceding chapters about 'nothingness' in three ways. First, he wants to encourage readers not to exaggerate the demonic or to become over-preoccupied by it, while recognising its reality. Second, he argues that, even though demons are not persons or subjects, it is legitimate to personalise them. Third, he argues that, as 'nothing', the character of evil is chaos and irrationality rather than organisation.[47] No credence is thus to be given to accounts of the demonic that describe a carefully structured demonic organisation with sophisticated strategies, even if the information about this supposedly comes 'from the inside', from what demons say themselves.

However, Wright does not draw conclusions for 'deliverance' from his perception that the Satan and associated demons are a projection of the human psyche. This indeed is a development of the second edition of the book, and most of his discussion of demon possession is carried over from the first unchanged. His guidelines seem, in fact, to fit better with his earlier

---

[45] Wright, *Theology of the Dark Side*, 113-121.
[46] Wright, *Theology of the Dark Side*, 125.
[47] Wright, *Theology of the Dark Side*, 112. Further, see Nigel G. Wright, 'Charismatic Interpretations of the Demonic' in Lane (ed.), *Unseen Powers*, 158.

thought that Satan and demons are fallen angels, created personalities who have fallen *into* nothing. Carrying through the proposal that Satan is a 'construct' of human personality would not undermine the objective reality of the phenomena, but might well lead one to be more cautious about talk of 'demonic strongholds' in the lives of individuals.[48] It might lead one to rely more on the language of healing than 'expulsion', even in the moderate form that Wright employs.

Wright observes that the charismatic movement has widened its interest in the 'dark powers', beyond the threat to individual persons to the discerning of the demonic in the structures of society.[49] Here there is a bridge to his interest in political theology and his explorations of the relation between Church and state from a nonconformist viewpoint. We have already seen that in his dialogue with Walter Wink, he insists that the language of 'powers' in the New Testament refers *both* to human structures and to 'superhuman agencies'. We can, for example, see this deliberate ambiguity in the three beasts of Revelation 12-13, where evil power takes form in the political and religious structures of the Roman Empire.[50] For Wright, the power structures of human life are vulnerable and open to 'invasion' by the powers of darkness which draw their strength from human self-exaltation. The structures of economic, political, cultural and religious life either enhance or distort human existence according to 'the power that is at work within them'.

The state is not intrinsically evil, but it can become 'demonised' when it goes beyond its proper function of serving humankind and makes itself of ultimate concern. In *Theology of the Dark Side*, the dual aspect of the powers is thus 'structure' and 'dark power'.[51] The spiritual forces can be dealt with by prayer; the powerful structures have to be tackled by political engagement. The notion of evil as 'nothingness' continues to be significant here. Since the dark powers are 'nothing', the only powers that can be redeemed are the human structures. Having been made by God, the structures will one day be redeemed and resume their proper function (Colossians 1:15-20). In the meantime 'they can be humanised ... and brought back into line in order to serve and not

---

[48] Wright, *Theology of the Dark Side*, 123.
[49] Wright, 'Charismatic Interpretations', 150-151, 159-163.
[50] Wright, *Theology of the Dark Side*, 144.
[51] Wright, *Theology of the Dark Side*, 142-143.

oppress'.[52] It is in accord with this logic that in Wright's later work on the powers of the state he shows less and less interest in the 'dark powers' that 'invade' them and can be 'expelled' from them. All concern is transferred to an analysis of the structures themselves, and to a different kind of duality in the powers. This is the duality of a state which both shares in human fallenness and yet manifests the signs of God's purposes in creation.[53] Corporate life is both alienated from God and an instrument of God's creative intentions. States are not creative ordinances as such, but they are provisional measures governed by divine providence to hold in check the human tendencies towards self-destruction and to restrain chaos.[54]

When we are sensitive to this duality of fallenness and 'created ontology',[55] Wright argues that we should thus be *both* Anabaptist and Baptist in our approach to the worldly powers of the state. We should hold an Anabaptist suspicion of the state and its lust for domination, while we must make a continuing search for social and civil justice through state agency, as in the Baptist tradition, and in common with the whole Reformed tradition.[56] Wright's thesis is that the state exists for the sake of the Church, to provide a framework of order, stability and justice within which the humanising and redeeming work of the gospel can run its course.[57]

It is striking that Wright can discuss the 'principalities and powers' in the context of the relation between Church and state without invoking 'dark powers' which are distinct from the structures. This seems a witness to their 'nothingness' and is entirely consistent with their being a 'construct' out of human personalities and the structures themselves.[58] It also shows that Nigel Wright has a lively theological mind which is always developing, which keeps faith with his past thought, but which is never trapped in previous positions and does not merely repeat

---

[52] Wright, *Theology of the Dark Side*, 145.
[53] Nigel Wright, *Power and Discipleship. Toward a Baptist Theology of the State* (Whitley Lecture 1996-1997; Oxford: Whitley Publications, 1996) 21. Cf. his *Free Church, Free State. The Positive Baptist Vision* (Milton Keynes: Paternoster, 2005) 235-245.
[54] Wright, *Power and Discipleship*, 22, 27.
[55] Wright, *Power and Discipleship*, 21; cf. Wright, *Free Church, Free State*, 240.
[56] Wright, *Power and Discipleship*, 13-16, 35-37.
[57] Wright, *Power and Discipleship*, 27; cf. Wright, *Free Church, Free State*, 238.
[58] So Wright, *Theology of the Dark Side*, 143.

them. This, of course, is why we are honouring him with this volume.

Inclusive representation revisited

Paul W. Goodliff

Writing in 1977, Neville Clark discussed the gulf between what Baptists believe about ministry and what they practice. On the one hand are the statements made about ministry, which tend to look to the past. On the other hand, the actual practices and beliefs held by Baptists reveal a different and more varied pattern. According to Clark, Baptists 'have in fact come to believe more and differently than their conventional words proclaim, more and differently than they are consciously aware.'[1]

In support of Clark's assertion, amongst the findings from a recent survey of Baptist ministers' beliefs about ordination and ministry was strong evidence that a representational understanding of ministry predominates at present. This view did not prevail in the older papers on ministry but has come to prominence in the last ten years. This change is in large part due to the influence of Nigel Wright's advocacy of Baptist ministry as 'inclusive representation'. In this paper I first of all want to pay tribute to Nigel's insight in putting his finger on the pulse of Baptist vernacular theology. Second, I want to take the argument a step further by integrating this discernment of the *Zeitgeist* with another theologically coherent position that makes space for a more sacramental understanding of ministry. Wright in some ways endorses this understanding of ministry that is already moving to a place of surprising significance amongst British Baptists at present. A more or less developed sacramentalism of the kind advocated by Paul Fiddes or John Colwell is emerging as a significant belief about ministry amongst more recently trained ministers. Third, I want to apply this sacramental understanding to the experience of ministers by reference to an extraordinary statement of Jesus in Matthew 10:40, and argue that above all else this gives confidence to pastors and evangelists as they minister in Christ's name.

A questionnaire

In the summer of 2007 twenty percent of Baptist ministers on the Register of Covenanted Persons Accredited for Ministry responded

---

[1] Neville Clark, 'On recognising what we believe', Paper for the Advisory Committee on Church Relations (Baptist Union of Great Britain, 1977).

to my request for participation in research for a doctoral thesis by answering a questionnaire on-line. One question asked the respondents to indicate their level of agreement with the statement 'Baptist ministry is a representative role in church and community'. Of those 316 respondents, 36.7% strongly agreed, 59.2% agreed, while only 3.5% disagreed and 0.6% strongly disagreed. Using a Lickert scale weighting tool to analyse the strength of agreement with this and seven other statements about Baptist ministry, the mean level of agreement was 3.3, where 2.5 indicates indifference, and 4.0 the maximum level of agreement. This was the highest score for any of the eight questions posed about the nature of Baptist ministry, indicating the greatest level of agreement with any of those statements.

Reports and papers

What does this statement about ministry signify? Nigel Wright's article 'Inclusive Representation: Towards a Doctrine of Christian Ministry'[2] was a more thoroughly worked out version of the paper he presented to the Doctrine and Worship Committee of the Baptist Union in 2000[3] and its theme was repeated in his 'presidential' book written as he was serving as President of the Baptist Union in 2002-2003, *New Baptists, New Agenda.*[4] These publications form the culmination of a decade-long debate about ministry in the period 1992-2002, which resulted in the establishment of the current Register of Covenanted Persons Accredited for Ministry in 2002.

The normative understanding of Baptist ministry in the twentieth century is best summarised as 'ministry of Word and Sacrament', even if many who held that view would have referred to the sacraments of baptism and the Lord's Supper as ordinances. This view continued throughout the second half of that century, albeit weakened as time elapsed. The roots of a representational view of ministry lie in the earliest period during which current practitioners of ministry trained, although at the time it was not named as such. It is implied in the emphasis in the two

---

[2] Nigel G. Wright, 'Inclusive Representation: Towards a Doctrine of Christian Ministry', *Baptist Quarterly* 39.4 (October 2001) 159-174. [Editor: In the present volume Christopher Ellis and Robert Ellis also interact with this article.]
[3] *Ministry: Towards a Consensus*, Doctrine and Worship Committee, Baptist Union of Great Britain, 2000/13.
[4] Nigel G. Wright, *New Baptists, New Agenda* (Carlisle: Paternoster, 2002) 112-130, esp. 127-129.

foundational documents about Baptist ministry, *The Meaning and Practice of Ordination*[5] and *The Doctrine of the Ministry*,[6] published in 1957 and 1961. These affirm that the ministry of Jesus Christ is the ministry of the whole Church and that in a significant way ministers represent that ministry. It is they who set the Word before the Church that is called to live under its authority and who administer the enacted words of baptism and eucharist. This view is endorsed by Paul Fiddes and others in an exposition of the nature of Baptist ministry, *Forms of Ministry among Baptists*, written in the context of debates about the theology of ministry in the 1990s. This report notes how the minister is 'the representative of the Universal Church' in the local scene.[7]

Earlier centuries of diversity in the understanding of ministry among Baptists came to focus in Arthur Dakin's *The Baptist View of the Church and Ministry*. Dakin's conviction was that if a Baptist minister were to cease to preside over a particular Baptist church,

> leaving him with no church over which to preside, he would for the time being cease to be a Baptist minister, just as a deacon ceases to be a Baptist deacon when he gives up the office. There is no sense in which a man can claim to be a Baptist minister when he is not the head of a Baptist church.[8]

Writing this, as Principal of Bristol Baptist College he was excluding himself from ministry and referred to himself as Principal Dakin rather than as pastor or reverend. Ernest Payne received this view with some alarm and quickly wrote a strong rebuttal that never saw the light of day. Because Dakin was about to be inducted as President of the Baptist Union, the General Secretary of the Union, M.E. Aubrey, did not want a controversy. Instead, Payne wrote a milder version of his concerns in *The Fellowship of Believers*.[9]

---

[5] *The Meaning and Practice of Ordination among Baptists. A Report submitted to the Council of the Baptist Union of Great Britain and Ireland*, 1957.
[6] *The Doctrine of the Ministry*, Baptist Union of Great Britain and Ireland, 1961.
[7] Paul S. Fiddes and others, *Forms of Ministry among Baptists* (Didcot: Baptist Union, 1995) 11.
[8] A. Dakin, *The Baptist View of the Church and Ministry* (London: Baptist Union, 1944) 45.
[9] E.A. Payne, *The Fellowship of Believers: Baptist Thought and Practice Yesterday and Today* (London, Kingsgate Press, 1944).

Wright's article

Wright notes that recent Baptist thinking did not follow Dakin. What has been consistent is a commitment to a pattern of office, either the minority three-fold order of bishop/messenger, elder/presbyter and deacon, or the normative two-fold order of bishop/pastor and deacon. In 'Inclusive Representation' he discusses more recent trends, including the gifts and callings emphasis of a functional approach to ministry, the influence of charismatic renewal and a marked reduction in deference to authority in wider society. He describes the current understanding as one of confusion. For all its best efforts, Wright concludes that the 1995 attempt to redefine ministry for the twentieth century, Fiddes' *Forms of Ministry among Baptists*, had failed to achieve the consensus it was seeking and that an alternative approach is needed.[10]

In a fuller way than in *Ministry: Towards a Consensus*, the same persistent sticking points are discussed: the priesthood of all believers; the opposition of leadership and service; uncertainty over the meaning of some terms (minister, leader, pastor); hesitation over the traditional term 'minister of Word and Sacrament' (Wright prefers the term 'ministers of the Gospel'); distaste for hierarchy; concern about ordination.[11] Significantly, while avoiding any sense of an automatic ontological change at ordination, Wright argues for change in the minister nonetheless:

> However, in that the ordained person is set apart for ministry with the prayers of God's people, those prayers must count for something, unless we believe that prayer in general counts for nothing. An enduement of the Spirit for ministry is surely our firm expectation and this must indeed mean a change. The act affirms that they are commissioned to represent God's people in an enduring way and with a degree of authority that is not shared by all. (...) *Forms of Ministry* called this .... a 'way of being' or 'order of life'.[12]

The classical view, where ministry takes precedence over the congregation, is contrasted with the communal model, where ministry emerges from the church. Wright argues for a combination of these insights.[13] He recognises validity in both ends of the

---

[10] Wright, 'Inclusive Representation', 161-163.
[11] Wright, 'Inclusive Representation', 163-169.
[12] Wright, 'Inclusive Representation', 169.
[13] Wright, 'Inclusive Representation', 170.

duality (ontology over function, separated ministry over ministry of all, etc.) and chooses a particular lens through which to view the problem. This lens is authority or weight of testimony. 'Those whose testimony is weighty are people of authority',[14] and this testimony is weighty to the extent that they bear the Word of God. Those who are called, gifted and sent by God to be bearers of his Word, and who do so in the Spirit of Christ, have authority to minister that Word. 'The weight of testimony is at its greatest when both forms of authority come together, when some minister for the sake of the ministry of all and all minister alongside the some.'[15]

Having utilised this lens, Wright establishes the understanding of ministry that he wishes to work with, 'inclusive representation'. Inclusive, in the sense that ministry does not exclude the competence and the right of others to baptise, to administer communion or to preach, because it is the Church that does these things; and representational, in that they are representatives of Christ, of the wider Church, and of the local church to itself. Ministers embody the life of the local church to itself, which is why they do not exclusively administer the sacraments and preach the Word, but they do so consistently. Here Wright refers approvingly to a Mennonite publication that uses the image of incarnation at this point.[16]

This understanding, which Wright claims gives due weight to both the ministry offered by the whole church and to the particular ministry offered by some, attempts to avoid any question of status being sought by those who are ministers. This robust doctrine of ministry is not offered 'in such a way as to undermine the vision of the ministry of all God's people'. But,

> the ministry of all will not be realised in its fullness without our recognition of the gifts that Christ has given to some, gifts which are in reality people being and doing particular things for the sake of the whole.[17]

This representational view of ministry is a deliberately irenic notion, attempting to find a new consensus where one had not existed. As we saw above, it is widely held today.

---

[14] Wright, 'Inclusive Representation', 171.
[15] Wright, 'Inclusive Representation', 171; original is in italics.
[16] Wright, 'Inclusive Representation', 172-173.
[17] Wright, 'Inclusive Representation', 173.

Sacramental turn

The older foundational documents about ministry, *The Doctrine of the Church*, *The Doctrine of the Ministry* and *The Meaning and Practice of Ordination* denied the legitimacy of an understanding of ministry that we might call sacramental, but in the past fifteen years the writings of Nigel Wright, Paul Fiddes and John Colwell have countered this denial with an advocacy of a sacramental understanding of ministry in either a 'soft' (Wright and Fiddes) or a more thoroughgoing variety (Colwell[18]). In their roles as college tutors charged with the task of enabling ministerial formation, these persons have influenced the most recent generations of ministers, adopting a sacramental alternative to a functional approach in the way that fifty years ago, ministry of 'Word and Sacrament' (but not in a sacramental sense) was the alternative to a pietistic and individualistic emphasis upon the call of the minister prevalent amongst 'low' Baptists. One of the most striking features of the research that I undertook in 2007-2008 was the way in which this aspect has moved from outright rejection among those who trained in the 1950s to widespread adoption by those trained in the first five years of the twenty-first century.

This sacramental turn has arisen because of the perceived inadequacy of a simply functional approach to characterise ministry as a way of life, or a 'way of being'. The ontological concentration is variously conceived, from a lifestyle appropriate to the minister added to an essentially functional approach (the weak case) to a thoroughgoing emphasis upon the ontological change that is wrought in ordination which sets the minister apart from other members of the Church, not in a sacerdotal sense, but in terms of a way of being that is the proper response to the call of God and Church to be a minister.

I believe this sacramental turn is based on three developments in the character of Baptist life in Britain over the past fifty years. The first development is the gradually increased influence of ecumenism, which has enabled the practice of ordination to recover its significance after its nineteenth-century demise in the face of the distance required by Baptists from the Tractarians. Ecumenical contacts have latterly enabled a fuller sacramentalism to become acceptable amongst Baptists as they engage with other, more sacramental traditions than their own.

---

[18] John E. Colwell, *Promise and Presence: An Exploration of Sacramental Theology* (Carlisle: Paternoster, 2005).

This development has been enhanced by the influence of a demotic ecumenism through pan-Evangelicalism and, especially, the charismatic renewal.

The second factor is this charismatic renewal, which has opened the door to sacramentalism through the expectation of divine action in response to prayer. This expectation lies at the heart of the charismatic experience. If the Holy Spirit acts in response to the invocation 'come, Holy Spirit' in the context of prayer ministry, why would he not do so in response to prayer in the context of the ordination of a minister? The understanding of the presence of God is more immanent in the charismatic movement than the utterly mediated presence in a sacramental understanding of ordination, but the emphasis upon what God does, as opposed to what humans do (viz., to witness and to make promises) in the 'real absence' alternative is what is significant. Baptists have embraced charismatic renewal with greater alacrity that almost any other historic denomination.

The third contributing factor is the transformation of Evangelicalism from a narrower Reformed and conservative movement to the current broad form of churchmanship that seeks to be inclusive rather than exclusive. This evolution has opened up Evangelicals to expressions of spirituality and theology previously considered suspect, especially those that predate the Reformation. The grounding of a more sacramental understanding of ministry and ordination in a deeper tradition, with greater ubiquity than its alternatives is also a significant factor in the sacramental *risorgimento*. Where the shallowness of prevailing forms of Evangelicalism is perceived, with their emphasis upon utilitarian and pragmatic values and their lack of a coherent theology, one reaction is to seek a fruitful interaction with an imported theology. Whereas Charismatics look to neo-Pentecostalism, those from a 'high' Baptist stream look to sacramental and catholic theologies to help them locate their Baptist identity within a broader context of the tradition of orthodox and catholic sacramental theology. This development also reflects a post-liberal or post-conservative theological move on the part of a movement that now almost entirely defines who Baptists are in their Evangelical beliefs.

Is this sacramental turn to be welcomed or resisted? Clearly there are those who resist its presuppositions and conclusions, and it remains an understanding of ministry that, while a majority view, has fewer adherents than other, less controversial views had in the past. Nowadays it certainly claims greater acceptance than the Dakin doctrine, which is as good as redundant. In my view, the sacramental understanding is to be welcomed for a number of theological reasons. It has greater coherence with the way in which God acts in the world as mediated presence. It is located in the wider traditions of the Church and it has greater capacity than its alternatives to resist those forces that erode the true value of ministry such as an obsession with numbers and 'the bottom-line', or a shallow emotivism. It resists the forces of romantic interiority, where ministry is all about 'my call'. It resists the unwelcome excesses of management theory which threatens to reduce ministry to the effective delivery of ministerial tasks. It also resists postmodern radical scepticism and individualism, which see ministry as an unknowable practice, with greater effectiveness than a purely functional model.

Its emphasis upon the promise of God to act in certain spaces, such as baptism, eucharist and ordination, and his presence in response to prayer and invocation, restricts the individualism of much current evangelical and Baptist experience. The actuality of God's action through the Church is less privatised than some contemporary Baptist emphasis upon the individual's sense of call, while allowing space for that personal element within the total process of being set apart for ministry. This reliance upon the promise of God rather than the individual's experience has the potential to give greater confidence and security to the ministerial call, which - if too closely linked to 'success' - remains at the mercy of the exigencies of ecclesial and personal life.

The sacramental view coheres adequately with the expectation that God's Spirit will be active and present in the experience of the believer. Within the missional priority of much contemporary Baptist thinking about the Church, it has an important role in pointing to a 're-sacralising' of the world for a culture that is spiritual but not religious.

In place of a presumed consensus about ministry in the 1950s there now exists a considerable diversity of beliefs about ministry among Baptist ministers, ranging from the charismatic, through the representational to the sacramental. The growing trend is to see ministry as inclusive representation with a sacramental form. For this move we have in large part Wright to thank.

Representation in practice
How might this theological move deepen the practice of ministry in the twenty-first century? One vital dimension is the confidence which it brings to ministry. In Matthew 10:40 Jesus says something utterly extraordinary about himself and about God, and also about those whom he calls and sends into his world: *'Whoever welcomes you welcomes me, and whoever welcomes me welcomes the one who sent me.'* Jewish notions of an authorised representative lie behind this claim: the idea that a person who is sent should be treated as equivalent to the one who sent him or her. They are sent with the same authority and should be welcomed as such.[19] While this concept might be familiar to Jesus and his disciples, what is outrageously new is the claim that it is also true of Jesus and God. Jesus has been sent by God and comes with the same authority and power, which is why he heals the leper in Matthew 8:3 and forgives sin in chapter 9, something only God could do, much to the dismay of the Pharisees, who mutter 'this man is blaspheming.' (8:3)

When we welcome Christ we welcome God. In later centuries the Church Fathers would come to frame this conviction in the doctrines of the Person of Christ and of the Trinity. These creeds say that Jesus is not just representing God, but is indeed God; but here Jesus simply but profoundly affirms that when he turns up, so does God.

But to this important theological statement about Christ something must be added about those whom Jesus sends. The entire discourse in Matthew 10 is addressed to the Twelve (10:1) and I suppose some might argue that this promise is limited to them. I think that it applies to all whom Jesus sends - and that is all of us who are his disciples -, but that it finds a particular focus in those whom he calls to ministry, who are representatives of all disciples and inclusive of them. The simple but extraordinary claim here is that when we go in Jesus' name, he goes too, and when he goes too, then so does God.

It is helpful to think of this view using a term borrowed from the Orthodox Church and applied to Mary the Mother of Jesus. She is called *Theotokos*, 'God-bearer'. We ministers too are Godbearers, not in the sense that we have the privilege of bearing

---

[19] Donald A. Hagner, *Matthew 1-13* (Word Biblical Commentary; Dallas: Word Books, 1993) 295-297; John Nolland, *The Gospel of Matthew* (New International Greek Testament Commentary; Grand Rapids: Eerdmans, 2005) 444.

the Son of God in our womb, but rather that where we go, we bear God with us. We carry the aroma of Christ, says Paul in 2 Corinthians 2:15, we carry the life of Jesus in our bodies, as it were. By his Spirit, we are agents of his presence, ambassadors of his Kingdom.

Of course, this says something about the way in which God works in the world, a way that we might describe as a thoroughgoing sacramental way of working, best illustrated by a story from that utterly absorbing piece of American television, the series West Wing. Early in series one the fictional President Jed Bartlet has to decide whether to commute a death penalty. He calls for his pastor, a Catholic priest, Fr Tom Cavanagh, to come and see him. Fr Tom tells the President this story:

> A man hears on the radio that the river is rising and he must evacuate his home. 'I am a Christian,' he tells himself, 'I pray, I love God. He will save me,' and he stays put. The river rises, and a man in a rowing boat comes by. 'Get in the boat, the river is rising. You will drown,' he says. 'I am a Christian,' the man replies, 'I pray, I love God. He will save me.' The waters keep on rising until the man is on the roof of his house. A helicopter arrives and the pilot says 'Grab hold of this rope, the river is still rising. You'll drown.' 'I am a Christian,' the man replies, 'I pray, I love God. He will save me.' Soon the waters rise above the roof and the man drowns. Arriving at the Gates of Heaven, the man, by now angry and disappointed, demands an audience with God. 'I prayed,' he tells God, 'I love you. I believed that you would save me. Why did you not hear my cry?' God replies, 'I sent you a radio report, a man in a rowing boat and a helicopter pilot. What are you doing here?'

Generally God works through his people, and not just on those spectacular occasions when every thaumaturge from Oral Roberts to Tod Bentley 'strut their stuff'. How does God feed the hungry, bring freedom to the oppressed and proclaim good news? Through those whom he sends: 'whoever gives even a cup of cold water to these little ones in the name of a disciple', says Jesus (Matthew 10:42 NRSV). His presence is mediated through others, just as his grace is mediated through the waters of baptism or the bread and wine of the Lord's Supper. Each one of us is a *theotokos*, a God-bearer, by the Spirit. This confidence is expressed in three aspects of ministry: pastoral encounter, evangelistic endeavour and the exercise of leadership.

Pastoral encounter
It is often in the pastoral encounter that ministers most question their competence. In the place of bereavement or of marriage breakdown, what can the pastor do but speak words and pray? Often that seems quite inadequate when what we want is to make things better, to cure the sick, to resolve the dispute and to bring the dead back to life. Yet, it is the experience of those who welcome the pastor to their bedside or living room filled with anguish and sorrow that somehow their presence brought hope and comfort. When the minister came it made the presence of Christ seem that more real and vital. Matthew 10:40 was in action. This is why the elderly want the pastor to visit, wonderful though the pastoral care deacon might be. Resist it as folk religion if you like, but actually I think something else is at work that we refute at our peril. God goes with the pastor in her work of pastoral care, Christ is present when the minister visits to comfort the bereaved and he is present in a particular way when the pastor visits his congregation.

Evangelistic endeavour
Of equal importance in the minister's work is leading God's people in their mission, or rather, enabling them to participate in the mission of God to his world. Here again, confidence is forged when Matthew 10:40 is understood. That conversation with the stranger, that work of co-operation with the local civic community in relieving the plight of the homeless, that personal encounter that explains the gospel to an unbeliever and calls for faith and repentance, all are done with God present and active. The minister is not just using finely honed skills, the evangelist is not merely rehearsing a familiar story and appeal, for Christ by his Spirit is present to work and act. 'If they welcome you, they welcome me,' says Jesus. Confidence and faith is built when we realise this is his work first and foremost, not simply ours, dependent upon how spiritual we feel or how competent we are.

Leadership
Wright explains how the New Testament and Baptist practice at its best affirm the ministry of all and the leadership of some. Using ministry in this way is slippery, as too profligate a use of the term

'ministry' can too easily diminish the importance of those called and set apart to minister in a surge of egalitarian zeal that owes more to the 1960s than to Scripture. I prefer to use the word 'service'. However, the point Wright makes is that the ministry or service that all are called to exercise, the fruit of responsible discipleship to which all are called, does not negate the necessity that some are to lead the people of God. The manner of that leadership must echo Christ, of course, and will be mostly by example; one of Paul Beasley-Murray's descriptions of the minister is 'exemplary pilgrim'.[20] It will eschew all power play and manipulation for personal gain. Nonetheless, leadership is called for, its exercise vital for the well-being of the Church and its purpose the edifying of the Body of Christ. Who is competent for such things? Well, probably no one, unless Christ empowers and enables the leader. It is just such confidence that Matthew 10:40 brings, even if always subject to the wider affirmation and discernment of the Church. When the minister leads in Christ's name and in his way, then God is present to change human hearts and to empower the whole Church.

Christian ministers represent Christ to a watching world and bring the blessing of Christ as they visit people in their homes, lead church meetings, conduct worship and proclaim the Word. Not just when they feel like it, not just when their morning devotions were particularly intimate, not just when the sermon was particularly well-crafted, but simply as and when they go at the command of Christ. This is inclusive representation with a sacramental character in practice. Ministry is no longer simply down to the skills and persona of the minister, but it is an active encounter with the God who works in and through the created world to build his kingdom and Christ's Church. It is just such a vision that Nigel Wright sets before us as he explores inclusive representation, and for that we should all be grateful.

---

[20] Paul Beasley-Murray, *A Call to Excellence* (London: Hodder and Stoughton, 1995) 196-226.

The radical ecclesiology of Nigel Wright

Stephen R. Holmes

Nigel Wright was the first person ever to try to teach me any theology, when he was doctrine tutor and I a new student at Spurgeon's College in 1992. When he returned to the college as Principal, I had the privilege of working with him as a colleague in teaching theology to new generations of students. Through his career Nigel has straddled the worlds of academy and Church more successfully than most of us; it was rapidly clear to the newest student that, for Nigel, theology was (in the ancient formulation) 'the Church's science': a subject that existed not for the sake of knowing more, or demonstrating our cleverness, but for the sake of the Church, that the body of Christ might be shaped and built up.

Perhaps because of his experience in the 'real world' of pastoral ministry, it is also noticeable that 'the Church' was and is, for Nigel, a far more concrete entity than it is for many theologians. The Church is not a vague and idealised metaphysical construct, possessed of and defined by certain marks and notes which requires the repeated use of words like 'pure' and 'right' without explanation or qualification; rather the Church is the odd and broken collection of misfits that gathers Sunday by Sunday in local congregations. It is fairly easy, and largely useless, to pontificate about the entity where the Word is purely preached and the sacraments rightly administered; it is much more challenging, and much more interesting, to do as Nigel did, and focus on lived reality.

I have chosen the word 'radical' to characterise Nigel's ecclesiology; it is a word that is characteristically his - I would be surprised if it is not used elsewhere in this collection. Two of Nigel's publications use the word in the title, *The Radical Kingdom* and *The Radical Evangelical*.[1] Further, when he studied the

---

[1] Nigel G. Wright, *The Radical Kingdom: Restoration in Theory and in Practice* (Eastbourne: Kingsway, 1986); idem, *The Radical Evangelical: Seeking a Place to Stand* (London: SPCK, 1996).

ecclesiologies of Moltmann and Yoder for his doctoral thesis,[2] it carried the tagline on the front cover 'A radical Baptist perspective on Church, society and state'. Again, perhaps the fullest statement of Nigel's constructive ecclesiology, *Free Church, Free State* begins with a section entitled 'The Radical Way'.[3]

What does this word 'radical', almost ubiquitous as it is in Nigel's published writings on the Church, actually mean? He himself often determines it with a footnote referencing G.H. Williams's groundbreaking study, *The Radical Reformation*.[4] 'Radical' here opposes 'magisterial' and denotes the quite diverse groups within the ferment of sixteenth-century Reform who rejected the idea that the political community was co-terminus with the ecclesial community. For the most influential and long-lived of these groups, the rejection of indiscriminate infant baptism and the recovery (as they saw it) of the biblical and ancient practice of baptising only those who had made personal profession of faith was one determining mark of their radicalism. Others were a pacifist commitment that led them to refuse state offices which implicated the holder in violent coercion, and a belief that Christian discipleship could not be demanded by the state, but instead was enforced only by the threat of exclusion from the Church community.

In Nigel's first book, however, although the appeal to the sixteenth-century Anabaptists was fairly central,[5] 'radical' was parsed in a different way. Its first chapter is an extended play on the ambiguity of the word in English, reflecting its etymology (a return to the 'roots' of something) and its common connotation (a decisive breaking away in new, surprising and challenging directions). The charismatic movement, particularly its 'Restorationist' wing, is presented as 'radical' in both these senses. It is both a return to primitive Christianity (meeting in houses; looking for visible signs and wonders; expecting counter-cultural discipleship) and a new and transformative expression of Church

---

[2] Published as *Disavowing Constantine: Mission, Church and the Social Order in the Theologies of John Howard Yoder and Jürgen Moltmann* (Carlisle: Paternoster, 2000).
[3] Nigel G. Wright, *Free Church, Free State: The Positive Baptist Vision* (Carlisle: Paternoster, 2005) 2.
[4] George H. Williams, *The Radical Reformation* (London: Weidenfeld and Nicolson, 1962, third ed. 1992).
[5] Wright, *Radical Kingdom*, e.g. 29-45.

life. In books such as *Free Church, Free State*,[6] however, 'radical' is entirely determined by Williams's usage and there is little or no emphasis on this idea of restoration or on the charismatic renewal of the church more generally.[7]

In this paper I want to explore the connection between these two different views of what it might mean to be radical: radicalism-as-believers'-church and radicalism-as-charismatic-restoration. Is this merely a linguistic coincidence, serving mainly to disguise slightly the fact that Nigel's ecclesiology has moved away from Restorationist emphases to a different vision founded in the Anabaptists? Or is there deep connection here, suggesting that, properly understood, a Restorationist church should embrace believers' baptism, the separation of Church and state, and the particularly Anabaptist strain of pacifism hinted at above, and that a fellowship consciously influenced by the Anabaptist tradition should be charismatic and restorationist in its practices of worship and discipleship?

Clearly, if one holds to standard baptist and charismatic positions concerning the mode and subjects of baptism and the use of spiritual gifts in the New Testament Church, then a radicalism which sees the proper orientation of Church praxis as merely the purest possible return to the primitive apostolic church will embrace both. I think it can be shown, however, that Nigel has not operated with quite so naïve an ecclesiology and that, in his appropriation of the Anabaptist tradition, he has increasingly focused on political theology, which is not so easy to reduce to a simple appeal to the New Testament witness.

Back to the New Testament?

On the first of these points, the refusal to embrace a crude notion of the normativity of the New Testament church, I think there is a development in Nigel's published work. In *The Radical Kingdom*, whilst there is passing acknowledgement of the imperfection of the New Testament church,[8] and a warning against a too-rigid attempt

---

[6] See also Wright's *New Baptists, New Agenda* (Carlisle: Paternoster, 2002).
[7] Ideas recognisably derived from charismatic renewal are not wholly absent from either book, but they are not at all central. In both, the major implicit reference to renewal is in the use of the language of charismatic gifting as a key motif for developing a theology of ministry. Wright, *Free Church, Free State*, 14; *idem*, *New Baptists, New Agenda*, 115-116.
[8] Wright speaks of 'the shortcomings which Scripture does not seek to disguise', *Radical Kingdom*, 22.

to read a complete ecclesiology from the pages of the New Testament,[9] the fundamental position of this book is that the New Testament describes a vision of church life to which we should aspire, a model to which we should actively conform our own fellowships.

By the time we reach *New Baptists, New Agenda*, however, the position is seriously altered. The ecclesiology there is nowhere based on an appeal to conformity to New Testament practice; it is biblical in a more sophisticated way, appealing to scriptural principles concerning the nature of God, the nature of humanity and the nature of salvation, and deriving ideas about the Church from them. More strikingly, however, the opening chapter, entitled 'Legends of the Fall', advances the thesis that 'the true church has yet to come',[10] decrying any appeal to a supposedly-perfect past. The examples in the chapter are drawn from appeal to more-recent supposed 'golden ages', it is true, and the 'Restorationist' impulse is nowhere mentioned, but the implications of the logic are sufficiently clear.

In *Free Church, Free State* the shift is explicit: '... the Bible does not lay down a blueprint valid for all times ...' To be sure, Scripture is not indifferent on the matter of Church life: it gives us 'an enduring vision of the church, and a whole host of images and metaphors by which we can navigate'.[11] The controlling metaphor here, however, is 'growth', the sense that the New Testament witness plants a seed which grows and develops in a variety of ways, many of them equally appropriate. Why the change? No doubt there are biographical reasons: when Nigel recalls his encounter with Restorationism in *Charismatic Renewal* he is (this reader senses) considerably more critical in his retrospective consideration of the movement than in *The Radical Kingdom*, although the seeds of the later critique are certainly present in that text as well. In *Charismatic Renewal* he also points to meeting with Mennonites as a decisive experience,[12] but, strikingly, the language of that chapter is still rather 'Restorationist': there is a disagreement over the church order the New Testament demands,

---

[9] Wright, *Radical Kingdom*, 19, talks about treating 'the Scriptures like the blueprint for the tabernacle given to Moses on the mountain'.
[10] Wright, *New Baptists, New Agenda*, 4.
[11] Wright, *Free Church, Free State*, 2.
[12] Thomas A. Smail, Andrew Walker and Nigel Wright, *Charismatic Renewal: The Search for a Theology* (London: SPCK, 1993) 26.

but still the sense that it does in fact demand a particular church order and that there is a need to discover it.

I suspect, however, that the key reasons for the development are not biographical but theological. The nuanced appeal to Scripture found in *Free Church, Free State* is very reminiscent of Nigel's description of Yoder's account of the biblicism of the Anabaptists in his early writings. There Nigel suggests that 'Yoder's ecclesiology is ... uneasy and arguably implies that the church he aspires to has never existed.'[13] The Church is to be a creative, traditioned response to the normative scriptural texts, attempting faithfulness to their inner coherence rather than slavish imitation of their partial descriptions of particular local moments. Insights such as these began to inform Nigel's own perception of how the Church should be shaped by the Scriptures.

The startling claim in *New Baptists* that 'the true church is yet to come' owes more to the other key figure in Nigel's doctoral research, Jürgen Moltmann. Moltmann's early project, the 'theology of hope',[14] stressed the priority of the future. He explicitly worked this out in connection with a radical ecclesiology: the Church must reject the temptation to become the 'public cult' of Christendom or the private club of pietisms in modernity; rather it must live in the expectation of its own future life as a radical and incomprehensible community.[15]

The local congregation

Nigel's ecclesiological hermeneutic developed, then, through engagement with Yoder and Moltmann. At the same time, it would seem, these two thinkers helped him to develop a distinctive political theology. This is expressed most clearly and positively in *Free Church, Free State*. Somewhere near the heart of the ecclesiology expounded in that book is a conviction about the active lordship of Christ; this defines practices of church life, and the proper relationships between Church and state.

In the Church, Christ's active lordship removes the possibility of any other authority structures.[16] All Christian traditions confess Christ as Lord, of course, but the baptist distinctive is to see a real and present activity in Christ's lordship.

---

[13] Wright, *Disavowing Constantine*, 60-63; quote from 61.
[14] Advanced not just in *Theology of Hope* (ET London: SCM, 1967) but in all Moltmann's writing until *The Crucified God* (London: SCM, 1974).
[15] Moltmann, *Theology of Hope*, 304-325.
[16] [Editor: For what follows see also the essay by Took in this volume.]

Christ rules in the congregation, and because Christ rules, no-one else can claim final authority. Every decision or direction flowing from whatever leadership structures are in place is in principle open to correction. The baptist conviction, further, is that Christ chooses to make his directions known through the whole body of the gathered church. In Nigel's thought, and in classical Free Church ecclesiology, this has two implications:

On the one hand, it implies that leadership within the congregation carries only moral authority. Christ does not speak definitively and finally to those who are ordained in a particular place or to those who are entrusted with particular ministries of leadership. We expect, of course, our leaders to pray, study, and seek guidance, and we suppose that they will hear from the Lord in the course of this; but after they have sought and shared insight, their ideas remain provisional and corrigible until confirmed by the gathered fellowship. Christ's active lordship, as understood by Baptists and others in the Free Church / Believers' Church tradition, decisively relativises the authority of ordained clergy.

On the other hand, this belief locates the ability and the duty to discern the mind of Christ within the local fellowship. Each gathered church is able to govern itself in communion with the triune God without any other intervention. Baptist churches rejoice in their fellowship with other congregations locally and across the world; but they do not need that fellowship to be, authentically, church. The local covenanted community of believers is Church, regardless of its history and its external relations.

This point is, well, 'radical', in the Christian tradition and so bears examination. The local ecclesial community finds its legitimacy not in continuity with the church down through the ages, nor in being able to trace its lineage back to the apostles, nor in fellowship with the Church across the world, in being in communion with other Christians in other places. Its own life is sufficient for it to be Church.

This point has decisive missional implications. It happens that today I heard of a (smallish) group of Christian believers in an Islamic country who each, individually, had made a commitment to Christ, and who had begun worshipping together.[17] They have no minister who has been ordained and/or authorised by a wider or higher body; they have no real fellowship or connection with the

---

[17] I presume that they were each baptised, although the point was not explicit in the report.

wider body of Christ. Is what is happening there, today, church? The baptist ecclesiology that Nigel has championed would insist yes; I think he is simply right on this point.

This does not remove the fact that it is both good and right for churches to be in fellowship with one another. Neither Nigel's own ecclesiology nor the wider baptistic ecclesiology in the mainstream of its development has ever questioned this point. Nigel cites the famous Abingdon doctrine of association: 'there is the same relationship between one church and another as there is between the members of one church'.[18] In a baptistic ecclesiology, this is an astonishingly strong statement: members of one church are covenanted together in such a way that their discipleship is mutual - if one falls, all fall. So it is with the churches of Christ. There is a positive duty to be in fellowship with other Christian churches, but not a need. If there are no other local Christian churches or if the possibilities of fellowship are restricted by distance, difficulty, or persecution, that does not affect the ecclesial reality of the isolated local church. Its status as a true Church of Christ, a true and complete instantiation of the universal Church, is guaranteed by its local internal life, regardless of its relationship, or lack thereof, with other ecclesial bodies or with translocal ministries.

Political theology
Nigel's account of the ecclesiology of a free church is clear and compelling, but fairly standard. It is his relationship of this to political theology that explores new ground. In the Reformation debates there were basically two options: the magisterial reformers, together with the Roman theologians, held that the state was ordained by God alongside the Church, and so tried to develop a sophisticated theology of both; the Anabaptists held that the perfection of Christian discipleship was simply incompatible with the necessary compromises, particularly with the power of the sword, into which the state had to enter, and so there was no serious theology of the state - theology taught how to live counter-culturally, not how to understand the culture.

The English Free Churches, from Helwys, through Owen, and down to today, have wanted to maintain the Anabaptist witness to the radical nature of true discipleship, but to align it with a theology of the state that is not merely negative. This is, in a

---

[18] Wright, *Free Church, Free State*, 188.

sense, a further rejection of Augustine. In the *Civitas Dei* Augustine had argued that the 'City of humanity' had no interesting or lasting ethical insights. It offered a merely pragmatic account of how to maximise peace (understood in a fairly reductionist way, excluding almost any notion of justice); because a peaceable city offers the most fertile ground for the propagation and spread of the gospel, this 'earthly peace' is to be welcomed by the churches as providing the most amenable context for their life to flourish.

For the Free Church ecclesiology of which Nigel is an able representative, this is not enough, in at least two ways. On the one hand, the church simply demands more space than this account can offer it. We do not wish simply to propagate a gospel of individual salvation; we want to live out a model of redeemed (or at least being-redeemed) human sociality. The existence of gathered churches, if they are true to their calling, will always be a challenge, mute perhaps, but eloquent, to the culture of the day. Churches will live in a way that models different commitments about the place of human beings in the world - commitments at once more realistic, in their grasp of the truth of human sinfulness, and more optimistic, in their awareness of the wonderful truth that Christ has conquered all sin.

But the account that Nigel develops is not merely a negative rejection of certain errors, but a positive embracing of certain themes that generate a baptist theology of the state.[19] This is the distinctive political theology I mentioned earlier. The argument would seem to go roughly like this: God's call on the Church is to maintain a distinctive and counter-cultural witness, seeking to shape society through persuasion and through evangelism. Given this, the state must either be seen as inevitably demonic, opposed to Christ's activity in and through the Church (a view sometimes held amongst the continental Anabaptists) or there must be a proper ethic of statehood, which consists primarily in providing the space for the Church to be true to its calling. Nigel locates the state within the order of preservation, the gracious divine sustaining of the world after its fall as it waits for its final redemption.[20] The state is not the way God will graciously redeem the world; nor is the state the way the world was originally created to be. *Society* is part of God's good ordering of the world, but the

---

[19] [Editor: For what follows compare the essays by Colwell and Took in this volume.]
[20] Wright, *Free Church, Free State*, 236.

state is a permissive ordinance designed to limit the damage caused by the fall. The state does this, on Nigel's telling, by fulfilling three callings: the delivery of justice, the maintenance of peace, and the protection of freedom.

The Church will honour and support the state in its attempts to live out these callings. It will call the state to faithfulness and witness to the impermanence of the state by its life. It will not, however, form an alliance with the state. God's work of redemption cannot be accomplished by an agent of the order of preservation. The state's characteristic posture is coercion, which is an appropriate act in its sphere: the state coerces those who would threaten justice, peace or freedom to maintain those goods. The Church cannot attempt to coerce unbelievers to accept the gospel: to do so would be to trespass on ground where Christ alone is King. The Church's characteristic posture is therefore persuasion.

This political theology is developed in *Free Church, Free State* in dialogue with the biblical witness, particularly with Romans 13, but it is hardly the straightforward reading off of New Testament practice that marked the ecclesiology of *The Radical Kingdom*. This is a sophisticated theology of a radical Church life recognisably in continuity with the patterns of Reformation described by Williams. Does it, however, relate in any way to the radicalism of the earlier book, found in uncompromising discipleship and an expectation of God's present miraculous action in the life of the Church?

The commitment to discipleship is easier to understand: the believers' Church tradition, represented by Yoder, found part of its distinctiveness in the expectation of serious discipleship amongst members of the churches. Moltmann's major direct appeal to Yoder in his work (as far as I am aware) is on precisely this point: the 'perfect obedience' of Christ is, in Yoder's formulation, not merely the condition for salvation but the model for Christian life.[21] Christian ethics is not about finding plausible ways of living in the world, but about following Jesus, even if that should be offensive, useless or incomprehensible in the eyes of the world.

This, however, is a very particular model of serious discipleship, and one that is different from that usually associated with the restorationist strand of the charismatic movement. There, discipleship was often defined in legalistic terms (a fault not absent

---

[21] Jürgen Moltmann, *The way of Jesus Christ: Christology in messianic dimensions* (London: SCM, 1990) 118.

from Anabaptist expressions, it must be said), and it was developed within a context of strong structures of authority, usually involving close personal accountability to a particular pastor, the practice known as 'covering' or 'shepherding'. Discipleship thus became a matter of referring all decisions to a human ecclesial authority for approval. In *The Radical Kingdom*, this is the one area of restorationist tradition that Nigel criticised most heavily.[22] He developed instead a view of authority which is shaped by the 'servant leadership' of Jesus and an account of the role of the apostle that stresses mission, not imposition, as the core and defining activity of the calling/gifting. The account is visibly 'restorationist' in that it still appeals to a normative and timeless pattern of Church life found in the New Testament; it merely disagrees with other, contemporaneous, restorationist accounts of what that pattern looks like.

This criticism is re-affirmed, more strongly, in *Charismatic Renewal*, to which Nigel contributed three chapters. The first, some biographical reflections, returns to the criticisms of patterns of authority in Restorationism, this time with explicit appeal to the Anabaptist tradition.[23] The two later chapters are critiques, clearly friendly, although sometimes sharp, of the practices and teachings of a different strand of charismatic renewal, one that also influenced Nigel deeply, that associated with the name of John Wimber.[24]

Both chapters can be read as a criticism of a dualistic worldview which sees God at work in the spectacular and immediate but not in the ordinary. The first explicitly identifies this dualism, and then mainly deals with healing.[25] The argument is largely that a better theology of creation and the goodness of this world is necessary for a right understanding of Christian healing, which may take place as well through the skilled hands of a surgeon as through the shaking hands of a prayer-ministry team. The other chapter, although very brief, is more interesting for my argument.[26] It addresses the question of prophetic ministry, firstly

---

[22] Wright, *Radical Kingdom*, 82-116.
[23] Nigel Wright, 'A Pilgrimage in Renewal' in Smail, Walker and Wright, *Charismatic Renewal*, 22-32.
[24] [Editor: See also Smail's essay in this volume.]
[25] Nigel Wright, 'The Theology and Methodology of "Signs and Wonders"' in Smail, Walker and Wright, *Charismatic Renewal*, 71-85.
[26] Nigel Wright, 'The Rise of the Prophetic' in Smail, Walker and Wright, *Charismatic Renewal*, 117-122.

through a consideration of Paul Cain, but then by arguing that Martin Lloyd-Jones and Martin Luther King had at least as much right to be considered Christian prophets, through a commitment to proclaiming scriptural truth (Lloyd-Jones) and an uncompromising witness to biblical patterns of justice (King). This places the question of political theology on the agenda.

Revelation
Political theology had not, in fact, been absent from *The Radical Kingdom*, in which Nigel had demanded that the new churches should be agents for social change, an idea not common in charismatic circles at the time.[27] The authentically 'restored' Church will be politically radical, in three ways: It will model an alternative lifestyle, living out a community vision that is incomprehensible, or at least hopelessly idealistic, to the world around; it will witness to 'the principalities and powers'; and it will involve itself in service where it can, and remain separate from the evil world where it must. It is striking that, in some contrast to the rest of the book, the appeal in this chapter is not to the practices of the New Testament church, but to deep theological themes. The question of the relationship of Nigel's two ways of being 'radical' was, in that sense, already present in the book.

There are two major differences between this chapter and the more developed visions in *Free Church, Free State*. Neither is directly related to my argument but both are interesting enough to highlight. One concerns the developed theology of the state in the later book, which is entirely absent from the earlier work. The other, perhaps more interestingly, concerns an account of the spiritual reality of the world. In *The Radical Kingdom*, society is shaped by the 'principalities and powers', unseen spiritual forces; these are wholly absent from *Free Church, Free State*, where we are told, surprisingly perhaps, that the New Testament language of principalities and powers refers to human rulers and that '[t]here is, of course, no state "as such", no metaphysical entity of independent existence outside the people who compose it.'[28] I suspect a developed political theology will need more of the understanding of the spiritual reality of the state suggested by the 'principalities and powers' language and the imagery of the book of

---

[27] Wright, *The Radical Kingdom*, 117-132, the chapter entitled 'Restoration and Contemporary Society'.
[28] Wright, *Free Church, Free State*, 229, 236.

Revelation, whether in the 'mythological' form of active spiritual forces or in the idea of a 'collective ethos' or some such.

Can a radical political theology and a radical ecclesiology, that seeks primarily faithfulness to the New Testament, be coordinated? I suspect that they can, through attention to a text which is surprisingly rarely appealed to in Nigel's corpus: the Book of Revelation. There, the writer offers us (in highly symbolic form) a vision of the spiritual realities that underlie the sweep of human history. The Church of Jesus Christ is seen to be the decisive reality around which the history of nations will break and flow; but the task of the Church is merely to witness, to suffer in faithful devotion to God as Jesus Christ first suffered. There is powerful political theology here, very similar to that which Nigel developed through his reading of Yoder and Moltmann, and built, simply, on the practices and self-understanding of the New Testament churches.

There is not space for much exegesis to demonstrate this point; any worthwhile commentary will confirm it repeatedly. Let me, however, offer one striking, if disputed, illustration in closing. In the vision of the risen Christ in Revelation 1 we are told he holds seven stars in his right hand. These stars are identified as 'the angels of the churches'. The precise import of 'angels' here need not detain us; suffice to say that all the various theories stress that the angels can virtually be considered identical with the churches. Why seven stars? One idea in the literature suggests an allusion to the then-current traditions of astrology, which saw in the seven known moving stars (the Sun, Moon, Mercury, Venus, Mars, Saturn and Jupiter) the forces which shaped the destiny of humans and nations. John's image offers a radical reversal: it is faithful, broken, suffering, failing, little local church fellowships that will cause the rise and fall of empires and rulers. They will overcome, not through force of conquest or compulsion, but 'by the blood of the Lamb and the word of their witness' (Revelation 12:11). Free churches, witnessing to the coming of a radical kingdom, and so creating and shaping free states. Here, I suggest, is the missing exegetical link in Nigel's ecclesiology.

Church planting, peace and the ecclesial minimum

Stuart Murray

Introduction
Free Church, Free State[1] is an accessible, attractive and winsome introduction to both the internal dynamics of church life and the church's relationship with the social order. In this book, Nigel Wright presents and commends a distinctive baptist[2] ecclesiology and distinguishes this, carefully but not polemically, from ways in which other traditions have understood the church.

In his introductory discussion of the significance of various characteristics of the church (especially pages 18-20)[3] Wright employs the phrase 'ecclesial minimum' to tease out those elements he regards as essential, without which he would be reluctant to regard any community as authentically church. These elements include (with particular reference to Matthew 18:20 and Acts 2:41-42) a covenanted community of disciples, their confession of faith in Christ, the doctrine of Christ rooted in the apostolic testimony, the practices of baptism and the Lord's Supper (19-20).

At the end of this discussion (20) Wright buttresses the notion of an ecclesial minimum with terms that are more familiar to Catholics and Anglicans: *esse, bene esse* and *plene esse*. Some things pertain to the very essence of the church and so equate to the ecclesial minimum (*esse*); others are important for its well-being (*bene esse*); and others characterise the church in its fullness or maturity (*plene esse*). While it may sometimes be necessary to identify those aspects of the church that are essential – and salutary to realise how many familiar and precious features of church life are not essential – this results in a rather thin description. So *Free Church, Free State* proceeds to explore other

---

[1] Nigel G. Wright, *Free Church, Free State: The Positive Baptist Vision* (Milton Keynes: Paternoster, 2005).
[2] Throughout the book, 'baptist' is used for the broader tradition stemming from the radical wing of the European Reformation to which 'Baptist' churches belong. This tradition, according to Wright (*Free Church, Free State*, xxiii), includes Mennonites, Brethren, Pentecostals, Disciples of Christ and others, although whether these groups would welcome cooption into the category of 'baptist' is not explored. The same usage of 'Baptist' and 'baptist' will be employed here.
[3] Numbers in brackets refer to pages in Wright, *Free Church, Free State*.

dimensions of church life that may not be absolutely essential but are vital if a church is to participate faithfully and effectively in the mission of God and press on towards maturity.

My intention in this chapter is to explore two issues that are dealt with only briefly in the book: the practice of church planting and a commitment to peace. Wright affirms both without indicating how these relate to the *esse*, *bene esse* and *plene esse* framework, although as they do not appear in his summary of the ecclesial minimum, they must presumably be allocated to one of the latter categories. He investigates briefly (246-249) some of the implications of the church embracing a commitment to non-violence and suggests (252) that there are features of baptist ecclesiology that may facilitate effective church planting. But neither subject is afforded the attention given to other topics in the book, such as church government, ministry and ordination, associating or the place of children in the church. I believe both subjects warrant further attention as components in a baptist ecclesiology, as aspects of the *bene esse* or *plene esse* of the church. One or both might also lay claim to inclusion in the ecclesial minimum or *esse* of the church.

Church planting

A graph representing the incidence of church planting initiatives between 1990 and the present day in most British denominations would show a peak in the mid-90s, followed by a trough during the latter part of that decade and the early years of the next, before a slowly rising line indicating that church planting is increasing again. Although there are exceptions to this picture (and plausible explanations for these exceptions), this has been the shared experience of Anglicans, Baptists, Methodists, Assemblies of God, Salvation Army and others.[4]

During the period represented by the trough on the graph, there was sustained reflection in several denominations on issues that had not been adequately addressed in the previous years when church planting had been widely endorsed and enthusiastically practised. Not least among the questions demanding attention was why many new churches had failed to thrive or had already closed. Was this the result of inadequate research, preparation and training, coupled with poor leadership?

---

[4] For details, see George W. Lings and Stuart Murray, *Church Planting: Past, Present and Future* (Cambridge: Grove, 2003).

Were expectations of numerical growth and the speed at which this might occur unrealistic? Did these new churches have deep enough spiritual and theological foundations to persist beyond the initial enthusiasm?

If the primary question at the start of the 1990s was 'how many churches can we plant?', conversations at the end of the decade revolved around the question: 'what kind of church should we plant?' or even 'what do we mean by church?' The rise of the phenomenon we now know as 'emerging church' and the subsequent authorisation of 'fresh expressions of church' (especially but not exclusively in Anglican and Methodist circles) in the wake of the *Mission-shaped Church* report[5] have provoked many others to ponder these questions and have ensured that few church planters today ignore these ecclesial issues.

An exercise I have often used to help practitioners and their sponsors think through and articulate their ecclesiology involves a chart listing features of church life. Participants are invited to designate each item as 'non-negotiable' or 'negotiable' as they reflect on their contexts and planting plans. There is also an 'unsure' option. Groups of three then reveal their convictions to one another and explore areas of divergence – which usually results in animated conversations. Subsequent plenary discussions have elicited the following conclusions:

- In no threesome, let alone an entire group of participants, has there been complete agreement on what is negotiable or non-negotiable. In every case an element that one participant has deemed essential, another has perceived as non-essential.
- This lack of unanimity on essentials has surprised, and sometimes disturbed, those who had assumed they were agreed on such foundational issues. Chastened, they have determined to reflect further together on what they are planting and why.
- There has been growing appreciation of the influence of contextual factors, with some participants arguing that certain aspects may not be essential everywhere but are vital in their particular community. Many participants ticked the 'unsure' box for this reason.

---

[5] *Mission-shaped Church* (London: Church House, 2004).

- Some participants have commented that they had never even considered certain items on my list, but in some cases they now perceived these as non-negotiable.

Although I tend to avoid the use of Latin tags, this exercise encourages practitioners to consider which (familiar and apparently less familiar) ecclesial features constitute the *esse*, *bene esse* and *plene esse* of church. It invites them to identify what they perceive as the 'ecclesial minimum' as a starting point for planning a new church.

To practitioners wrestling with these issues in various local contexts and to those who are responsible for equipping, deploying and supporting these practitioners, *Free Church, Free State* offers both resources and challenges. Some of these are especially pertinent to Baptist (or baptist) church planters; others have wider relevance. For baptists especially, it is an accessible primer that investigates – in much greater depth than is possible in this exercise – key issues that they should consider as they move forward. They may not agree with all of its emphases and conclusions: not all will be convinced by Wright's arguments for ordained ministry, and some may be disappointed that the section on 'the priority of mission' (16-17) is very brief and does not seem to lay the foundations for a more missional ecclesiology in the rest of the book. Indeed, if 'mission has to be seen ... as the defining essence of the church' (16) it is strange that mission is not included in the characteristics that make up the 'ecclesial minimum' and reappears only sporadically.

Together

A further weakness of church planting in the 1990s, particularly apparent among baptists, was the absence of any coherent mission strategy. That the vision, energy, personnel and funding for church planting initiatives arose almost entirely from local congregations is unsurprising, given the baptist emphasis on what many refer to as the 'autonomy' of the local church, but which Wright helpfully prefers to call the 'competence' of the local church (183). But the result of this reliance on entrepreneurial local initiatives was that new churches were planted where there were sufficient resources rather than where the greatest mission needs or opportunities were identified. Putting this bluntly, most church planting was into the relatively comfortable suburban and small-town neighbourhoods in which baptist and other churches were already flourishing. Not only did this ignore the needs of poorer communities, marginalise the inner cities and rural communities, and avoid the challenges of cross-cultural mission; it exacerbated the unequal distribution of churches and reinforced the perception that the church is a middle-class institution.

So what are the alternatives? Centralised planning and national church planting strategies are unlikely to generate much enthusiasm among baptists; furthermore, denominations that have adopted this approach have not been conspicuously effective in planting churches. But baptist church planting need not succumb to the inevitability of localism. There is a middle way that is much more congruent with baptist ecclesiology, to which Wright points (albeit without explicit reference to church planting) in the chapter entitled 'Relating and Resourcing' (183-203). 'Churches', he writes, 'freely choose to relate to other congregations in order to express life together as the body of Christ more fully and for common purposes in the service of mission' (186). These 'common purposes in the service of mission' are not limited to church planting, of course, but church planting is a significant means by which they may 'express life together as the body of Christ'.

Associating with others beyond the local church – whether through regional structures, such as Baptist Associations, or informally – opens up new possibilities for baptist church planting:

- Regional research and consultation can identify opportunities and priorities that will probably not be considered by a single local church because they are beyond their geographical or cultural range.
- Associating with others enables a church planting team to be assembled out of several congregations, endangering the health of each church less[6] and providing a broader support base for this new initiative.
- Such church planting teams bring with them diverse experiences of church life and so are less likely to clone an existing model and more able to think creatively and contextually about the church they are planting.
- Lessons learned from church planting initiatives can be shared more widely than when only a single church is

---

[6] Some churches have been seriously, even terminally, weakened by over-ambitious planting initiatives.

directly involved, enabling experience to grow and expertise to be developed.

There were very few examples of 'church planting through associating' in the 1990s, but there were some, including some officially sponsored by regional Associations within the Baptist Union and relational partnerships (such as the Cornerstone group in the Cotswolds[7]). It has been encouraging to hear of conversations in several Associations during 2008 about developing church planting strategies. Perhaps baptist church planting in the coming years will embrace this more strategic and cooperative approach, which continues to endorse the competence of local churches but sets this within the broader framework of associating. For this to be the case, a deeper understanding of the concept of association – which Wright insists (187) has been present among English Baptists since their beginnings in the sixteenth century[8] – is essential.

Wright in this chapter also rehearses a case he has made elsewhere[9] for baptist 'bishops', arguing that such translocal ministry is necessary for the *bene esse* and *plene esse* of the church and 'almost necessary' (198) for its *esse*. Reflecting on why Anglicans have in the past few years launched several hundred 'fresh expressions of church' while baptists have been involved in far fewer missional initiatives of this kind, I strongly suspect that the permission-giving role of bishops is at least part of the reason. Fresh expressions of church are potentially threatening to inherited forms of church, implicitly critical of their culture, practices and missional capability. Gaining support from local churches for such initiatives can be problematic. But permission and support from and accountability to a bishop has allowed many fresh expressions to flourish. There might be an analogous role for translocal ministries within baptist denominations.

Whether 'bishop' is the best term for translocal ministry among baptists is a moot point. Wright advocates this in preference to the historic 'messenger' or arguably pretentious 'apostle' (203), partly on the grounds that the term is widely recognised. What is much more important – if translocal ministry is to fulfil its missional potential, including the development and

---

[7] See www.cornerstone-churches.org.uk.
[8] [Editor: See also the essay by Brown in this volume.]
[9] Especially in Nigel G. Wright, *Challenge to Change: A Radical Agenda for Baptists* (Eastbourne: Kingsway, 1991) chapter 7.

oversight of strategic church planting initiatives – is having suitably gifted men and women in translocal roles (which has implications for selection criteria), providing appropriate induction and training for them as they move out of local ministry, and releasing them from onerous administrative and pastoral responsibilities.[10]

Renewal
The paragraph in *Free Church, Free State* which introduces a brief discussion of church planting is worth quoting at length (252):

> It may be said then that the baptist tradition is inherently progressive in that it expects to learn and change. To be true to the tradition is to be oriented towards the future and to be aware of a pilgrimage in which we will both learn new ways and adapt old ways to the new circumstances in which we live. This open flexibility is one reason why the baptist way of being church has proven to be highly effective in the mission of the church. It also has the capacity to adapt itself to future needs.

As Wright explains, this 'open flexibility' is not only the basis for engaging in church planting *per se*, but in contextually sensitive and culturally appropriate forms of church planting (252-256). Baptist church planters need to take careful note of this. Too many churches planted in the past twenty years have replicated rather than adapted old ways. Many have eschewed new ways, paying inadequate attention both to their circumstances and to the 'inherently progressive' nature of their own tradition. This will not do. If the church is to demonstrate the capacity to adapt itself to an emerging culture that is diverse and changing more rapidly than at any time in history, baptist church planters will need to be more deeply rooted than ever in their baptist tradition so that they have the resources, instincts and reflexes to be missionary pilgrims.

In several ways, then, *Free Church, Free State*, despite mentioning church planting only occasionally, offers vital insights, challenges and resources for church planters and those who deploy them. Indeed, the paragraph quoted above suggests that the baptist tradition itself provides a particularly helpful framework for church planting. And yet, church planting is mentioned only occasionally, and no indication is given of its ecclesial status.

---

[10] See further Stuart Murray (ed.), *Translocal Ministry: Equipping the Churches for Mission* (Didcot: Baptist Union, 2004).

There is surely reason to include it within the *bene esse* of the church: not only does this practice often (although not always) facilitate the church's participation in the *missio Dei*, but it is a primary means by which the church refreshes itself, reassesses its heritage and adapts to changing circumstances. Practised in the context of associating, church planting has the potential not only to increase the number of congregations but to offer the wider church opportunities for missional reflection and ecclesial renewal.

Should church planting be included within the more restricted company of features of church life that comprise its *esse*? A persuasive argument against inclusion is that church planting is not always contextually appropriate: in some situations there are already more than enough congregations and their nurture and renewal seems preferable to efforts to establish more. But this may be to succumb again to the perspective of localism. A glut of congregations in one region or neighbourhood does not mean that church planting is not necessary elsewhere or that churches in the saturated area cannot participate in this work in other ways than planting a new church nearby. Until the gospel fully penetrates all communities, and while cultures continue to mutate and evolve, church planting will remain a crucial aspect of the church's mission. If the *plene esse* of the church is to be reached, church planting is essential.

So might reproduction and constant renewal be a dimension of the *esse* of the church, as George Lings suggested at a church planting conference in the mid-1990s? Following his lead,[11] I argued several years ago that 'a healthy church does not just develop internally and expand in size and social impact, but naturally expresses its life in new forms and structures'.[12] If Wright is correct that 'the baptist tradition is inherently progressive in that it expects to learn and change', maybe church planting should be included within the *esse* of what the baptist tradition means by church.

Peace

This chapter has followed Wright's heuristic device of using 'baptist' to embrace what is often described as the 'believers'

---

[11] He has continued to pursue this line of thought in doctoral research due for completion before this book is published.
[12] Stuart Murray, *Church Planting: Laying Foundations* (Carlisle: Paternoster, 1998) 57-58.

church' tradition and 'Baptist' to identify the narrower stream within this tradition that emerged from the seventeenth-century English Baptists. There are advantages to this nomenclature, but there are also risks – not least that Baptist convictions may be predicated onto the wider baptist tradition or that emphases found in other streams of the baptist tradition may not be adequately represented if they are less amenable to Baptists. Perhaps this is why the issue of peace receives rather less attention than it might warrant in a discussion of baptist (rather than Baptist) ecclesiology.

Free Church, Free State includes within the baptist tradition the following movements: Mennonites, Brethren, Pentecostals, Disciples of Christ and unspecified others (xxiii). Wright also identifies the sixteenth-century Anabaptists as forerunners of this tradition (32-37) and of the English Baptists, 'certainly in spirit and possibly also by ancestry' (32).

Although not all early Anabaptists were unequivocally committed to non-violence, within a few years of the beginnings of this variegated movement principled commitment to the way of peace became a central characteristic. Anabaptists and Quakers together comprise the 'historic peace churches'. As Wright notes, early Anabaptists rejected violence (34), denied the legitimacy of enforcing religious conformity (36) and regarded the power of the 'sword' to be at variance with the way of Christ (37). They accepted the role of the civil authorities and recognised that those authorities would use violent means to keep order, but for most Anabaptists this precluded their involvement.

Mennonites, descendants of the branch of the Anabaptist movement associated with the Dutch pastor, Menno Simons, have generally retained this commitment to non-violence. There is some diversity of conviction and practice among contemporary Mennonites, but the weight of the tradition is firmly behind a commitment to pacifism.[13] In recent years the emphasis has shifted from non-violence to active peacemaking, as Mennonites have explored creative alternatives to violence.[14]

It is not clear whether the 'Brethren' in Nigel Wright's enumeration above are the Plymouth Brethren, Brethren in Christ or Church of the Brethren. The latter two denominations

---

[13] Article 22 of the Mennonite Confession of Faith (1995) clearly affirms the historic position on peace.
[14] Examples include Christian Peacemaker Teams, conflict resolution and mediation programmes and restorative approaches within the criminal justice system.

acknowledge their Anabaptist heritage and both are explicitly committed to the way of peace, not only in their official statements of faith but in the visibility given to the issue of peace on their websites.[15] If Wright has the Plymouth Brethren in view, while this movement would not trace its roots to Anabaptist forebears, peace witness was a significant concern of the early Brethren[16] and pacifism was 'widely held by early members',[17] although contemporary Brethren have not shown much interest in this issue.

Although Pentecostalism is generally associated with other features, such as baptism in the Spirit, speaking in tongues and healing, commentators were particularly struck by the dismantling of racial barriers in the early years of the movement and the reconciliation between black and white Christians. Many Pentecostals were also committed to pacifism, although (as with the Plymouth Brethren) this commitment gradually disappeared as the movement developed.[18]

As for the Disciples of Christ, the Encyclopaedia of the movement affirms categorically, 'Pacifism has been a central issue in the Stone-Campbell movement worldwide.'[19] This is unsurprising in light of the interest in peace of one of its founders, Alexander Campbell,[20] although the primary contemporary expression of this visible on their website relates to ministries for racial reconciliation.[21]

The picture emerging from this necessarily brief survey of the groups Wright names as representatives of the wider baptist tradition is that they all, at least in their early and formative years, emphasised what they variously referred to as peace testimony, peace witness and commitment to non-violence, pacifism or reconciliation. For some this became an enduring and central ecclesial conviction; others either de-emphasised or rejected the

---

[15] See www.bic-church.org and www.brethren.org.
[16] See Peter Brock, 'The Peace Testimony of the Early Plymouth Brethren', *Church History* 53 (1984) 30-45.
[17] Tim Grass, *Gathering in His Name* (Milton Keynes: Paternoster, 2006) 89.
[18] See Jay Beaman, *Pentecostal Pacifism: The Origin, Development, and Rejection of Pacific Belief among the Pentecostals* (Hillsboro, KA: Center for Mennonite Brethren Studies, 1989).
[19] Douglas A. Foster and Anthony L. Dunnavant, *The Encyclopedia of the Stone-Campbell Movement: Christian Church (Disciples of Christ), Christian Churches / Churches of Christ Churches of Christ* (Grand Rapids: Eerdmans, 2005) 586.
[20] See Craig M. Watts, *Disciple of Peace: Alexander Campbell on Pacifism, Violence and the State* (Indianapolis: Doulos Christou Press, 2005).
[21] See www.disciples.org and www.reconciliationmission.org.

stance of their forebears as the movement spread. But the ubiquity of interest in the issue of peace in these baptist denominations does seem to demand greater attention in baptist ecclesiology than it receives in *Free Church, Free State*.

In fact, the Baptist tradition is alone among the denominations named here in *not* having a historic commitment to peace. There have, of course, been individual Baptists who have embraced pacifism or advocated a peace witness, and the experiences of World War I led many more Baptists to reject the use of violence as incompatible with the way of Christ. Pacifism seems, for example, to have become quite widely embraced by Welsh Baptists. But this has not been a position most Baptists have adopted, or indeed an issue on which most Baptists have reflected greatly. The Baptist Peace Fellowship has attempted to keep the peace witness alive within the movement,[22] many regional ministers have received training in conflict resolution from the Mennonites,[23] and the Baptist Union Council from time to time passes motions challenging militarism, but a proposal that the Baptist Union of Great Britain should celebrate the year 2000 by declaring itself a 'peace church' received little support and attracted minimal interest. It is not surprising, then, that peace does not feature prominently in Baptist ecclesiology, but there is a stronger argument for it to feature prominently in baptist ecclesiology.

However, although the topic of peace may not feature prominently or frequently in *Free Church, Free State*, when it is mentioned, its significance is clear. We read that 'God's saving activity, revealed through Christ and the Spirit, is directed through the church towards the recovery of God's peace, of *shalom*' (235). Peace is the goal towards which redeemed humanity and restored creation are heading, and the church is caught up in the saving activity of God that has this end in view. But how this relates to the church's *esse*, *bene esse* or *plene esse* is unclear.

Wright acknowledges the mandate of the state to maintain peace along with justice and freedom, affirming its policing function to uphold social order and differentiating this from making war against other nations. He warns, though, that fallen structures can only ever deliver limited peace, justice and freedom, and he

---

[22] See www.baptist-peace.org.uk.
[23] See www.menno.org.uk/bridgebuilders.

recognises that questions remain about where the boundary between policing and making war should be drawn (238).

What is the role of the church vis-à-vis the state? Moving beyond the Anabaptist stance of separation, Wright advocates various forms of engagement that allow the church and individual Christians to play constructive and creative roles in society but do not invest unwarranted hope in fallen structures or ideologies (243-245, 270-279). One crucial role is faithfully being the church so that 'the justice, peace and freedom which are the responsibility of the state receive definition and are protected from distortion, in part, through the witness of the church' (243-244). Another role, which both baptists and Baptists have consistently fulfilled, is to argue for toleration rather than persecution or the championing of one faith over others in society (215-220).

The strongest statement on the subject of peace seems to align Wright with the broader baptist tradition and its Anabaptist forerunners: 'It needs to be asserted unambiguously that Christians are called to a non-violent life in imitation of Christ. God's redemptive purposes are not achieved through violence' (246). But in the discussion that follows, he notes that Baptists have dissented from the Anabaptist conviction that this unambiguous assertion precludes involvement in the state and participation in violence in the name of the state. This carefully nuanced argument (246-249) proposes distinctions between war and policing, between force and violence, and between the conscientious decisions of individual Christians and 'the peaceful way embodied in the Christian community as a whole' (248). Wright suggests that the state's use of force can be 'a possible sphere of Christian action', but only 'within the overall belief that it is the duty of the Christian to work for the reduction and minimisation of all forms of violence and coercion' (248).

This conclusion, and the argument that leads towards it, is undoubtedly representative of the best of Baptist thinking on the way in which Christians might communicate their commitment to peace and their concern to be actively and faithfully involved in society. Together with sections of the book that investigate other aspects of the relationship between church and state, this not only extends the scope of ecclesiology beyond its often narrow bounds, but offers a distinctive and attractive approach, neatly summed up in the book's title. What is less clear is the extent to which this represents baptist thinking and practice. Certainly not all the groups named as baptist in *Free Church, Free State* would be willing to accept the nuances and distinctions in Wright's argument here, however much they too are wrestling with the social and political outworking of their primary commitment to peace.

We return again to the question of whether such a commitment to peace belongs within the *esse, bene esse* or *plene esse* of the church – at least within a baptist ecclesiology. The eschatological dimension of peace noted above, namely the recovery of God's peace as the goal of God's saving activity, suggests that peace should be included within the *plene esse* of the church, especially if, as Wright argues, this saving activity is directed through the church to the establishment of *shalom*. It is a short step from here to the proposal that a commitment to peace should also be located within the *bene esse* of the church, both for the sake of its mission and for the sake of its internal health.

What about the *esse* of the church? Are other baptist traditions correct in placing greater emphasis on the issue of peace than most Baptists, or is the Baptist perspective a helpful corrective that precludes its inclusion within the *esse* of the church? One further strong statement in *Free Church, Free State* might point towards some mention of peace in any account of the ecclesial minimum. Wright insists: 'non-violence and active peacemaking are at the heart of the gospel and of the church's task' (246). If this is so, surely what is at the heart of the church's task and, indeed, of the gospel the church is commissioned to embody and proclaim, should be regarded as an aspect of its *esse*.

This is not to propose that pacifism should be affirmed as non-negotiable for members of baptist or other churches. Although pacifism has been a distinctive stance of many baptist communities over several centuries, there are enough dissenting voices to resist including this in the ecclesial minimum. But *Free Church, Free State*, however we interpret certain qualifications and enduring questions, presents a powerful case for the church to embrace non-violence and practise active peacemaking as central aspects of its participation in the mission of God to restore peace throughout creation.

Conclusion
The argument of this chapter is not primarily concerned with locating church planting or a commitment to peace within a particular ecclesial category. I have proposed that there might be sufficient grounds, including convictions expressed within *Free*

Church, Free State itself, to consider locating one or both of these practices within a baptist account of the ecclesial minimum. But whether or not this proposal is persuasive, if these practices are at least to be located within the *bene esse* of the church, I suggest that they warrant greater attention than many baptists give to them. Church planting is not just one mission strategy among others but an essential process whereby churches and traditions renew themselves. The commitment to peace is not just a special interest for a fringe group of baptists but adoption of ways of being and living that enable us to share in the peace-restoring mission of God and that invite us to anticipate this vision of *shalom* in our own communities. *Free Church, Free State* lays strong foundations for further exploration of these issues.

Part of a movement: Nigel Wright and Baptist life

Ian M. Randall

Writing a 'Presidential Postcard' in the *Baptist Times* of 30 May 2002, soon after having taken up the presidency of the Baptist Union of Great Britain, Nigel Wright affirmed a comment he had heard after the Baptist Assembly, that it was good to feel part of a 'movement'. 'This surely is better than feeling part of an institution or even a denomination', he commented.

> Movements are heading somewhere: they have purpose, intention and goal. They are dynamic, creative and energetic. Sometimes we need to be part of a movement because it will carry us when we can't carry ourselves.[1]

This comment illustrates something of the relationship that Nigel Wright has had with the Baptist denomination. He has spoken candidly about this. Before assuming the presidency of the Baptist Union he recalled that in his earlier days he regarded institutions as 'slow and lumbering', 'self-protective and self-interested', and 'obsessed with rules and regulations, not initiatives and action'. He added that he still believed we should 'watch them like hawks' but that he had 'come to see that they too have a place' and that people not rooted in a tradition had a tendency to become eccentric.[2]

In this essay I wish to explore aspects of the relationship that Nigel has had with Baptist life since his Christian conversion in the 1960s, when he first joined a Baptist congregation.[3] In the early 1970s he trained for ministry at Spurgeon's College. Since then he has been a pastor in two congregations, Ansdell Baptist Church and Altrincham Baptist Church, both in the North-West; has been the Tutor in Christian Doctrine and then later the Principal of Spurgeon's College; and has served as President of the Baptist Union, as well as fulfilling many other roles within the national and world-wide Baptist community. Here I will not be examining his Baptist and ecumenical involvement at European

---

[1] *Baptist Times* (30 May 2002) 5.
[2] Nigel Wright, 'From Poacher to President', *Talk. The Mainstream Magazine* (Spring 2002) 26
[3] As a close friend of Nigel's I find it too artificial to refer to him as 'Wright'.

and global level, important though these have been. Nigel's closest relationship has been to Baptist life in this country and I will look primarily at some of the distinctive contributions – as I see them – that Nigel has made to this particular Baptist community.

The charismatic dimension

The first contribution is in the area of charismatic spirituality. This is how Nigel described his first encounter with charismatic thinking:

> The mid-1960s were the years when charismatic renewal was making inroads into the mainstream Church. No soon was I converted, therefore, than I came up against the charismatic movement.

He read David Wilkerson's book, *The Cross and the Switchblade*, which talked from a pentecostal point of view about baptism in the Spirit and speaking in tongues. 'I was both attracted', Nigel commented, 'by the vital spiritual life and repelled (theologically ignorant though I was at this stage) by the theological language in which it was packaged.'[4] During his years as an undergraduate at Leeds University, Nigel was challenged by friends who had already entered into charismatic experience, including Judy, his future wife, and he discovered personally 'the gift of tongues'.[5] His reflection on what happened is significant: 'I see that this experience had more to do with assurance of salvation than with spiritual power.' He goes on:

> I am of the opinion that the experiences which are often called 'baptism of the Spirit' might properly be understood within the context of the doctrine of assurance. They are heart-warming moments when the knowledge of salvation wells up within the heart. To know that I too was not excluded from God's grace but made its object, did a lot for me, giving me a spiritual importance which was to lead me to a vocation in the ministry on completing university.[6]

---

[4] Nigel Wright, 'A Pilgrimage in Renewal', in Tom Smail, Andrew Walker and Nigel Wright, *Charismatic Renewal: The Search for a Theology* (London: SPCK, 1993) 24.
[5] For the charismatic movement of that period see P. Hocken, *Streams of Renewal: The Origins and Early Development of the Charismatic Movement in Britain* (Carlisle: Paternoster, 1997).
[6] Wright, 'Pilgrimage', 24-25.

This vocation took Nigel to Spurgeon's College to train, and then, in 1973, to his first pastorate – Ansdell Baptist Church, Lytham St Anne's. There were clear signs of new life and growth in a number of Baptist churches in England in the 1970s and in certain cases this was directly linked with charismatic renewal. Among the Baptist churches in the North which grew in this period was Ansdell, which went from 62 to 198 members under Nigel's leadership.[7] In the early period of his charismatic experience it seemed as if renewal brought personal spiritual benefits with no obvious implications for the corporate life of the church. But as a minister he had a growing conviction that the church needed to be renewed and restored, that the new wine of spiritual experience demanded new wineskins of reformed structures. There were, however, acute tensions in some Baptist churches about how this should be achieved. The House Church movement or Restorationism (expressing the belief that a New Testament model of the church could be restored) was growing rapidly.[8] In 1976 Bryn Jones, in Bradford, launched the Dales Bible Week, Harrogate, which was soon attracting 9000 people. Another Restorationist leader, Arthur Wallis, had written: 'I see no future for denominations, but a glorious future for the body of Christ.'[9] Nigel later spoke of a 'haemorrhaging of churches and pastors' out of the Baptist Union into Restorationist networks.[10] He himself was attracted by the emphasis on the 'apostolic' dimension of ministry stressed in these networks, but felt very uneasy about the authority of apostolic figures and the call for submission to them.[11]

A consultation at Ansdell Baptist Church in July 1981 drew together fifty Baptist ministers, through the initiative of a small group of ministers in the North-West affected by charismatic renewal. This group had been developing a 'covenant' relationship

---

[7] Ian Sellers (ed.), *Our Heritage: The Baptists of Yorkshire, Lancashire and Cheshire, 1647-1987* (Leeds: Yorkshire Baptist Association and Lancashire & Cheshire Baptist Association, 1987) 152.
[8] Andrew Walker, *Restoring the Kingdom* (London: Hodder & Stoughton, 1985).
[9] *Renewal* 52 (1974) 16.
[10] Nigel Wright, 'Becoming a denomination worth joining', *Talk. The Mainstream Magazine* (Summer 2001) 18. By the 1980s there were at least ten distinct Restorationist networks: Nigel Wright, 'The Nature and Variety of Restorationism and the "House Church" Movement', in Stephen Hunt, Malcolm Hamilton and Tony Walter (eds.), *Charismatic Christianity: Sociological Perspectives* (Basingstoke: Macmillan Press, 1997) 60-76.
[11] Wright, 'Pilgrimage', 26.

in order to pastor one another. The purpose of the larger meeting at Ansdell was to

> discuss, pray and explore together concerning the ways in which ministers involved in the present move of the Holy Spirit in renewal can grow together, work together, and discover new depths of commitment to one another.[12]

This development, in which Nigel was fully involved, was to be significant as a vision for renewal in the denomination took shape. Members of the Ansdell congregation were taken into unexpected dimensions of charismatic renewal a year later. Nigel had heard that the Anglican charismatic leader, David Watson, had been hosting John Wimber and a team from California, and this team was then invited to Ansdell for a Renewal Weekend on 'power evangelism'. When an associate of Wimber's, Lonnie Frisbee, climbed into the pulpit and said 'Come, Holy Spirit', the results were remarkable. As Nigel described it, 'Within seconds the Spirit of God had fallen upon a large proportion of the congregation.' Many of those present began to tremble, speak in tongues and prophesy.[13]

By 1983 the initial group of ministers in the North-West had expanded and for a time Douglas McBain, from Lewin Road Baptist Church, Streatham, gave what was described as 'apostolic input'.[14] McBain had been a pioneer of charismatic renewal in Baptist life and would later become London Baptist Superintendent.[15] In 1986 Nigel resigned his pastorate, and spent a year in theological research.[16] A year later he was appointed Tutor in Christian Doctrine at Spurgeon's College, a post which gave him significant opportunities to contribute to the development

---

[12] *Renewal* 96 (December 1981/January 1982) 13-14; cf. Nigel G. Wright, 'Gleanings from the North West', *Mainstream Newsletter* (January 1982) 4-6.
[13] Wright, 'Pilgrimage', 27; see also Nigel Wright, 'A Baptist Evaluation' in David Pytches (ed.), *John Wimber: His Influence and Legacy* (Guildford: Eagle, 1998) 244-256. [Editor: See also the essay by Smail in this volume.]
[14] M. Beaumont, 'Growing together in committed covenant relationships', *Mainstream Newsletter* 13 (April 1983) 3.
[15] For his account of Baptist renewal, see Douglas McBain, *Fire over the Waters: Renewal among Baptists and others from the 1960s to the 1990s* (London: Darton, Longman and Todd, 1997) 50.
[16] Nigel's theological thinking in this period produced his book *The Fair Face of Evil: Putting the Power of Darkness in its Place* (London: Marshall Pickering, 1989), which was later revised and published as *A Theology of the Dark Side* (Carlisle: Paternoster, 2002).

of Baptist ministers. Nigel was determined by this time to seek to stimulate serious theological engagement with renewal. 'It appears to me', he commented later, 'that a feature of the aftermath of renewal is a deep hunger for understanding, and that this is a mark of its authenticity.'[17] In a key book, *The Radical Kingdom* (1986), Nigel probed Restorationist thinking. It was now clear that he was emerging as the foremost Baptist thinker dealing with ecclesiology and spirituality in relation to renewal. He was critical of the 'rigid and slavish attempt' by some Restorationists 'to decode the New Testament and to bring life into a sterile conformity with it', and argued for a view of renewal that embraced the whole church.[18] It was such inclusive renewal that he would continue to advocate and that many Baptists would welcome.

In fact a survey at Spurgeon's College in 1989 showed that 80% of the students saw themselves as charismatic in their spiritual experience.[19] Thus Nigel was in touch with the spirituality of a younger generation of Baptists in a way that was unusual for Baptist leaders of that period. Paul Beasley-Murray, the College Principal, considered that Nigel's commitment to charismatic renewal would bring a healthy balance to Spurgeon's. The College, he emphasised, had connections with all areas of Baptist life and work – Baptist Union and non-Union, including charismatic groups.[20] Nigel's thinking about Baptists and renewal was expressed in 1991 in his highly influential book *Challenge to Change* in terms of 'renewed Baptist' identity, which took full account of the Spirit's work and re-appropriated Baptist values.[21] The trajectory of Nigel's own thinking was indicated in 1993 when he wrote that

> it does appear to me that charismatic renewal is merging again with the primary traditions of the Church's life and becoming less an entity in itself and more a seasoning and a dimension in the totality of the Church's life. (...) In more theological terms, having emphasised the Spirit and sought

---

[17] Wright, 'Pilgrimage', 29.
[18] Nigel G. Wright, *The Radical Kingdom* (Eastbourne: Kingsway, 1986) 19, 140.
[19] *Baptist Times* (21 December 1989) 10.
[20] Minutes of a Spurgeon's College Council Conference, 9-10 January 1987; see Ian M. Randall, *A School of the Prophets* (London: Spurgeon's College, 2005) 55.
[21] Nigel G. Wright, *Challenge to Change: A Radical Agenda for Baptists* (Eastbourne: Kingsway, 1991) 21-22. David Coffey wrote the foreword.

to give him place, there is now an entirely consistent and appropriate need to become fully trinitarian.[22]

Baptists for Life and Growth

An important vehicle for the articulation of Nigel's thinking to the wider Baptist constituency in the 1980s was Mainstream. Informal discussions about needs within Baptist life led to a meeting in February 1978 between Raymond Brown, then Principal of Spurgeon's College, Douglas McBain and Paul Beasley-Murray, then minister of Altrincham Baptist Church. The launch of a new movement, with the title 'Mainstream', was agreed. The sub-heading was 'Baptists for Life and Growth'.[23] The evangelicals who came together in Mainstream wished to avoid separatism (in the early 1970s a number of conservative evangelicals had left the Baptist Union) and also charismatic divides. The early Mainstream leadership included Raymond Brown as president and David Coffey, who was minister of Upton Vale Baptist Church in the 1980s, as secretary. Mainstream was publicly launched at a late night extra at the 1979 Assembly and attracted 700 people.[24] Nigel was one of those who was attracted to this new movement and in 1998 he wrote:

> I think I can claim with justification to be one of the few people still involved with Mainstream in an official capacity also to have been involved, albeit modestly, in its beginnings twenty years ago.[25]

Soon Nigel was writing regularly for the *Mainstream Newsletter*.

One of the strategies of Mainstream was to seek to influence the Baptist Union through publications. In 1980 an address given by B.R. White, Principal of Regent's Park College, at the first Mainstream Swanwick Conference in January 1980, was published. This argued for an appreciation of the Holy Spirit's activity in both the liturgical and charismatic movements.[26] In the same year Nigel addressed the challenge to Baptists of the House

---

[22] Wright, 'Pilgrimage', 31. By this time Nigel, together with Tom Smail (Anglican) and Andrew Walker (Russian Orthodox), was involved in leading ground-breaking seminars in different parts of the UK to reflect theologically on charismatic renewal. [Editor: See the essay by Smail in this volume.]
[23] *Mainstream Newsletter* 1 (March 1979) 1.
[24] *Baptist Times* (5 May 1979) 4.
[25] *Mainstream Newsletter* (September 1998) 33-35.
[26] B.R. White, *Opening our Doors to God* (Ilkeston: Mainstream, 1980) 16.

Church movement. He was concerned that the Union should have leaders 'of extraordinary wisdom, prophetic vision and spiritual effectiveness'.[27] A few months later he spoke in the *Newsletter* about the story of Ansdell, which had changed, he said, under the ministry of his predecessor, W.A.D. Whyte, from 'a middle of the road Baptist church into one of strong evangelical emphasis and thrust'. Nigel outlined the lessons being learned at Ansdell: the importance of warmth of fellowship, committed workers, 'charismatic renewal which has deepened the experience of many although not without alienating others', willingness to make structural changes such as introducing house groups, and a desire to reach out in many different ways. Growth had been mainly through conversions. He also spoke of struggles that had been experienced.[28] A vision for vibrant local evangelical churches was being expressed.

Mainstream members, Nigel among them, were also involved in wider debates. In 1981 a collection of essays was produced by a group of Baptist ministers, *A Call to Mind*. In an essay, 'On Being the Church', Brian Haymes, later Principal of Northern Baptist College and then Bristol Baptist College, commented: 'Theological reflection is ... not a luxury for the few but a necessity for all. It may be difficult, even uncongenial and disturbing at times, but it is essential for the life of the Church'.[29] The group that produced *Call to Mind* became convinced, like Nigel, that a crucial issue for Baptist identity was authority. In 1983 Paul Fiddes, one of the group, who was Tutor and later Principal at Regent's Park College, Oxford, produced a study of leadership, *A Leading Question*.[30] As the group considered authority, they concluded that a crucial problem was the loss of the concept of 'covenant' – a concept which had become important (as noted above) for the ministers in the North-West. *Call to Mind* was followed by *Bound to Love* (1985) and then by *A Question of*

---

[27] Nigel Wright, 'The Challenge of the House Church Movement', *Mainstream Newsletter* (September 1980) 5-7.
[28] Nigel Wright, 'Ansdell Baptist Church', *Mainstream Newsletter* (January 1981) 8-9.
[29] Brian Haymes, 'On Being the Church', in Keith W. Clements *et al*, *A Call to Mind: Baptist Essays Towards a Theology of Commitment* (London: Baptist Union, 1981) 35. For a full account of this group, see Paul S. Fiddes, *Doing Theology in a Baptist Way* (Whitley Publications, Oxford, 2000).
[30] Paul S. Fiddes, *A Leading Question* (London: Baptist Publications, no year [1983]).

Baptist Identity (1986), by Brian Haymes.[31] In response, Mainstream convened a consultation to consider these reflections, and a booklet, *A Perspective on Baptist Identity*, was produced. In this collection, Nigel examined 'The Baptist way of being the Church'. He urged a reassessment of Baptist heritage to take seriously the ecclesial life of the sixteenth-century Anabaptists and Reformation centralities: Scripture, faith and grace. 'Baptists', he claimed, 'are by definition evangelical. A departure from evangelical theology entails a fatal loss of Baptist identity.'[32] This was a theme to which he would frequently return.

However, Nigel and others were advocating an evangelicalism of a particular kind. A report by Nigel in the *Mainstream Newsletter* in January 1982 on the group in the North-West spoke about how they had been

> nurtured in the evangelical faith and are grateful for its heritage stressing, as it does, the doctrines of grace, the sinfulness and helplessness of men [this was prior to inclusive language], the importance of conversion, the authority of the Bible.

Nigel commented:

> All of these doctrines we adhere to most firmly although our expression of them belongs to an evangelicalism of a newer and more open kind than former varieties.[33]

The idea of 'open evangelicals' was to be taken up within Anglicanism, but the expression 'radical evangelical' was to be more common in Baptist life, in part because of the way Nigel commended this expression. Writing in the April 1982 *Mainstream Newsletter* he observed that to have been called 'radical' would at one time have seemed suspect to most conservative evangelicals. He warned against 'radical' becoming 'the next shibboleth' and also talked about 'the trap of believing that because it's radical it must be right'. Nonetheless, he insisted that this was 'a good word'. He argued:

---

[31] Brian Haymes, *A Question of Identity* (Leeds: Yorkshire Baptist Association, 1986) 1.
[32] David Slater (ed.), *A Perspective on Baptist Identity* (Mainstream, 1987) 41-44.
[33] Nigel Wright, 'Gleanings from the North West', *Mainstream Newsletter* (January 1982) 4-6.

> The true Baptist heritage is a radical heritage calling the church back to a demanding conformity to Scripture; it is a heritage which ought to teach us to be restless with both the social and the ecclesiastical status quo.[34]

The case for a radical evangelical position was one that Nigel continued to advocate in the 1990s. In 1995 he moved from teaching at Spurgeon's College back to the North-West, to become senior minister of Altrincham Baptist Church. In the following year, in the face of claims that the Baptist Union's Declaration of Principle held together Baptists with 'widely differing theological understandings', Nigel argued that 'diversity', if true to the Declaration, had to be within the boundaries of commitment to the deity of Christ, the Trinity, the absolute authority of Christ, scriptural authority, the doctrine of baptism, and conversion.[35] The same year saw his thinking on these questions articulated in *The Radical Evangelical*.[36] 'Post-evangelicalism' was being promoted in this period by David Tomlinson, a former House Church leader. Nigel became involved in the post-evangelical debates, like others such as Derek Tidball, Principal of London Bible College,[37] and Nigel's view was that post-evangelicalism was a dead-end term offering no constructive way forward. Like Derek Tidball, he wanted a renewed commitment to evangelical faith and the development of forms of evangelicalism that would take account of valid criticisms while maintaining continuity with the tradition.[38]

In the early twenty-first century, as Nigel reflected on Mainstream, he expressed his thankfulness for what it had achieved and for the opportunities it had given him and others through the Mainstream conferences and the range of friendships. He has often said that Mainstream operated in a very limited way, yet had been able to address the 'acute anxiety about the spiritual and numerical decline of the Baptist Union' felt by many in the 1970s.[39] He noted that the new or Restorationist churches which had seemed so attractive had not fulfilled their early vision. He

---

[34] Nigel Wright, 'Who's Radical Now?', *Mainstream Newsletter* (April 1982) 4.
[35] *Baptist Times* (29 August 1996) 6.
[36] Nigel Wright, *The Radical Evangelical: Seeking a Place to Stand* (London: SPCK, 1996).
[37] Now London School of Theology; for a history see Ian M. Randall, *Educating Evangelicalism* (Carlisle: Paternoster, 2000).
[38] Nigel Wright, 'Re-imagining Evangelicalism' in G. Cray et al., *The Post-Evangelical Debate* (London: Triangle, 1997) 109.
[39] Wright, 'Worth joining', 18.

commented that the 'denominations over which they were prepared to write "Ichabod" have not withered on the vine' and he continued: 'One of Mainstream's aspirations has been achieved. The Baptist Union is worth staying in.' However, he added, it would be wrong for Mainstream to take the credit, since that lay with David Coffey and his team and with many Baptists throughout the country who had made cumulative decisions pointing in a new direction. The next step, he suggested, was to show that the Union could be a home for Baptist-compatible churches not at present in the Union.[40] Surprisingly, given what was by then a widely-accepted radical evangelicalism within the Union, Nigel argued in 2004 that the Union would benefit from having within it more 'right wing' evangelicals, people who 'take the Bible with extreme seriousness and believe in filling it with the content of good Christian doctrine'.[41] A robust evangelicalism has been central to Nigel's theological vision for Baptist life.

Anabaptist perspectives
Another theological stream that has nourished Nigel is Anabaptism. In 1977, when Nigel was recognised as a fully accredited Baptist minister, he received the handshake from Ernest Payne, former General Secretary of the Baptist Union and President in that year. Payne had a great interest in the radical sixteenth-century Anabaptist movement,[42] and Nigel's own interest in the Anabaptist-Mennonite tradition was aroused in this period as a result of contacts made through one of his church members. Sources of radical thinking about spirituality and ecclesiology were being widely explored. The Mennonite Centre in London, founded in 1953, became increasingly influential in the 1970s through the work of Alan and Ellie Kreider. An Anabaptist study group, convened by Alan Kreider and Nigel, met in the 1980s at the London Mennonite Centre. In the later 1980s Nigel's *The Radical Kingdom* introduced Anabaptist ideas to a wider evangelical and charismatic audience and these ideas were dealt with more fully in his *Challenge to Change* (1991), in which he argued that Anabaptism was one of those movements in which 'something

---

[40] Wright, 'Worth joining', 18.
[41] Nigel Wright, 'Looking for a right wing', *Talk. The Mainstream Magazine* (Autumn 2004) 27. Nigel was on the Council of the Evangelical Alliance in this period, and was well aware of intra-evangelical differences that were being aired.
[42] W.M.S. West, *To be a Pilgrim: A Memoir of Ernest A. Payne* (Guildford: Lutterworth Press, 1983) 66.

hugely creative breaks into our world and unleashes a creative force'.[43]

In his work on Anabaptism, Nigel operated in two somewhat different modes. As he put it himself, the story of the emergence of Anabaptism had 'a romantic power' and he used it as a source of inspiration. Thus in *Challenge to Change*, which was his first major book seeking to set out an agenda for Baptist Christians, he outlined what could be learned from the Anabaptists about discipleship, evangelism, zeal and the way of peace.[44] This use of the Anabaptist story continued. In a subsequent programmatic book, *New Baptists, New Agenda*, Nigel spoke about how the Anabaptists,

> .... having rejected the notion that all of Europe was Christian, set out intentionally to win converts and to plant churches. They were enormously successful, despite the odds ranged against them. (...) Neither is it surprising that within the baptist traditions in particular there has been an enormous energy for mission which has led to rapid church growth in many parts of the world.[45]

He also noted that calls for religious liberty could be traced back to the Anabaptists.[46]

A parallel concern of Nigel's has been to undertake scholarly research into the Anabaptist tradition and to be part of the conversation about the interpretation of the tradition. In his PhD, completed in 1994 (King's College, London) Nigel examined 'Mission, Church and Social Order' in the theologies of John Howard Yoder, an American Mennonite theologian, and Jürgen Moltmann, a German Reformed theologian, then at the University of Tübingen. This contained a chapter on Anabaptism and also explored the concept of a 'Free Church in a Free State'. The work was published in 2000 as *Disavowing Constantine*.[47] This work brought Nigel into the political arena, at least to some extent. He gave evidence in 1999 to a Royal Commission on the Reform of the House of Lords.[48] The analytical exposition of Free Church

---

[43] Wright, *Challenge to Change*, 213.
[44] Wright, *Challenge to Change*, 228-232.
[45] Nigel G. Wright, *New Baptists, New Agenda* (Carlisle: Paternoster, 2002) 60.
[46] Wright, *New Baptists, New Agenda*, 57.
[47] Nigel G. Wright, *Disavowing Constantine. A Radical Baptist Perspective on Church, Society and State* (Carlisle: Paternoster, 2000).
[48] John Ioannou to Nigel Wright, 29 June 1999.

theology was taken further in the most recent of Nigel's books on ecclesiology, his seminal *Free Church, Free State: The Positive Baptist Vision*. In each of his books on these themes he builds on and extends his previous thinking and in *Free Church, Free State* the programmatic and the scholarly approaches to a large extent converge.[49]

As well as using his writing to influence attitudes to Anabaptism, Nigel has continued to support initiatives commending Anabaptist perspectives. He spoke warmly in 1992 about the formation of an Anabaptist Network and a new journal *Anabaptism Today*.[50] Emerging out of this network, an Anabaptist Theological Study Circle was started, with drew together about fifteen people for discussions from 1996 onwards. The co-chairs were Keith G. Jones, Deputy General Secretary of the Baptist Union, and Alan Kreider. At a meeting in June 1996, Brian Haymes gave an introduction to the thought of James Wm. McClendon, Jr., and study sessions were devoted to responses to McClendon.[51] In February 1997 Nigel introduced 'questions from McClendon'. From the 1980s, McClendon had been exploring a new understanding of 'the Baptist Vision',[52] but until the 1990s his work was not well known in Britain. Nigel promoted McClendon's idea of using 'baptist' rather than 'Baptist',[53] in recognition of the fact that Baptists are part of a broader 'baptist' movement (including the Anabaptists) in which common perspectives are widely shared although diversely expressed – believers' baptism, religious liberty, separation of church and state and the self-governing congregation held in common.[54] The Study Circle was

---

[49] Thus Nigel draws from his own research, for example his articles, '"The Sword": An example of Anabaptist Diversity', *Baptist Quarterly* 36.6 (1996) 264-279; 'Baptist and Anabaptist Attitudes to the State: A Contrast', *Baptist Quarterly* 36.7 (1996) 349-357.
[50] *Baptist Times* (24 September 1992) 10. The Anabaptist network grew to about 1200 members. Those involved belong to a wide range of denominational backgrounds: Roman Catholic, Anglican, Mennonite, Quaker, Baptist, Presbyterian, Methodist, United Reformed, Pentecostal, Independent and House Church. Baptists are the largest group.
[51] Anabaptist Theological Study Circle Programme, 17-18 June 1996. The file is in the possession of Keith Jones, Rector of IBTS, Prague. I am grateful to him for his help.
[52] See James W. McClendon, 'What is a "Baptist" Theology?', *American Baptist Quarterly* 1.1 (1982) 16-39.
[53] James W. McClendon, *Systematic Theology: Ethics* (Nashville: Abingdon 1986) 19-20. [Editor: Cf. the essay by Murray in this volume, esp. note 2.]
[54] Donald F. Durnbaugh, *The Believers' Church: The History and Character of*

instrumental in arranging for McClendon to visit Britain and speak at Baptist Colleges and at the London Mennonite Centre.[55]

Yet Nigel was not an uncritical participant in the attempt to draw from Anabaptist thought. In 2003 he wrote about the idea that along with the rejection of the Christendom idea of the church (as Anabaptists do), being at 'the margins' of society was something the church should welcome. Nigel suggested an alternative approach: 'The persuasion that Christendom was a bad idea is now commonplace but in being rejected the issues surrounding "Christendom" are often oversimplified and unclear.' He posited the possibility of re-inventing Christendom, pointing out that if the loss of Christendom meant public policy was determined by a secularist world-view, he found it hard to rejoice in that. In a key passage in terms of the debate about mission in post-Christendom he wrote:

> Are we to abandon the powers to idolatry? Sometimes I gain from Anabaptist friends the impression that they are so keen to be free from Christendom that a godless state is exactly what they would prefer. By contrast, I want to contend that the vision of a non-sectarian state can actually be a Christian vision for the state.[56]

As with charismatic issues and with evangelical identity, while arguing for openness to what was new, Nigel remained rooted in classical Christianity.

Renewing Baptist identity

The last decade of the twentieth century saw significant developments taking place within the life of the Baptist Union. Nigel Wright wrote in the *Mainstream Newsletter* in January 1990 that the 1990s could be an opportunity 'for Baptists to turn a corner in their experience of denominational life' and look at 'extensive change in the largely Edwardian structures of the Union'. He hoped to see the Union cultivating a new spirit of warmth and personal affirmation, reforming its structures and engaging in sustained decentralization, and acting as a resource agency. He suggested a plan to be implemented by the year 2000.[57] In March

---

Radical Protestantism (London: Macmillan 1968).
[55] Report by Keith Jones to Members of the Study Circle, 16 March 1998.
[56] Nigel Wright, 'Re-inventing Christendom', *Anabaptism Today* 33 (June 2003) 7.
[57] Nigel Wright, 'An Agenda for Baptist Christians', *Mainstream Newsletter* (January 1990) 2-4.

1990 the Baptist Union Council nominated forty-eight year old David Coffey and thirty-nine year old Keith Jones, then Secretary of the Yorkshire Baptist Association, as General Secretary and Deputy General Secretary.[58] The scene was set for new directions. Nigel elaborated on his ideas in his widely-read *Challenge to Change* (1991), in which he suggested ways to renew church meetings – for example by less use of voting procedures and more reliance on consensus – and to foster more meaningful Association and Union life.[59] He had forged many of these ideas, and expressed them in embryonic form, within Mainstream.[60]

On the crucial issue of the church meeting in relation to Baptist identity, Nigel suggested that the church meeting was criticised as unbiblical, as unspiritual, treating all church members as if what they had to say was equally important, and as impractical, since it had an inbuilt conservative bias which prevented churches from responding imaginatively or swiftly to any initiative.[61] These were powerful arguments, he said, and there were too many examples of church meetings working badly. Pastors from other networks and traditions may admire many things in Baptist churches, he suggested, but the church meeting was rarely one of them. He commended the church meeting as a 'discernment process'. All had a part to play but pastors, together with others who are mature, prayerful, live close to God and know and understand people, will have particularly weighty contributions to make to the process. 'Thus, church meetings properly understood and led, are occasions for sharing wisdom, not for airing prejudices or defending preferences.'[62] This discussion shows how Nigel was able to face up to the problems in Baptist life and to suggest ways forward which were transformative in local situations.

Wider reform was also in the air. A Denominational Consultation was held in September 1996 and the major question was: 'What kind of Baptist Union is required to respond to God's call to mission as we enter a new millennium?' A Denominational Conference Reference Group was set up with Tony Peck, Secretary of the Yorkshire Baptist Association and later General

---

[58] *Baptist Times* (15 March 1990) 1.
[59] Wright, *Challenge to Change*, chapters 4-6.
[60] See *Mainstream Newsletter* (January 1984) 2-4; *ibidem* (September 1985) 5-7.
[61] Wright, *Challenge to Change*, 97-98.
[62] Wright, *Challenge to Change*, 103.

Secretary of the European Baptist Federation, as convenor.[63] A Task Group pursued the over-riding theme of reform of the Associations that had come out of the Consultation. This group was chaired by Nigel. It produced a report, *Relating and Resourcing*, which went alongside a report on superintendents, *Transforming Superintendency*. The call was for 'a radical revision of our Associating'.[64] It is clear that thinking which had been formulated by Nigel was influential. *Relating and Resourcing* envisaged mutually supportive 'relationships, clusters and networks'. Having introduced the word 'cluster' to 'Baptist Speak', Nigel wondered later if it had become a cliché.[65] A crucial recommendation in *Relating and Resourcing* was for the merging of the existing Associations and the Areas in order to create regional associations. Each of these would be served by a regional team comprising a variety of ministries - pastoral, evangelistic and others. Another radical recommendation was that regional ministers would be employed and paid locally. The regional leaders, together with senior staff at Baptist house, Didcot, would form a national leadership team.[66] Almost all these proposals put flesh on ideas in *Challenge to Change*.

Nigel presented *Relating and Resourcing* to the Baptist Union in Spring 1998 and its main themes were affirmed.[67] The 1998 Assembly saw a spirited debate on restructuring.[68] The thinking in *Relating and Resourcing* was commended by Nigel through Mainstream channels. 'The Union', he wrote, 'has within its grasp to reform itself and enter into the next millennium with God's help as a substantially renewed body'.[69] In March 1999 the Council agreed a new framework for Associations. Associations would facilitate clustering. Regional team leaders would be appointed and regional teams would have responsibility for mission and pastoral care.[70] As part of the process of engaging the churches, a Baptist Leaders' Day was held at Wembley Conference Centre in March 1999 and attracted 2600 people.

---

[63] *Baptist Times* (27 November 1997) 4.
[64] *Relating and Resourcing* (Didcot: Baptist Union, 1998) Appendix 1. [Editor: On this report see also Brown in this volume.]
[65] *Baptist Times* (10 October 2002) 7.
[66] *Relating and Resourcing*, 10-15; *Baptist Times* (26 March 1998) 1 and 8.
[67] *Baptist Times* (2 April 1998) 1; *ibidem* (16 April 1998) 4-5.
[68] *Baptist Times* (14 May 1998) 1.
[69] Nigel G. Wright, 'Time to Associate', *Mainstream* (May 1998) 10.
[70] *Baptist Times* (1 April 1999) 7.

There were a number of speakers, each of whom took up key issues, with David Coffey as the keynote speaker. Nigel, not surprisingly, spoke on renewing relationships.[71]

Yet Nigel was not content with an approach to the reform of Baptist life which was inward-looking. Addressing the Baptist World Alliance Heritage and Identity Commission at the 18th Baptist World Congress, Melbourne, January 2000, he looked beyond the Baptist denomination and welcomed the breaking down of denominational barriers.[72] Denominations, he observed, were 'a somewhat ambiguous phenomenon'. He argued that separatism might sometimes be inevitable, but it was also frequently a symptom of narrowness of the human mind and spirit. He suggested that Baptists were likely to find that they needed the enrichment of other ecclesiologies which informed, challenged and to a degree complemented their own. Questions about the nature of the church, he observed, persisted.[73] This larger vision of theological interchange motivated Nigel in his hope that the Baptist Union in Britain would become a denomination worth joining. For this to happen, he suggested,

> it would have to argue *theologically* that inter-church communion is not an option extra for any church but a necessary expression of the church's interdependence and catholicity. It would have to develop *institutionally* in such a way that it could cope with variations within stated parameters in the way churches organize and govern themselves. It would have to develop *ecclesially* so as to make membership of the Union meaningful.[74]

Denominational directions

From the 1970s onwards Nigel was seeking to bring 'challenges to change' into Baptist life and his insights had a significant impact. The beginning of the twenty-first century saw him becoming President of the Baptist Union. In his earlier days, said Nigel in *Talk* in Spring 2002, he 'would not have believed it possible'.[75] Here I will outline briefly some aspects of Nigel presidency, as part

---

[71] *Baptist Times* (18 March 1999) 1, 2, 5, 7, 10.
[72] Nigel is a member of the Council of the Baptist World Alliance and was chair of its Study Commission on Christian Ethics, 2000-2005.
[73] 'New Baptists, New Opportunities', later included as chapter 4 of *New Baptists, New Agenda*, see 47-52.
[74] Wright, 'Worth joining', 18.
[75] Wright, 'From Poacher to President', 26.

of his contribution to the denomination. At the Assembly at which he became President, his presidential address was on a four-fold conversion: to Christ, to the church, to the world and to the future. As before, his intention was to communicate a direction to the Union. After the Assembly, he reported in the *Baptist Times* that his first task had been to contribute to a Mainstream North Theology Day at the 'much loved' Blackley Centre, West Yorkshire, a centre run by Blackley Baptist Church. In the first of a weekly series of 'postcards' in the *Baptist Times* during his presidential year, he observed:

> This is my idea of a good time! For a start, it was in the North. Secondly, it involved Mainstream, which has long been a home for me. And then it involved that irresistible combination of theology, in particular the theology of ministry, and the fellowship of fellow ministers whom I admire. Call me sad and tell me I need to get out more, but it works for me.[76]

An important part of his year was meeting with ministers. Another aspect of his work was communicating with the constituency. He had been a regular writer in the *Baptist Times* before, and now he used his 'postcards', which gave a fascinating insight into the varied experiences he had as President, as a means of communication. The presidential year also included many visits at which he spoke at local churches and Associations. He visited England, Scotland, Wales and Ireland, and each of the Associations in membership with the Baptist Union. There were also responsibilities abroad, such as the Baptist International Conference of Theological Educators and meetings of the Baptist World Alliance.[77] Nigel was enthusiastic about a visit to the Baptist Leading Edge holiday week, noting that many Baptists did not go to the Assembly but that Leading Edge attracted many families and young people.[78]

During this period Nigel reflected on his thinking about renewal and the place of denominations. He explained that in his early days he had seen denominations as institutions that 'got on board with movements of the Spirit about twenty years after they happened, i.e., twenty years too late'. So, he asked, 'has the

---

[76] *Baptist Times* (16 May 2002) 5.
[77] *Baptist Times* (18 July 2002) 7.
[78] *Baptist Times* (29 August 2002) 7.

poacher turned gamekeeper?' He had, he explained, come to see that institutions too had a place. For him there were various dimensions to this. 'One is theological. It has to do with the Body of Christ as a corporate, translocal reality.' Although believing firmly in the local church, he considered that 'local churches that are not open to other congregations of God's people are frankly defective. They are violating the universal nature of the church.' Denominations, he argued, provide networks and communities which offer a wider dimension of Christian solidarity, while allowing freedom for distinctive identities. This state of affairs is provisional – one day all distinctions will perish. Nigel added that over time his own instinct had been to be more deeply rooted in the centre – the doctrinal centre expressed in the doctrine of the Triune God and also in the wisdom of the church. In conclusion, he acknowledged that he had become something of a denominationalist, seeing 'a charism, a gift of grace, that God imparts through the communion of churches'.[79]

In line with his long-standing concern for 'life and growth', Nigel reiterated the case for Baptist bishops that he had first made in *Challenge to Change*, stressing that they should be concerned, above all, with mission.[80] Following up later on the theme of mission, he called for greater emphasis on evangelism in the Union. 'The time is ripe', he wrote, 'for the Baptist Union to think again about how it stimulates and focuses the evangelism of Baptist churches.' He applauded the commitment to holistic mission, but argued that it was possible for evangelism 'to get lost in a concept of mission which is so broad it just becomes a synonym for "what churches do"'. Nigel's theme was the gospel as 'the power of God for salvation' and his call was for the Union to take a somewhat new direction – to train some of its best people as evangelists.[81]

His desire - fed by Anabaptist perspectives - for authentic ecclesial life was also evident. He took the view that particular expressions of church life, with their distinctives, had often played a prophetic role, reminding the church of part of its legacy. He continued: 'I here advance the claim, which some might regard as pretentious', that a reason why denominational boundaries are

---

[79] Wright, 'From Poacher to President', 26.
[80] Nigel Wright, 'Still a case for Baptist bishops', *Talk. The Mainstream Magazine* (Autumn 2002) 26.
[81] Nigel Wright, 'Power to change', *Talk. The Mainstream Magazine* (Summer 2004) 27.

less evident is 'because *by default or design the church at large has begun to adopt values for which baptist Christians have historically stood.*'[82] Alongside that, he argued in January 2003, in the context of tensions in inter-church and intra-church relationships in some quarters: 'If Baptists can learn to be welcoming, generous and affirming (and this surely isn't beyond us), we will surprise ourselves about how much more effective we become.'[83] On the same ecumenically-orientated theme, he reported in March 2003 that the big event of the week had been the enthronement of Rowan Williams as Archbishop of Canterbury: 'Rowan Williams' sermon delighted me. It was based upon Christ as the only one who knows the Father and who makes the Father known. It was Christ-centred and church-affirming.'[84]

Finally, in this period Nigel continued to press for deeper reflection on how to express Baptist identity, and he addressed specific issues related to this topic. At many of his local church visits there were evening meetings when 'cluster' churches came together. This, he believed, was to be encouraged, and his perception was that clustering was really working.[85] Commenting on the roles of churches of differing sizes in the Union, Nigel observed: 'Our denomination is a mixed economy of large and small churches, and none the worse for that. All have something to offer to the whole and are to be judged not according to their size but by faithfulness to the mission they have been given. What we most need to learn is a new quality of co-operation and mutual service.'[86] The final presidential postcard was from Prague, from the International Baptist Theological Seminary, where in-depth exploration of issues of Baptist and Anabaptist identity was taking place. Nigel wrote:

> This is a great place to be. (...) IBTS has prospered under the leadership of Keith Jones who has done a remarkable job in re-establishing it. The place is buzzing with life and students who will be the leaders of tomorrow.[87]

---

[82] Wright, *New Baptists, New Agenda*, 56; italics his.
[83] *Baptist Times* (16 January 2003) 7.
[84] *Baptist Times* (6 March 2003) 7.
[85] *Baptist Times* (10 October 2002) 7.
[86] *Baptist Times* (2 January 2003) 7.
[87] *Baptist Times* (1 May 2003) 7.

Conclusion

Nigel Wright has contributed enormously to English Baptist life since the 1970s. He has exhibited a remarkable ability to take the best of a wide range of influences and, over time, to jettison the unhelpful.[88] He has been an advocate of charismatic renewal, but has called for theological reflection on the charismatic movement:

> Beyond the glow of shared fellowship there are still the hard questions of theological discourse. (...) Integral to these are questions about the nature of the church itself which lie at the root of so much denominational proliferation.[89]

Part of his aim has been to achieve a greater wholeness and completeness – to think hard but also to avoid the over-intellectualising of the faith and the neglect of the heart and emotions. He has advocated, especially through Mainstream, robust evangelical convictions, while also calling for a generous spirit. He has come increasingly to the view that denominations can incarnate a way in which the catholicity of the Church may be expressed. Nigel has brought to many Baptists and to others a vision of radical church life that he discovered in Anabaptism, but has also been rigorous in his evaluation of this strand of Baptist life. As he has involved himself in seeking the reform and renewal of the Baptist Union, he has been inspired by a vision of the Union as a body that is worth joining. He has also consistently stressed the priority of mission.

Nigel has been deeply shaped by Baptist tradition and the movement of which he has been a part, and he has also played a highly significant leadership role in the shaping of that movement. Indeed it could be argued that an episcopal ministry among Baptists (Baptist bishops), for which Nigel has been an advocate, is a ministry that he himself has exemplified through his many creative, prophetic and missional insights.

---

[88] I am indebted to my colleague, John Colwell, for this phrase.
[89] Wright, *New Baptists, New Agenda*, 51.

When Wright was right

Thomas A. Smail

For me, looking back, the blessing of the charismatic renewal not only consisted in the gifts of the Spirit that it enabled us to rediscover, but even more in the rich new relationships with other Christians that our shared experience of the Spirit enabled us to enter into. For generations we had tossed our hand grenades of theological polemics across seemingly insuperable barriers of denominational separation and contradictory doctrinal traditions. Yet these barriers tumbled down as the Spirit revealed us afresh to one another as people who were basically united in a warm commitment to and dependence upon the Father who had saved us in his Son and was now uniting us in faith, hope and love in his Spirit. This certainly did not mean that we agreed about everything, but it did mean that our confrontations changed from being battles to the death against denounced opponents to still often passionate exchanges in which we learnt not only to speak but to listen to Christians who were different from us but who had become respected and even affectionate friends.

It is in this context of charismatic *koinonia* that I was introduced to the Baptist tradition in general and to Spurgeon's College in particular. Shared charismatic experience brought me first into a close, forty-year friendship with the late Douglas McBain (1933-2007) in which our God-given love for each other held us together when the differences of our personal profiles could easily have driven us apart. More recently I have been enriched by a more theologically orientated but no less warm ongoing interchange with John Colwell as he has been seeking to relate his Baptist inheritance to the catholic tradition. It was in the midst of all this that I first came into contact with Nigel Wright and I am honoured to be able to contribute to this birthday tribute to his person and his work, just as I was honoured to be invited to be the preacher at his installation as Principal of Spurgeon's College in 2000 – itself a sign of how far an ex-Presbyterian Anglican has been allowed to penetrate the Baptist heartlands!

The love of power and the power of love

My initial collaboration with Nigel in the early nineties was explicitly charismatic. Together with Andrew Walker we were involved in a three-man twenty-four hour seminar that toured the country. We invited church leaders of all shapes and sizes who had been involved in the charismatic renewal to reflect critically on what had happened to them. We encouraged them to make some theological judgements on the whole renewal movement to discern where it was and where it was not a faithful contemporary expression of the biblical gospel on which it said it was based. At the time we claimed that this was the first attempt at an organised assessment of the renewal and the responses on the day suggested that it was timely and appreciated; at least some renewal leaders had reached a point of maturity at which they were ready to do some hard thinking about it. The seminar went under the title 'The love of power or the power of love' and the papers we gave were later published under the title *Charismatic Renewal*.[1]

Wright on Wimber

Nigel's main contribution to the book was a paper entitled 'The theology and methodology of "Signs and Wonders"' which offered an assessment of the work and ministry of John Wimber. Nigel and the Lancashire church of which he was then minister were exposed to Wimber during a memorable weekend in June 1982 (27-28). Wordsworth once defined poetry as 'emotion recollected in tranquillity'[2] and that could serve as a subtitle for Nigel's paper in which he seeks from a reflective distance to discern what had really happened to him and his people in the heady excitement of these days with Wimber and his team.

What I want to do now is, as it were, to reflect on Nigel's reflection. In reading it all again more than ten years later it seems to me that, although Wimber is now history, the methodology with which Nigel assesses his contribution contains such a combination of generous appreciation, theological acumen and sheer down-to-earth wisdom as to make it an excellent hermeneutical model with which to approach contemporary and future manifestations of the charismatic revivalism that Wimber represented twenty-five years

---

[1] Tom Smail, Andrew Walker and Nigel Wright, *Charismatic Renewal* (London: SPCK, 1993, 1995). Page numbers in brackets refer to this book.
[2] William Wordsworth, Preface to the second edition of *Lyrical ballads* (1800).

ago. In the central characteristics of the approach he adopted, Wright was right then; if we follow his example, we shall not go far wrong now.

Affirmation and discernment

What comes over first is that Nigel is at heart an irenic theologian, more concerned to hold things together than to tear them apart, much more inclined to say 'both - and' than 'either - or'. He is deeply disinclined to reach 100% verdicts which would hold that Wimber was either all good or all bad. He sees that one of the chief gifts of the Spirit is a discernment that eschews both undiscriminating affirmation and unqualified condemnation. In what happened when Wimber was around there are things to be received with gratitude as gifts from God that have upon them the authentic seal of approval of the biblical gospel. Yet these co-exist, like the wheat and the tares in the same field, with other things that stand in tension with or sheer contradiction to that gospel. You will do the gospel no service if, either positively or negatively, you confuse the one with the other.

Nigel wants to affirm both the positive and the negative ends of the spectrum. Wimber is both a blessing and a danger and we shall get him wrong if we affirm the one at the expense of the other. If that leaves an unresolved tension, then that is the way things are in a world that is both created and fallen and in a church where the grace of the second Adam and the legacy of the first Adam are both at work.

In the end, Nigel gives priority to the positive over the negative because the grace that makes Wimber a blessing is more ultimate and powerful than the faults and failings that still make him a danger. Even if we are wary of the defects, we can still give thanks for the manifestations of life and grace in Wimber's ministry. It is that affirmation of the priority of grace that makes Nigel the irenic theologian that this piece of writing proves him to be. Evangelicals and charismatics of all shapes and sizes would do well to take note of this combination of warm affirmation and wary insight, because one of their persistent vices is to demand 100% verdicts at points where they are quite inappropriate. To insist that everything in the evangelical or the charismatic tradition is a pure unalloyed work of God so that to question any of it is equivalent to rejecting all of it, suggests that loyalty to the tribe has taken priority over loyalty to the gospel. Such insistence suggests that we are seeking to find our security in a human tradition that is no longer open to reform and correction in the light of the scriptural revelation which we profess to be ultimate. On the other hand, to latch on to the negative in a Christian ministry that we find threatening - either because of its unfamiliarity, its emotional intensity or its weird and dramatic accompaniments - can easily become a protective strategy in which we hide behind the facade of a congenial *status quo* and so insulate ourselves from the wind and the fire of the Spirit which could bring us a life and energy that we sorely need.

For Nigel's congregation Wimber was weird. Yet he describes their risky exposure to that weirdness as 'our first experience of spiritual power' which

> opened our eyes to the meaning of Pentecost. (...) The months following this event were times of intense spiritual ministry, much of it in the area of inner healing and deliverance. There was a sense of people being purged and prepared ... and it felt as if we were on the boundaries of the spiritual life (28).

How easy it would have been to put out these pentecostal fires with a bucket of cold evangelical orthodoxy and how much would have been missed if that had been allowed to happen! If we are exclusively positive or exclusively negative to Christ-centred movements of the Holy Spirit in a way that either misses the blessing or is blind to the dangers, it is likely to be because we are seeking security and safety in the wrong place.

Many charismatics are disproportionately upset by any criticism of the movement because they have invested too much spiritual capital in the experiences it has brought them; too many traditional evangelicals turn their backs on what they see as unruly manifestations of spiritual revival because they in turn have invested too much capital in a doctrinal orthodoxy that wants to confine the activity of the Spirit within the tight limitations that their scheme imposes. The latter easily forget that the Spirit to whom the Scriptures bear witness blows where he wants and refuses to be confined to the safe traditional boxes of our own devising that keep him safely under our control. The Spirit will not be shut up either in evangelical pulpits or catholic altars where we think we can cope with him. These are indeed places where he has promised to be, but if we become insensitive and unresponsive to what he wants to do there, he is liable to jump out at us through people such as Wimber. We will miss him if we seek shelter in the familiar hiding places when fresh winds are blowing all around.

The ultimate commitment
Nigel can be realistic about Wimber because he has not become over-dependent on him. His ultimate commitment is not to any charismatic experience, however powerful and enlivening, but to the length and breadth and depth and height of the scriptural gospel of the triune God, the gift of the Father incarnate in the Son made available to us in the Spirit. That commitment gives him a norm by which to measure Wimber and all claimed manifestations of the Spirit. In this way he can appreciate all that Wimber brings and is authenticated by the gospel and witnesses to the fact that the gospel is not just a first century story but a contemporary reality. At the same time Nigel's commitment to the gospel enables him to spot where Wimber falls short of that gospel and thus to identify the dangers that surround but do not nullify the blessings that the Spirit brings through Wimber.

Theology to the rescue
It is interesting how this position is borne out in Nigel's account of his personal pilgrimage in the autobiographical section of *Charismatic Renewal* (22-32). After demanding years of coping with the release of the Spirit which the Wimber visit initiated, he tells us how 'In the midst of all this activity a profound urge was reawakened within me. It was to do with theology' (29). As a result he spent a year (1986-1987) concentrating on the theology of Karl Barth (30). This is significant because Barth's understanding of the function of theology is highly relevant to Nigel's situation as he emerges from his years of engagement with the heady charismatic revivalism initiated by the Wimber visit.

For Barth one of the basic functions of theology is to expose the life and witness of the contemporary Church to the given biblical gospel so that it can be assessed, corrected and readjusted to give a fuller and more balanced expression of it. For example, the typical charismatic preoccupation with exotic and dramatic religious experiences needs to be corrected by a New Testament understanding of the person and work of the Holy Spirit as the one whose primary function is to relate us to the Father and the Son and to induct us into their purpose for the renewal of the whole created order which the Father's love initiates and the Son's incarnation, death and resurrection inaugurates. Such a theological grasp of the whole extent of God's purposes for us and for the world delivers us from a concern with what Nigel calls a privatised and domesticated personal religious experience. It turns us outwards in ministries of evangelism and compassion that include commitments to issues of social justice in the world.

Towards a trinitarian renewal
Nigel himself expresses this process in trinitarian terms:

> [H]aving emphasised the Spirit and sought to give him place, there is now an entirely consistent and appropriate need to become fully trinitarian. (...) Ultimately our concern is with God, and how we conceive him shapes our attitude to all other realities. To maintain its health and develop its impetus the [charismatic] movement must avoid unitarianisms of the Spirit and of the Son and explore the depth of the Church's trinitarian heritage (31).

In other words, the charismatic renewal must become a trinitarian renewal and biblically orientated theological study will enable us to map out the road that leads from the one to the other. Of course the map is not the journey. The theology that tells us where to go next will not itself provide the impetus and energy to make the adjustments to which it is pointing. That is the work of the Spirit and because he is the Spirit of the Father and of the Son, when we are open to him he will move us, perhaps through the immediacy of charismatic experiences, to a fresh openness to the Father and the Son because he will keep on crying *Abba* (Romans 8:15) and 'Jesus is Lord' (1 Corinthians 12:3) at the depths our being. Thus, as the third person of the Trinity, he will lead us into relationship with the other two persons, to appropriation of all that they give us and to obedience of all that they require of us.

To put this for once in the language of pentecostalist theology, the initial evidence that believers have been baptised in the Holy Spirit is not tongues or healing. It is the fact that they have come as his adopted children and heirs into a new filial relationship with their heavenly Father because they have been given a new access to him by trusting in the reconciling work of his incarnate, crucified and risen Son. The initial evidence that we are in the Spirit is that we echo his twin confession of God as *Abba,* Father and of Jesus as *Kurios,* Lord. All who make that confession are charismatic Christians whether or not they have spoken in tongues, prophesied or been 'slain in the Spirit'. It is our induction into these trinitarian relationships that opens the door to an engagement with the whole breadth and depth of God's boundless purposes for the world.

To say this is not to depreciate contemporary Christian experience. Those of us who, like Nigel, have experienced the personal revivification of faith that the charismatic renewal brought, could never for a moment write that off. The contemporary work of the Spirit is as necessary as the historic once and for all work of the Son. The work of the Spirit moves from a point of origin to a point of delivery as the words of Jesus show: 'All that the Father has is mine. For this reason I said that he will take what is mine and declare it to you' (John 16:15 NRSV). The work of the Spirit consists of taking what he has received from the Son in his historical context and demonstrating that it is still relevant and effective in our very different historical context. To put it very simply, the work of the Spirit is to show that what Jesus did then works now; or better, that what Jesus did once and for all for us in his flesh in Galilee and Jerusalem he continues to work out in us through his Spirit here and now. This 'here and now' dimension of the gospel is the realm of the Spirit. Without this element of immediacy the gospel would retreat into memory of acts of God done on our behalf long ago, to be trusted, no doubt, but without expectation of being so joined to Christ that we have personal and corporate experience in the Spirit of his saving grace and of its transforming consequences for our relationships with God and with one another.

Faithfulness and relevance
Thus the Holy Spirit whom we encounter in the gospel has an equal concern for faithfulness to what happened then and for the effectiveness and relevance of what is happening now. The work of the Spirit will be frustrated if it loses either its dependence on the work of Jesus ('He will take what is mine') or its manifestation among his people ('He will declare it to you'). The Wimber phenomenon in particular and the charismatic renewal in general are one way – I would not say the only way – in which the Spirit shows that the gospel still delivers what it promises. Nevertheless, we still need to see how much of what we experience is derived from and consonant with the gospel as we have received it. In doing so we may affirm everything in the renewal that authentically witnesses to Jesus and distance ourselves from everything that distracts or detracts from that witness. In this process of normative

assessment we are helped by a commitment to theological study that marshals all the resources of insight and wisdom that the Church has acquired down the ages in its attentiveness to the biblical gospel. In this way, as Nigel rightly saw, theology can be a powerful tool in the Spirit's hand.

The Spirit uses such tools, but does not need them, because he is inherently in his own being and nature orientated to the Father and the Son. When we take our starting point with him, he will begin to lead us in the direction of Father and Son, so that churches that were excited and absorbed with charismatic experiences are ultimately led back to a more balanced response to the gospel. This response will be based on a deep engagement with the Scriptures and result in a more fully orbed worship, in evangelistic outreach to the community around them, and in compassion with the needy and justice for the oppressed. The way the Spirit led Nigel personally is the way he has been leading us all corporately so that - even if we are less emotionally intense than we were at the start - we are nevertheless making a more securely based response to the purposes of the triune God.

As Nigel pursues his critique of the Wimber phenomenon in the light of his deepening theological engagement with the biblical gospel (73-85), some of that critique is indeed critical. Yet in irenic mood he prefaces his reservations with a positive affirmation of Wimber's ministry as a genuine work of the Spirit:

> [A]ll the elements to be found in the Vineyard movement have their rightful place in the landscape of Christian thought and experience. (...) Therefore, at no point shall we suggest that the signs and wonders movement is anything other than a work of God (73).

That said, there emerge a number of areas in which the presentation and what Nigel calls the focus of Wimber's ministry are not only inadequate to the gospel but tend to distort and misrepresent it. Because I think that these distortions are not specific to Wimber but characterise a great deal of charismatic revivalism, it is worth looking at a few of them in more detail.

The truth about healing

The first area of concern are the sweeping rhetorical claims about results achieved, especially in the realm of healing and deliverance. Here Nigel speaks not just in terms of statistical studies but out of personal experience of what actually happened when Wimber came, and - more importantly - after Wimber left. Here is what he says:

> We cannot help but feel, with others, that the vast majority of claimed healings are in the area of the placebo effect. It must of course be conceded that just as sickness is complex, so is healing. But it does not appear to be the case that there is much evidence for miraculous healing taking place such as we see in the ministry of Jesus and such as can be called 'signs of the kingdom'. The rhetoric about miraculous healing far exceeds the reality (76).

This verdict is confirmed by many other sympathetic observers of Wimber's ministry and its results, and the implications of it for Wimber's integrity, are perhaps more serious than Nigel in his generosity allows.

This tendency to over-claim goes far beyond Wimber and is almost endemic to a great deal of revivalism, charismatic or not. It fails to honour the Holy Spirit as the Spirit of truth. The Spirit clearly demands from Christian leaders an accurate and disciplined account of what actually happens as a result of their ministries, including the many times when prayers for healing are not answered and illness takes its fatal course. Such things are agonisingly familiar to most churches that have struggled in prayer over the illness of a much-loved member to whom no healing has come. To refuse to admit that this happens, or to blame a lack of faith when it does, is to sin against the truth - yet the Spirit is the Spirit of truth. Here if anywhere it is important not to reach 100% verdicts. The truth seems to be that there are far fewer healings than triumphalistic charismatics allege.[3] Yet here and there, for reasons ultimately beyond our discerning, hidden in the mysterious providences of God, in a way that defies sceptical doctors, however evangelical, people are prayed for and wonderfully restored to health in a way that does signify that the healer from Galilee is indeed risen from the dead and is at work by his Spirit among his people.

The Spirit and the cross
The ambiguity of the results signals the fact that we live in the time between the times, the period of the first fruits of the Spirit rather

---

[3] Cf. Andrew Walker's essay 'Miracles, strange phenomena, and holiness' in *Charismatic renewal*, 123-130.

than in the period of his final fullness. This means that in our day and age healing is selective rather than universal. We need not just a triumphant theology of resurrection in which the new life breaks through into the old. We need a theology of the cross that recognises that God is at work in the darkness of Good Friday as well as in the brightness of Easter. We are often called to follow Jesus through the sharing of his suffering as the appointed path to an ultimate sharing of his glory. Charismatic triumphalism in its obscuring of the truth can easily distort the gospel by refusing to come to terms with the cross.

If we do not come to terms with the cross in our theology, we shall be made to come to terms with it in our ongoing Christian experience. That is perhaps the best way to understand what Nigel says about the aftermath of Wimber:

> We also encountered the phenomenon of burnout, that intense spiritual experiences can give way, perhaps must give way, to a barrenness of spirit. After mountain-top experiences, where is there to go but back into the valley? And perhaps this must be so, since God is always greater than the experiences we have of him and therefore our experiences need to drop away so that we are dealing with God himself (29).

After the affirmation of the baptism in the Jordan, there was the demanding agony of the wilderness temptation; after the glory of the transfiguration on the mountain, there was the almost impossible requirement of the cup offered in the garden. All is summed up in the man on the cross who in utter forsakenness still cries out 'My God, my God'. Only after and because of all that, there is the Easter victory and the Ascension glory. If that is the way of the Lord, it will also be the way of his disciples. The dark nights of the soul are an integral stage of the journey to the kingdom; we are justified by faith in what God has done in Christ in the darkness of Calvary rather than by uplifting experiences of what he is doing in us. A revivalism that does not know about our sharing in the cross is not a reliable guide to our sharing in the resurrection.

The need for the natural
One of Nigel's most creative contributions to this discussion is the way in which he deals with the dualism of Wimber's approach in which everything that happens in the realm of spiritual experience

tends to be seen in supernatural terms as unambiguously demonic or unambiguously divine. In response to this incipient revivalist Gnosticism, Nigel reminds us again and again of the dimension of the natural, the created, which the triune God never by-passes but always affirms in all his dealings with us. Just as in the Son the uncreated divine comes to us in inextricable connection with the created humanity that he assumes, so in our experiences of the Spirit the divine action comes to us in the closest connection with the human reaction to it. Writing about the dramatic manifestations that accompanied Wimber's ministry, Nigel puts it like this:

> The category of 'the natural' enables us to assert that these phenomena are essentially varied human responses to the approach of the transcendent God. As such they should not be over-valued. If they are seen as the direct workings of God, such that he deliberately makes persons tremble or laugh uproariously or weep, we are left with the question why he does these things to some and not to others, and are led to the possible but faulty conclusion that absence of phenomena means absence of divine activity. More seriously, we might make superficial judgements about the work of God based upon the occurrence of the dramatic rather than on the evidence of a holy life. It is far more accurate to say that different individuals will respond to the divine in different ways and that there is little or no spiritual significance in the exact manner of their response (82).

This is not only sound common sense; it is consonant with the Christian belief in God's affirmation of his creation that comes to a climax in the incarnation of his Son. We never encounter naked divinity, but divinity clothed with humanity at every step of the way. In Jesus the humanity is hypostatically united to the divinity as its perfect and reliable mode of its expression. With us it is different because we have but the first-fruits of the Spirit; our humanity has a long way to go before it becomes the accurate mirror of Christ's. For that reason our reactions to the work of the Spirit in us may be more or less adequate to the nature of that work. The authentic work of God in us can be masked and even marred by reactions that are inappropriate to it. It is therefore important that we should be able to discern that inadequacy so that we do not divinise it and make it universally normative.

In other words, in all manifestations of the Spirit there will be the constant factor of the one gift of God imparting revelation, power and holiness to his people, but different people will react in different ways that have to do with their personality profile, the culture and tradition by which they have been shaped and the state of their psychological health and balance at any given moment. All these differences have to be recognised and some of them have to be corrected. We are not to universalise any individual's or any group's experience so that it becomes demanding and threatening for others who, for all these reasons, may react to the Spirit in quite different ways. There is not one standard renewal experience that fits all and that can be described as '*the* baptism in the Holy Spirit' – in that form, a quite unbiblical phrase. Instead there are many ways of being baptised in the Spirit, only some of which reflect the pentecostal paradigm. There are quiet undemonstrative Christians who have never fallen on the floor or even spoken in tongues, yet in whom the same Holy Spirit has unmistakably been at work. Charismatics - with their own cultural preoccupations - must not, in an unfounded claim to superiority, fail to recognise what the Spirit has been doing in a quite different way among others in the body of Christ.

Conclusion
In its recognition and affirmation of the above issues, Nigel's approach to Wimber offers an excellent model for contemporary discernment of where and how the Spirit of God is at work among us. It is irenic and comprehensive, affirming rather than criticising wherever it can. For that very reason, it recognises the ambiguity and incompleteness of all our experiences of the Spirit and so leaves open the door to an ongoing process of spiritual transformation that is not yet complete in any of us, however life-changing and dramatic our previous experience may have been. What Nigel has written is a faithful contemporary application of what Paul wrote to the Corinthians,

> And we, who with unveiled faces all reflect the Lord's glory, are being transformed into his likeness with ever-increasing glory, which comes from the Lord, who is the Spirit (2 Corinthians 3:18).

For all these reasons my considered judgement is that Wright was right about Wimber; whether I have been right about Wright only Wright himself has the right to say!

The Radical Evangelical. A critical appreciation

Derek J. Tidball

I am delighted to join with others in paying tribute to Nigel Wright on the occasion of his sixtieth birthday. In many respects God has led us on parallel paths in ministry. We have both served in the ministry of two local Baptist churches, both chaired Mainstream for a period, both served as Presidents of the Baptist Union of Great Britain and served the Baptist Union Council in various ways. We have both been members of the Evangelical Alliance Council and chaired subgroups of its *Faith and Nation* Enquiry. For much of our time we have served as theological college tutors and both ended as Principals of the colleges where we trained. In the latter capacity it was not only good to be able to share our common joys and woes at the responsibilities we bore (and he still does!) but also to bury the unhealthy rivalry that existed between Spurgeon's College and London School of Theology and to recognise our common vision to train men and women to serve the Gospel of Jesus Christ.

While gratefully acknowledging Nigel's major contribution to the Baptist denomination and theological education, this paper seeks to acknowledge with equal gratitude his contribution to the wider evangelical movement, where his acute theological mind and courage to probe issues deeply and his refusal to be content with pat answers have been greatly respected. It does so by revisiting his 'tract for the times', entitled *The Radical Evangelical: Seeking a place to stand.*[1]

Situating *The Radical Evangelical*

Evangelicals are frequently spoken of as undergoing 'an identity crisis'. Throughout my ministry I have heard such talk and heard it so frequently that I have come to believe that such a 'crisis' (overused word!) is a settled hallmark of the movement. There are several ways of addressing one's search for identity. One way is to trace our roots and by looking to the past see what has shaped us in the present. That is what David Bebbington did in his seminal

---

[1] Nigel Wright, *The Radical Evangelical: Seeking a Place to Stand* (London: SPCK, 1996).

work *Evangelicalism in Modern Britain*.[2] It is also what I was seeking to do, in a much more modest way, in my introductory historical survey *Who are the Evangelicals?*[3] The danger is, as with that book, that the story stops short just when it is getting exciting! No sooner had I written than the full impact of the transition to postmodern culture on evangelicalism began to be apparent, and the question of how the evangelical tradition would adapt with integrity to the new cultural situation became crucial. The past gave some good, indeed, essential, bearings, but these were uncharted waters.

Another way of addressing the question is to investigate the distinctive features of the evangelical subculture, or, rather, the various subcultures that identify themselves as evangelical, and to compare and contrast these with other Christian subcultures. This is the approach most brilliantly adopted by Christian Smith[4] but the task is still to be done in the United Kingdom. Such an approach can be illuminating but is confined to description as opposed to prescription.

However, since evangelicalism is essentially a doctrinal movement, the most significant contributors to the recent debate about its identity are neither historians nor sociologists but theologians.[5] Shortly after I published *Who are the Evangelicals?* Nigel published his more focused and adventurous theological tract *The Radical Evangelical* in which he advocates a kinder, thinking evangelicalism than the one often encountered. It may be helpful to briefly situate it by comparing it to a similar work also written by a Baptist theologian, Stanley Grenz. His *Revisioning Evangelical Theology*[6] was published three years before *The Radical Evangelical*. Both authors were reacting against the more fundamentalist streams of evangelicalism which were often based

---

[2] David W. Bebbington, *Evangelicalism in Modern Britain: A History from the 1730s to the 1980s* (London: Unwin Hyman, 1989).
[3] Derek Tidball, *Who are the Evangelicals? Tracing the roots of today's movements* (London: Marshall Pickering, 1994).
[4] Christian Smith, *American Evangelicalism: Embattled and Thriving* (Chicago: University of Chicago Press, 1998).
[5] See David Wells, '"No Offense: I Am an Evangelical": A Search for Self-Definition' in A. James Rudin and Marvin R. Wilson (eds.), *A Time to Speak: The Evangelical-Jewish Encounter* (Grand Rapids: Eerdmans, 1987) 22, and J. I. Packer and Thomas C. Oden, *One Faith: The Evangelical Consensus* (Downers Grove: IVP, 2004).
[6] Stanley Grenz, *Revisioning Evangelical Theology: A Fresh Agenda for the 21st Century* (Downers Grove: IVP, 1993).

on a priori assumptions⁷ which no longer held currency and which led to a restrictive, legalistic lifestyle. Grenz wondered if the word 'evangelical' was meaningful anymore as the era of modernity gave way to the culture of postmodernity.⁸ But both authors were convinced that the term still had currency and Nigel, somewhat against current fashion, rightly defended the use of labels in his opening chapter.

Using Bebbington's by now familiar quadrilateral,⁹ Nigel describes evangelicalism as a tradition marked by shared theological convictions but also heir to 'cultural forms and predispositions' inherited from Puritanism and Pietism.¹⁰ By contrast, Grenz argues that the ethos of evangelicalism, especially outside the academy, is more significant than its body of beliefs, a view that he developed when he subsequently defined evangelicalism as chiefly characterised by 'convertive piety'.¹¹ Even so, both are essentially concerned with the theology of the movement rather than its practice, although the two cannot be separated.

The differing emphases of the books are instructive. Grenz is writing out of a North American context, Nigel out of a British context. Grenz's theology is birthed more in philosophical theology; Nigel's is more shaped by trends in systematic theology. Grenz, still perhaps unconsciously betraying the legacy of the reaction against the social gospel, is concerned about the community of the church, whereas Nigel, reflecting the radical reformation tradition (and his own personal commitments!) is concerned about an evangelical social and political agenda.¹² Grenz gives the impression that evangelicalism needs to undergo a paradigm shift whereas Nigel, rightly in my view, is more cautious about such shifts. Not only is he justifiably dismissive of those who claim to have made such a shift but also, I detect, he would argue there is the need for constant revision and re-expression of the authentic

---

⁷ See the comment on the Bible in Wright, *Radical Evangelical*, 11.
⁸ Grenz, *Revisioning*, 13-14.
⁹ Bebbington identified the key characteristics of evangelicalism as conversionism, activism, Biblicism and crucicentrism, in Bebbington, *Evangelicalism in Modern Britain*, 5-17.
¹⁰ Wright, *Radical Evangelical*, 3.
¹¹ Grenz, *Revisioning*, 31, and Stanley Grenz, *Renewing the Center: Evangelical Theology in a Post-Theological Era* (Grand Rapids: Baker, 2002) 46-47.
¹² This is not to say he is unconcerned about the church, as many of his other publications demonstrate, starting with *The Radical Kingdom: Restoration in Theory and in Practice* (Eastbourne: Kingsway, 1986).

Christianity as changes occur in the wider pattern of thought and enquiry.[13] All theology has to be contextual if it is to make sense but the context can be engaged in a number of ways. Grenz has a self-conscious postmodern agenda while Nigel is more concerned about a contemporary rediscovery of authentic, if radical, orthodox Christianity.

Evangelicalism: a constellation around a living tradition

Some find a discussion of evangelical identity unnecessary. To them it has been settled for all time in the writings of Jonathan Edwards, George Whitefield, John Wesley, J.C. Ryle, C.H. Spurgeon or whoever. So before looking at some particular aspects of Nigel's contribution to the discussion, some comments on the nature of evangelicalism might be useful, not least because they demonstrate the validity, and the difficulty, of the debate in which he and others are engaging.

First, evangelicalism has always been a constellation of different movements, churches and institutions gathered around a common set of convictions about the gospel. In musical terms, the movement has always been characterised by its members singing in harmony rather than unison. In the early days, Puritan, Pietist and Holiness streams were its main tributaries; out of them has flowed a variety of emphases which have been catalogued in various ways (Nigel refers to one such analysis[14]), including the charismatic movement and social activists. They have their own heroes (and villains!), their own emphases and liturgies, their own customs and festivals, their own networks and institutions. The boundaries between them are far from watertight and evangelicals from the different streams spill over into one another, often quite happily.

Family arguments arise, and can become quite fierce, when insufficient recognition is given to the inherent diversity of the evangelical movement. When one stream wishes to draw the definition of evangelical so tightly that only its own tributary is recognised as genuinely evangelical, trouble occurs and the resulting fragmentation enfeebles the movement as a whole. But the diversity of the movement makes it inevitably open to boundary disputes. If no one can speak for all Baptists, neither can someone claim to speak for all evangelicals.

---

[13] Wright, *Radical Evangelical*, 15-22.
[14] Wright, *Radical Evangelical*, 6-9.

Nigel is well aware of this diversity and humbly argues that *The Radical Evangelical* 'represents a legitimate hue in the evangelical rainbow' which may enrich other evangelical believers.[15] The particular voice he brings to the wider evangelical movement is that of a theologian who is an avowed Free Churchman[16] of Baptist persuasion who has been blessed by the charismatic movement and influenced by the Anabaptist tradition of the radical reformation.

Secondly, although it is common to criticise evangelicalism for being rigid and inflexible, the accusation is false, as any knowledge of its history shows. Far from being a fossilised tradition, an insufficiently recognised aspect of its genius is its ability to adapt to the culture in which it is situated whilst being true to its own identity. David Bebbington has shown how the movement, which had its conception in the Reformers, in Puritanism and Pietism, came to birth during the Enlightenment and was subsequently configured and reconfigured by cultural movements such as Romanticism and Modernism.[17] Theology never takes place in a vacuum. As culture mutates, so the theological expression of the gospel has to change to engage with that culture. The current discussion of the identity of evangelicalism is part of the on-going task of shaping a movement that is contemporary and not merely historical.

Of course, some churches and institutions will live in the past and give the impression of inflexibility. One can step into some churches and feel like stepping back fifty years as one listens to their vocabulary, observes the outward marks of a past age, sings the music of yesteryear or fights the battles of a bygone age. The only preachers valued in some churches are dead preachers – the preachers of departed generations! But this is the exception rather than the rule. One only has to look at the use of

---

[15] Wright, *Radical Evangelical*, 12.

[16] See further Nigel G. Wright, *Disavowing Constantine: Mission, Church and the Social Order in the Theologies of John Howard Yoder and Jürgen Moltmann* (Carlisle: Paternoster, 2000) and *Free Church, Free State: The Positive Baptist Vision* (Milton Keynes: Paternoster, 2005). His anti-Constantinian stance was particularly helpful in discussing the relationship between Faith and Nation during the Evangelical Alliance enquiry which led to a major report being published in 2006.

[17] For criticisms of his thesis, see Michael A. G. Haykin and Kenneth J. Stewart (eds.), *The Emergence of Evangelicalism: Exploring Historical Continuities* (Nottingham: Apollos, 2008). Although the criticisms may require some modifications to Bebbington's thesis, they do not substantially undermine it.

electronic music, film and PowerPoint, especially when compared with churches of other traditions, to see how adaptable evangelicalism is.[18] And these are no superficial and insignificant changes; the media we use in communication are not innocent vehicles for messages but they have an inevitable shaping influence on the message itself, as Marshall McLuhan taught us.[19] Both in respect of the movement as a whole and in respect of many of its local expressions, evangelicalism seems an enormously pliant movement even if holding true to certain fundamental beliefs regarding the Bible, redemption and salvation.

A third feature of evangelicalism makes the task of defining its identity both crucial and complex at the same time. Evangelicalism is driven by its desire to make the gospel of Jesus Christ available to people in terms they can understand, so that they can respond to and enjoy God's grace. Its concept of mission has become more comprehensive in recent years, after the Great Reversal of the early twentieth century when 'saving souls' for heaven, rather than a wider kingdom agenda, was all that really mattered. Yet herein lies a danger. Evangelical history demonstrates that the passion to make the gospel relevant or intelligible to people carries with it the hazard of altering it beyond recognition simply to make it appealing. History is littered with the wrecks of people and movements whose evangelicalism has floundered on the rock of relevance. It is demonstrated most notably by the experience of SCM which grew out of the Student Volunteer Movement with its genuine passion to reach the world for Christ. As the sociologist, Steve Bruce, has said, their 'desire to build bridges to the secular world' and take 'religion out of the cloisters and put it back where people were' was 'organisational suicide', for

> the bridges that were built to the secular world did not serve to bring new blood into SCM or the Christian church.

---

[18] Research shows that the vast majority of Christian input on the Internet, at least in its early days, came from Evangelicals who characteristically saw an 'opportunity' and exploited the medium for their own mission ends quicker than other sections of the church; see 'Evangelicals and the Web' in Kevin J. Christiano, William H. Swatos Jr. and Peter Kivisto, *Sociology of Religion: Contemporary Developments* (Walnut Creek: Alta Mira, 2002) 245-246.
[19] Marshall McLuhan, *Understanding Media* (London: Routledge Classics, 2001) 7.

Instead, these bridges served as paths of defection for SCM members.[20]

But many have floundered in less dramatic ways. They were concerned to engage culture for the sake of Christ only to find that culture becomes all-embracing and eclipses Christ. Care needs to be taken that the compulsion of mission is not fulfilled at the price of having no genuine gospel to communicate. The mission impulse requires us to critique culture not merely address it.[21] A true engagement with culture means taking its values seriously enough to evaluate them, not just imitate them. William Willimon rightly warns,

> The gospel is not simply about meeting people's needs. The gospel is also a critique of our needs, an attempt to give us needs worth having.[22]

As Willimon is fond of saying, our task is to convert the world not merely converse with it.[23] The passion for mission and the desire to translate the gospel and evangelical tradition into contemporary terms present us with particular challenges. When is our 'translation' of the gospel genuine and when is it a transmutation into something else? When is our translation so free that it has lost touch with the original 'text'? When are we engaged, to use Lancelot Andrewes' terms, in legitimate 'renovation' and when in illegitimate 'innovation'?[24] Evangelicals often differ as to where they will draw the line between these positions, making any attempt to express the evangelical tradition in fresh terms risky.

Combined, these three factors – evangelical diversity, flexibility and mission-heartedness – highlight the difficulty of constructing a contemporary evangelical identity. Will it be truly evangelical or merely sectional? Will it hold firm to the tradition while re-expressing it or transform the tradition into something it is not? Will it connect to contemporary culture without betraying the revealed gospel? But they also highlight the validity and necessity

---

[20] Steve Bruce, *Firm in the Faith* (Aldershot: Gower, 1984) 91.
[21] An example of critique, albeit of intellectual positions, is found in Wright, *Radical Evangelical*, 23-24.
[22] William Willimon, *Pastor: The Theology and Practice of Ordained Ministry* (Nashville: Abingdon, 2002) 96.
[23] E.g. William Willimon's blog on 7th Nov 2007 entitled 'On NOT reaching our culture through preaching'. See http://willimon.blogspot.com/
[24] Cited by John Stott, *Christ the Controversialist: A Study in Some Essentials of Evangelical Religion* (London: Tyndale Press, 1970) 40.

of the task and we should be grateful to Nigel and others who have sought to do so.

The Radical Evangelical
It is impossible to do justice to the wide-ranging and carefully argued presentation Nigel offers and so what follows raises a number of key issues selectively.

1. The Trinitarian starting point
In line with the widespread theological trend of the day,[25] Nigel's exposition begins with the Trinity which he uses as a corrective to what he sees as the excessively negative tendency of traditional evangelicalism.[26] Unlike John Stott,[27] who also uses the framework of the Trinity but never truly develops it as such, Nigel builds his positive evangelicalism around the community of self-giving love. 'Out of this loving, divine communion', he writes, 'there flows the love which first creates the world and then redeems it'.[28] Thus, the starting point is no longer sin and the fall, as in traditional evangelicalism, but God and creation. He pleads that we do not move too quickly to sin and redemption, and miss out on the goodness of God's creation. Nonetheless, he does not deny that people are sinful and in need of redemption. They are *'fallen* in that through self-exaltation they have alienated themselves from God and their true destiny'.[29] He returns to the subject of redemption later in the book.

Much contemporary theology reads too much into trinitarian doctrine, drawing all sorts of conclusions from it that go beyond anything Scripture asserts but Nigel is not guilty of this. It has often struck me as significant that the rediscovery of the community of the Trinity has occurred hand in hand with the breakdown of community and authentic relationships in society. But here, Nigel uses the Trinity to offer a right corrective to a traditional evangelicalism that has often been unbalanced in its bias towards the negative.

---

[25] Colin Gunton, *The One, the Tree and the Many* (Cambridge: Cambridge University Press, 1993) and John Zizioulas, *Being as Communion: Studies in Personhood and the Church* (London: Darton, Longman and Todd, 1985) are particularly influential in this regard.
[26] Wright, *Radical Evangelical,* 28.
[27] John Stott, *Evangelical Truth* (Leicester: IVP, 1999).
[28] Wright, *Radical Evangelical,* 35.
[29] Wright, *Radical Evangelical,* 35.

2. The Bible

Wright next turns his attention to Scripture in keeping with the priority given to it in classical evangelicalism. He reviews a number of claims about Scripture which are valued by evangelicals, starting with the Reformation adage of *sola scriptura*. The truth is, he asserts, that while Scripture is 'the *supreme* authority for the church' it is not the *sole* authority. We can never come to it free from our presuppositions, traditions and contexts, all of which exercise a shaping authority over us. He argues that evangelicals have been too concerned about the form of Scripture and not sufficiently concerned about its content. We are intensely concerned about the historical trustworthiness of parts of it, while ignoring what the 'historical event' is there to teach. By contrast Nigel suggests

> ... that there is an essentially historical core to the biblical tradition but that the meaning and significance of that history is opened up to us through parables, sagas, poetry, allegories, symbols, prophecies, apocalyptic and even (when we understand the word properly) myth.[30]

Thus he is concerned to let the Bible speak in its own way through the various genres it embraces.

The concept of 'inerrancy', Nigel asserts, is not helpful for our understanding of the Bible. It should never be the judge of whether one is authentically evangelical or not. Those who are wedded to the word engage in contortions to uphold it and it is better to come clean about the difficulties we face within the Bible. But he wants to fully assert the '*reliability* and *sufficiency* of Scripture' as a witness to God and his saving actions, a witness that has been committed to writing through God's inspiration.[31] In many respects, this is a not dissimilar position to the one adopted by John Stott who, in debate with David Jenkins, commented,

> I confess that I have never myself been greatly enamoured of the word 'inerrancy', mainly because I prefer a single positive ('true' or 'trustworthy') to a double negative ('inerrant', or for that matter 'infallible', which is the historic British equivalent). These words could even obscure what

---
[30] Wright, *Radical Evangelical*, 51.
[31] Wright, *Radical Evangelical*, 52-53.

you rightly call 'the most important question about the Bible', which is 'whether it speaks the truth'.[32]

Nigel Wright then concludes by commending his namesake's view of Scripture in which it is seen as a drama in which we are invited to participate.[33] In this view, we understand Scripture not by excavating a set of timeless truths or propositions from the text but by entering into God's story. This story does not impose its authority on us but liberates us for living wisely in today's world.

Underlying these changes in the way Scripture is approached are changing cultural attitudes to literature and texts as well as to our understanding of authority. Wright, and Wright, articulate a position which is widely adopted in the emerging church where it is not the authority of Scripture so much as the usefulness of Scripture that is emphasised in line with the claim it makes about itself in 2 Timothy 3:16.[34] In doing so emerging church leaders claim to be more faithful to what Scripture claims about itself than some more traditional evangelical claims.

There is much here which is surely incontrovertible. I am of the generation who were taught how to defend the historicity of Jonah having been swallowed by a big fish but who were left ignorant of the scandalous message of grace that the prophecy of Jonah conveyed. A growing appreciation of the different genres within Scripture unlocks its riches rather than dilutes them. Unlocking the human side of Scripture helps us to see it in glorious technicolour rather than as a monochrome systematic textbook. The Bible does draw us into God's continuing story. Yet while this is a necessary corrective, for me these expositions of the doctrine of Scripture do not, as yet, go far enough. They are better at illuminating the human side of Scripture than its divine aspects. What is needed now is to place these arguments within the context of a thoroughgoing doctrine of revelation, which is where a true evangelical theology starts.[35] If we lose the sense of this book as

---

[32] David L. Edwards with John Stott, *Essentials: A Liberal-Evangelical Dialogue* (London: Hodder and Stoughton, 1988) 95.

[33] N.T. Wright, 'How can the Bible be authoritative?', *Vox Evangelica* 22 (1991) 18-23, and *Scripture and the Authority of God* (London: SPCK, 2005).

[34] E.g. Brian McLaren, *A New Kind of Christian* (San Francisco: Jossey-Bass, 2001) 53.

[35] Contemporary evangelical theologians need to engage more with James Packer's *Fundamentalism and the Word of God* (London: IVP, 1958) and Peter Jensen's *The Revelation of God* (Leicester: IVP, 2002) to ensure a truly

divine revelation, that in it and through it 'God has spoken', we end with a book of mere human testimony.[36] That may suit our pluralist age but is of no help when our world needs a voice from beyond to rescue it from the mess that human voices have created.

3. Atonement

The nature of the atonement has sadly been a storm centre of debate in recent years with Nigel's writing on the subject often referred to as one of the academic bases for the popular and controversial position adopted by others. For the most part Nigel's chapter on 'The Creative Redeemer' is wonderfully nuanced. He is well aware both of the complexity of the issue and the store put on one's interpretation of the cross by evangelicals. Much of the chapter covers well-trodden territory. There is a difference between the fact of the atonement and theories that seek to elucidate it.[37] Although harsh, he is surely right to say that since Scripture itself does not speak explicitly of 'penal substitution' as *the* interpretation of the cross this interpretation of the cross should not be given 'first-order' status.[38]

Far from jettisoning 'penal substitution' he wants to re-express it in more relational terms, setting it in the original forensic/legal context of Scripture, and avoiding the crass expressions of an angry father 'taking it out' on his son who appeases his wrath on the cross. The traditional penal substitutionary view owes too much, he thinks, to Anselm and the Reformers who were writing within their own particular cultural contexts. The Reformers 'rightly retrieved the biblical teaching concerning the wrath of God'[39] but it is their view of wrath that Nigel essentially questions. He admits a retributive element in this wrath but sees God's wrath as essentially restorative.[40] He writes,

> The wrath of God is fleeting by comparison with his love and the two are not to be seen as equally balanced

---

evangelical doctrine of Scripture where the initiative in communication as well as in grace lies with God.

[36] This is, of course, the major theme of Walter Brueggemann's *Theology of the Old Testament* (Minneapolis: Fortress, 1997) from which I have benefited immensely. But the 'status' of the testimonies involved needs confronting. Not all testimonies are trustworthy or of value.

[37] Wright, *Radical Evangelical*, 59.
[38] Wright, *Radical Evangelical*, 59.
[39] Wright, *Radical Evangelical*, 63.
[40] Wright, *Radical Evangelical*, 65.

attributes. God *is* love and it would be entirely wrong to claim that he *is* wrath.[41]

God solves the problem of our sin not by meting out his wrath on the cross but by resolving it within himself, forgiving those who are alienated from him, by a forgiveness which is inevitably 'painful and costly'.[42] Love and wrath, he rightly claims, are not opposites. God's wrath is an expression of his love and cannot be dispensed with because it 'manifests (his) ultimate resistance to anything and everything which tends to destroy the creatures who are the object of his love'.[43]

There is much to affirm in Nigel's writing and less discrepancy than is supposed between his position and that of a mature, as opposed to a crass, expression of penal substitution.[44] But there are also some things that cause me to say let's pause and think more carefully about that. To begin with, it is easy for critics of penal substitution to demolish popular expressions of the theory, countering them with their own sophisticated arguments, but to avoid engaging with more scholarly expositions of the approach such as that of John Stott.[45] Then, phrases like, 'The wrath of God is fleeting by comparison with his love' need careful consideration. It has become popular to claim that the wrath of God is not as major a theme in the Bible as traditionally taught, with scholars like Stephen Travis arguing that 'in Paul's understanding of divine judgement ideas of "punishment" or "retribution" lie on the periphery of his thought'.[46] But the evidence is not on their side. The God of the Bible is one, and the God who reveals himself in the Old Testament is certainly capable of moving in personal wrath against nations who practise evil. This is seen, for example, when those nations who serve as his instruments for the disciplining of Israel for their breaking of the covenant overreach themselves. The Bible shows no embarrassment about

---

[41] Wright, *Radical Evangelical*, 65.
[42] Wright, *Radical Evangelical*, 67.
[43] Wright, *Radical Evangelical*, 65.
[44] For an excellent recent discussion, see I. Howard Marshall, 'The Theology of Atonement' in Derek Tidball, David Hilborn and Justin Thacker (eds.), *The Atonement Debate* (Grand Rapids: Zondervan, 2008) 49-68.
[45] John Stott, *The Cross of Christ* (Leicester: IVP, 1986). Nigel, like other critics, affirms Stott's view of 'divine self-substitution', 59.
[46] Stephen Travis, 'Christ as the bearer of divine judgement in Paul's thought about the atonement' in John Goldingay (ed.), *Atonement Today* (London: SPCK, 1995) 21.

speaking of God's personal initiative and involvement in the act of punishment. God's opposition is more than the impersonal working out of the consequences of our alienation from him. The language of punishment, judgement, vengeance and wrath is also more common in the New Testament than those who want to present 'the acceptable face' of God to our generation would lead us to believe. Having studied the usage of such terms carefully, Howard Marshall concludes,

> There is a clear framework of thought in the New Testament which assumes a background of the future action of God against evildoers, an action of judgment in which God displays his wrath against sin and carries out judgment involving the destruction or death of sinners.[47]

Two other aspects of Nigel's exposition of the cross need more careful examination. Our view of the cross, as he rightly understands, stems from our view of God. As already quoted, he asserts rightly that God is love while it would be wrong to assert that God is wrath. He affirms, again rightly, that wrath is not opposed to love but an aspect of it. I agree. But perhaps insufficient attention is paid to other biblical statements about the essential nature of God. The very same letter that asserts 'God is love' (1 John 4:16) also asserts that 'God is light' (1 John 1:5). And the God of whom it was said that he is love is the God who says of himself, 'I, the Lord your God, am holy' (Leviticus 11:44-45; 19:2; 20:26). These sayings deserve more attention in seeking to understand the cross of Christ.

A further aspect of Nigel's exposition which requires thought is his insistence, following D.M. Baillie, that the cross is 'only' (?) an 'expression in time of the eternal reality which takes place in God's heart', and an 'outcrop' in time of God's eternal heart.[48] In so far as he is saying, with P.T. Forsyth, that, 'The atonement did not procure grace, it flowed from grace',[49] he is surely right. But Nigel seems to me to draw the wrong implication from this in using sentences like, 'It is not that the cross is necessary for God in order that he might overcome his wrath'; 'Forgiveness should not ... be seen as something which is made

---

[47] Marshall, 'Theology of Atonement', 52-53. See also his fuller exposition in I. Howard Marshall, *Aspects of the Atonement* (London: Paternoster, 2007).
[48] Wright, *Radical Evangelical*, 67.
[49] P.T. Forsyth, *The Cruciality of the Cross* (1909; reprint Carlisle: Paternoster, 1997) 14.

possible for God by the cross'; and 'God does not need an external, mechanical event to become capable of forgiving'.[50] He is surely on firmer ground when he speaks of the cross as the means by which the 'atonement becomes a completed reality'[51] – a claim I would love to hear explained further. Critics of penal substitution often complain that the theory is morally indefensible. But if the cross was only an expression of God's eternal love and not actually 'necessary', does it not make the crucifixion even more morally reprehensible? Is not Forsyth a surer guide in saying,

> It was a work that had to be done, and not merely a personal influence that was conveyed. Christ did not die simply to affect men but to effect salvation, not simply to move men's heart but to accomplish God's will?[52]

Bridging the eternal heart and the historical event Forsyth wrote,

> The atonement of the cross is the key that opens the door, but the house we enter is not made with hands. It is the very heart of God we have in Christ.[53]

4. Liberalism

The concluding chapters of *The Radical Evangelical* draw judiciously on the 'legacy of liberalism' to discuss the human side of the Bible and the humanity of Christ, to revisit hell and to construct what is called 'a kinder, gentler damnation', and to advocate a radical involvement in politics as part of our Christian calling. In none of these chapters is the impact of liberalism welcomed uncritically and its flaws are mentioned. Even so, its openness of spirit is welcomed as causing us to reflect more realistically on the doctrinal claims made about the Bible, Christ and hell in particular.

Once more, several claims made here are unobjectionable. First, contemporary evangelicals have to concede that critical approaches to the reading of Scripture that were anathema to their predecessors are now second nature to them.[54] Secondly, while there is an outright rejection of the classic liberal portrait of Christ,

---

[50] Wright, *Radical Evangelical*, 67.
[51] Wright, *Radical Evangelical*, 67.
[52] Forsyth, *Cruciality*, 18-19.
[53] Forsyth, *Cruciality*, 19.
[54] See Derek Tidball, 'Postwar Evangelical Theology: A Generational Perspective', *Evangelical Quarterly* (forthcoming).

evangelicals now generally shun their more traditional one-sided emphasis on the divinity of Christ, which was in truth docetic. Thirdly, many would feel more at home with Nigel's characterization of the torment of hell as 'beholding God at the last, looking upon his beauty, majesty and infinite love and knowing that through one's own deliberate fault all of this has been made forfeit and loss'[55] than with Spurgeon's portrayal of the human body in hell as made like asbestos 'so that it will burn for ever without being desensitised for all its raging fury'.[56] Fourthly, most, though sadly not all, would also accept that our calling is to engage in the politics of this world and not just to 'pass through' this world to the next.

Perhaps these 'advances' are due to the influence of liberalism, depending, as Nigel says, on how you define liberalism.[57] If defined as a broad cultural movement he is almost certainly right, since evangelicals have to make sense of their beliefs in the midst of the broader culture in which they find themselves and so, as argued before, changes are inevitable. These broad cultural currents have, I believe, helped evangelicals to work out their own tradition in a way that is truer to biblical revelation. But if the reference is to theological liberalism, I am not convinced. I would see it as more corrosive of true faith than does Nigel, even though he is not uncritical of it, and as having done grave damage to the church of Christ. Liberalism exalts human reason and acknowledges human beings and their experiences as supreme. It inevitably posits an anthropological starting point for theology, whereas evangelicals surely begin with the givenness of God's revelation which includes the wonder of his law as well as the magnificent initiative of his grace.

In a perceptive article, to which we shall return more fully shortly, John Stackhouse raises some disturbing questions about one area under consideration here, that of evangelical theologians and the Bible. He asserts,

> Evangelicals properly distance themselves from liberal methodology that feels 'free' to ignore, and even contradict, express teachings of Scripture in the name of the putative superiority of current opinion. And evangelicals continue

---

[55] Wright, *Radical Evangelical*, 94.
[56] Cited by John Blanchard, *Whatever Happened to Hell?* (Darlington: Evangelical Press, 1993) 313.
[57] Wright, *Radical Evangelical*, 73.

properly to wonder just how 'postliberal' postliberals really are in this respect. Do they stand under the authority of the Bible – even the awkward parts, even the parts that seem sexist or fantastic, or wrong – or are they still working with too much liberal freedom?[58]

I sometimes wonder if in a quest for academic recognition, our evangelical theological colleges are not sometimes in danger of drinking too deeply from the wells of 'liberal freedom'.

Conclusion
John Stackhouse has argued that 'Evangelical Theology should be Evangelical'. He defines the hallmarks of such theology as being Christocentric, biblical, conversionist and concerned with mission. To these he adds 'a robust trans-denominationalism' that promotes respect for differences over secondary matters and devotion to the central importance of Jesus Christ and his gospel.[59] Perhaps as much as transdenominationalism we need to add, as the evangelical movement becomes more diverse and fragmented, transpartyism. In these respects Nigel has offered a model of how to do evangelical theology. Although one might not always accept his conclusions, and although some consideration of the meaning of conversion in contemporary Britain would have been welcome, *The Radical Evangelical* demonstrates humility, a respect for others, a charity towards views he does not hold, an honest logic and a clear desire to uphold the essentials of the evangelical tradition and to work out the significance of Scripture for today. Nigel Wright's voice is one that has earned the right to be heard in the noisy, crowded and recurring conversation about evangelical identity.

---

[58] John G. Stackhouse, 'Evangelical Theology should be Evangelical' in John Stackhouse (ed.), *Evangelical Futures: A Conversation on Theological Method* (Grand Rapids: Baker and Leicester: IVP, 2000) 48.
[59] Stackhouse, 'Evangelical Theology', 58.

Crown rights of the Redeemer

Patricia M. Took

A fine old Baptist phrase?
In 1996 the Baptist Union produced an excellent pamphlet called *Something to Declare* in which its Declaration of Principle was explored by the Principals of the four Baptist colleges in England. In the chapter devoted to the first principle – 'That our Lord and Saviour, Jesus Christ, God manifest in the flesh, is the sole and absolute authority in all matters relating to faith and practice, as revealed in the Holy Scriptures, and that each church has liberty, under the guidance of the Holy Spirit, to interpret and administer his laws' – the comment was made that this 'is an affirmation that reaches back into the fine old Baptist phrase, "the crown rights of the Redeemer"'.[1]

This comment fascinates me; it seems full not just of historical resonance but also of unrealised potential, of an 'excess of meaning'.[2] While it might be said that the person who first uses a phrase should have the right to decide what colour it should have, there is also a legitimate exploration of fresh potential in all received communication which allows us to go beyond the struggle to recapture an original meaning, to find new significance for our own generation. I want to suggest that this expression, 'the crown rights of the Redeemer', can hold for us a historically nuanced, but still vital, meaning as well as a helpful, fresh dimension.

I decided first to see if I could track the phrase back to its source. It is described here as a Baptist phrase, and I have always associated it with Baptist churchmanship, assuming it to be an Anabaptist expression, or perhaps to have its roots in the polemic of Luther.[3] But my explorations took me back instead to the

---

[1] Paul Fiddes, Brian Haymes, Richard Kidd (editor) and Michael Quicke, *Something to Declare* (Oxford: Whitley Publications, 1996) 28.
[2] This subject has been widely explored but is splendidly opened up in the Introduction by David Ling to Hans-Georg Gadamer, *Philosophical Hermeneutics* (Berkeley: University of California Press, 1976) xxv.
[3] Most Anabaptists confessions and testimonies insist on Christ as King. They also contain the origins of much of our thinking concerning freedom of conscience. So e.g. Peter Riedeman, *Account 1542*: 'Wherever the government presumes to lay hands upon the conscience and to control the faith of man, there it is robbing God of what is his.' The words of Kilian Aurbacher (1534) foreshadow

Scottish Reformation and to that scourge of monstrous regiments, John Knox.[4] And on reflection it seems obvious that the use of the expression 'crown rights' indicates the political setting that arose out of those Erastian experiments at reform (or counter-reform) that followed the first generation of Protestant activists.

Crown rights

The expression seems to have begun life in the polemic of Knox against what he perceived as the blasphemous claim by Mary Queen of Scots to the obedience of her subjects in the conduct of religion:

> Mary: 'You have taught the people to receive another religion than that which their princes allow; but God commands subjects to obey their princes. Therefore you have taught the people to disobey both God and their prince.'
> Knox: 'Madam, as right religion receives not its origin nor authority from princes but from the eternal God alone, so are not subjects bound to frame their religion according to the tastes of their princes, for oft it is that princes are the most ignorant of God's true religion.'

Knox saw Mary's attempt to legislate for the souls of her subjects as a usurpation of the crown rights of the Redeemer. But his opposition appeared to threaten civil discord and the dissolution of the fabric of the state. The new world that emerged as a result of placing the movement for reform of the Church in the hands of the prince, a development particularly associated with Luther and the Diet of Augsburg, and summed up in the principle *cuius regio eius religio*,[5] had the potential to bring religious fervour into direct confrontation with the powers of the state.

To be a dissenter was no longer to be a heretic, someone who, having taken a stand against the Universal Church, had

---

our own Thomas Helwys: 'It is never right to compel one in matters of faith, whatever he may believe, be he Jew or Turk ... Christ's people are a free, unforced, and uncompelled people, who receive Christ with desire and a willing heart, of this the Scriptures testify.' Both in Walter Klaassen (ed.), *Anabaptism in outline. Selected primary sources* (Waterloo, Ont., & Scottdale, PA: Herald, 1981) 258, 293.

[4] While all the sources that I have looked at point to Knox as the originator of this expression, I have not been able to pin it down.

[5] 'Whose land, his religion', i.e. citizens had to adopt the religion of the local ruler.

stepped outside the body of Christ and was damned. In a fragmented Christendom in which the prince or city had assumed the right to control religious affairs, dissent became a challenge to political power and a threat to civil peace.

In England the Settlement of Elizabeth, with its deliberate ambiguity, quickly lost the support of many fervent souls. The rapid disenchantment of the returning Calvinist exiles with its compromises and disguises led to the development of the separatist movement and within that movement our own Baptist origins. Confronted with a civil authority whose demands ran counter to the individual conscience, we took our stand on the absolute right and duty to obey our conscience, and famously gave expression to the notion of the proper limitations of princely power in the sphere of religion by referring to the 'crown rights of the Redeemer'.

Mediated and unmediated authority

The issue at stake is not the sovereignty of God - that has always been a non-negotiable tenet of faith. To challenge God's sovereignty is to fall into the madness of King Nebuchadnezzar, whose sanity only returned when he blessed the Most High and praised and glorified the Ever-Living One, 'whose sovereignty is everlasting and whose kingdom endures through all generations' (Daniel 4:34-35, Revised English Bible). The issue is not that anyone would dream of challenging this fundamental principle, but that the crown was assuming the right, previously vested in the Pope, to mediate this authority. Yet can such authority ever be delegated or mediated? The Pope had at least the assumed scriptural warranty of St Peter's keys and the dogma that God would not allow the Church to go astray. To obey the Pope was to obey Christ - there was no remainder. Luther, however, came to the conviction that the Pope's claim to allegiance was usurpation of God's rule.[6] But while there had been some theoretical basis for the claim of the Pope, what justification was there to vest this power in the Crown?

---

[6] In the great Reformation Treatises of 1520 Luther inveighs against 'the Babylonian captivity of the Church' and, in 'The Freedom of the Christian' proclaims his famous paradox 'A Christian is a perfectly free lord of all, subject to none. A Christian is a perfectly dutiful servant of all subject to all.' The political dynamite let loose by these sentiments was later snuffed out by his own hand, but the Anabaptist and later Separatist traditions rooted themselves in this radical soil.

Clearly the Crown does have some rights. We must render to Caesar the things that are Caesar's (cf. Matthew 22:21).[7] We should normally pay our taxes and normally obey the law. We are called by Scripture to seek the peace of the city (Jeremiah 29:7) and to do whatever we are able to ensure the harmony and peace of the communities we live in. Even Anabaptists, who took a deeply pessimistic view of the role of the magistrate, insisted on obedience. Nevertheless we claim the right in certain circumstances not to obey the law, and to take the consequences, if we believe the law to be ungodly. The command to take up arms has been repeatedly resisted by men and women of conscience.[8] Martin Holloway, a peace activist in Missouri, writes:

> What is important is to avoid moral somnolence. It is precisely the false religion of blind obedience to human authority which must be resisted if we are to avoid a nuclear catastrophe. When the prison guard or the policeman or the judge issues the order, 'you must kill your neighbour', the Christian is called to say simply, 'No'.[9]

The baptismal declaration 'Jesus is Lord' has always proved to be profoundly revolutionary and subversive in its denial by the individual of any lords other than Christ. Once the lordship of Christ is vested in another authority it is no longer lordship. If the king has the right to decide in matters of religion, Jesus is no longer Lord. Christ commands our ultimate allegiance and no other power has final authority over us.

The authority of conscience
There is a sense in which this claim, that Christ in dialogue with the individual conscience has an ultimate authority in all matters of faith and practice, was a new phenomenon in the sixteenth century. Of course, there are forerunners in the renewal movements of the late Middle Ages.[10] But it was generally

---

[7] For Nigel Wright's reflections on the extent and limit of proper obedience to the state see his *Power and Discipleship. Towards a Baptist Theology of the State* (Whitley Lecture; Oxford: Whitley Publications, 1996) and *Free Church, Free State: The Positive Baptist Vision* (Milton Keynes: Paternoster, 2005).
[8] [Editor: See the essay by Murray in this volume.]
[9] In Geoffrey Bould (ed.), *Conscience be my Guide. An Anthology of Prison Writings* (London: Zed Books, 1991) 162-163.
[10] See John Hus, 'Letter to John Barbatus and the People of Krumlov' [1411] in Andrew Bradstock and Christopher Rowland (eds.), *Radical Christian Writings. A Reader* (Oxford: Blackwell, 2002) 52-54.

assumed that individuals stood within a community that shaped, informed and directed their conscience, and that they were accountable to that community for conforming to its truth. Since that community was coterminous with the body of Christ, the highest sacral authority bound the individual to the will of the group.

If we are to continue to challenge this view, in spite of the findings of psychologists and sociologists that the individual never stands alone - never determines in complete autonomy - we need to proceed with caution. Is there not great danger in equating the instincts of conscience with the will and purposes of God? After all, humanity is fallen. Our conscience has been shaped, perhaps warped, by the effects of our upbringing, the prejudices of our society, the anxieties of our own identity. We are blinded by ignorance, by folly, by egotism. My perspective is skewed by the obsessions of my age. Before I can put such final trust in my conscience I need the redeeming power of the Holy Spirit, so that I can be transformed in my mind. I need the wisdom of brothers and sisters who can see further and deeper than I can. So our first Baptist Union principle declares that 'each church has liberty, under the guidance of the Holy Spirit, to interpret and administer his laws.' This authority is not vested in individual Christians. It is a Baptist conviction that it is together that we seek and discern the mind of Christ. For us, the power that others have seen as vested in and mediated by the Pope or other sacral authorities is instead experienced directly in the living Christ who stands at the heart of each congregation and whose will can be discovered whenever that congregation earnestly seeks it. Surely the claim to stand alone is contrary to this understanding.

But what if I alone come to a clear conviction in heart and soul that the customs and understandings of my community are contrary to the will of God? Surely I must obey God rather than man? And is it not true that for all my fallen nature there remains a witness of God within my spirit, a deep knowledge of rightness, of the love that is owed to God and my neighbour, of what it means to be humane, which is not conditioned by my social setting, but is in some sense instinctual? If in the name of my community, whether family, race or church, I am asked to violate those deepest instincts, I must say no. As God is real, as God is truth, as God is incarnate, there can be no ultimate separation between the claims of God and the inner conviction of that which is good. If there is a dissonance between that deepest instinct and the accepted view of what God requires, it is more likely that it is the accepted view that is mistaken. It appears to me that it is essential for the protection of humanity that we insist upon the right to dissent where conscience is affronted. Baptists have always stood, and surely still stand, within the tradition that will challenge the crown rights, the ultimate claims, of any community or any king other than the Redeemer. All other allegiances are contingent. All others must bow before this ultimate allegiance.

Continued vigilance[11]

Over the centuries the need to dissent from political arrangements has ebbed and flowed according to the nature of those arrangements. At the moment most Baptists in England would not feel that their freedom of conscience and action was under great threat from the state. However we might be mistaken in this sense of security. There is evidence that the whole religious enterprise is becoming somewhat disreputable and the powers that be are beginning to give legal expression to their distaste for all religion. The wearing of a cross by an airline employee was an interesting example. It seems wise for us to continue to reflect on and to cherish our religious freedoms, and all those other freedoms that find their source in freedom of conscience. There has been plenty in the history of the last hundred years to suggest that standing guard over the sovereign rights of God will continue to be crucial for the freedom of humanity as long as there are people who would like to usurp his place. Two examples will show what is meant. In 1934, in response to the Nazi claim to govern in the Church and to have itself a revelation of God's purposes, the Barmen Declaration asserted:

> We reject the false doctrine that the Church could or should recognise as a source of its proclamation beyond and beside this one Word of God (Jesus Christ as attested in Scripture) yet other events, powers, historic figures and truths as God's revelation. (...) We reject the false doctrine that there could be areas of our life in which we would not belong to Jesus Christ but to other lords, areas in which we would not need justification and sanctification through him.[12]

---

[11] [Editor: See also the essay by Colwell in this volume.]
[12] Quoted from Bradstock and Rowland (eds.), *Radical Christian Writings*, 202.

In 1985, facing the timidity and conformism of the church in South Africa and the claims of the state to scriptural warranty for demanding unqualified obedience to unjust laws, the *Kairos Document* insisted that

> the South African State recognises no authority beyond itself and therefore it will not allow anyone to question what it has chosen to define as 'law and order'. However there are millions of Christians in South Africa today who are saying with Peter: 'We must obey God rather than man.'[13]

It is the perennial inclination of tyrants, whether individuals or parties, to want to control the thoughts as well as the actions of their subjects. In the face of all such tyranny the declaration that is foundational to the Christian faith – that Jesus is Lord – will have to be made again and again, always at great risk to those who own that allegiance.

King of the church

In the same way Baptists take their stand against ungodly expressions of power in the church. Our Congregationalist church governance stands guard against all oppressive and illegitimate expression of clericalism and prelacy, placing responsibility squarely with the gathered community. We believe that when people come together in the name of Christ, and in prayer seek his will and guidance, he does not fail to make himself known. This guidance is not something that can be discerned at arm's length by some other authority figure. It is only in the face to face life of prayer and listening that this dynamic is released for our guidance. The church must obey that immediate expression of lordship that Christ exercises at the heart of each community. This is a sacred space, and no-one has the right to trespass on it.

Ideally the same conviction of Christ's inalienable right to rule should govern our dealings with one another in the church. There should be among us no invasive or abusive forms of evangelism, no manipulation, no heavy shepherding, no abuse of the pulpit, no emotional blackmail, no bullying. Nothing that smacks of inappropriate pressure or domination. If individuals are to be able to exercise their freedom to follow Christ they must not be subjected to anything that disempowers them, either physically

---

[13] Quoted from Bradstock and Rowland (eds.), *Radical Christian Writings*, 298. The Scripture verse is Acts 5:29.

or spiritually. On the contrary we must labour to see each brother and sister come to a full and free maturity and independence, so that each can make their contribution to the wisdom of the whole congregation, and each can judge for themselves in matters of private conscience where God's will is to be found. Indeed, the involvement of Baptists and other Dissenters in the campaigns for the redress of slavery, poverty and all forms of oppression has always been driven not just by compassion and humanitarian impulses, but also by a concern to create for each human being the conditions in which they will be able to make a free and mature response to the call of Christ.

Neither may we impose upon one another our own notion of the agenda for transformation that this redeeming King might wish to enact in another person's life. It might seem to me that the first thing a sister should do is give up the heroin. But Christ might feel that being reconciled to her father comes first. And while we are encouraged to walk together and watch over each other, helping each other discern how we might be conformed to the mind of Christ, in the end it is Christ himself who knows best how to conform us.

As a believers' church we are bound to eschew all forms of domination. So we will continue to resist the cult of celebrity and the hankering after showbiz styles of leadership. And while we will want to honour those in positions of leadership and to recognise and encourage the gift of leadership within the church, we will strenuously refute the idea that any church of Christ is ever leaderless.

In our private lives we are under the same obligation to acknowledge that, whatever the dynamic of respect and care within the family, each of us has in the end only one ultimate allegiance - to God. Here too constant vigilance is required. The abuse of Scripture to justify ungodly and blasphemous domination, both in the church and in the home, is more prevalent today than it has been for several decades. With the rise of fundamentalisms around the world a concern to keep control over people's thoughts and behaviour has seen a serious erosion of freedom, even in our Baptist community. Here too we need to guard the sacred space. In the end, in the church and in our homes, each man and each woman must obey God rather than human beings

Excess of meaning

So much then for the heritage of dissent in which we stand – that opposition to all ungodly, abusive and destructive power which leads us, like John Knox, to take our stand on the crown rights of the Redeemer. Such usurpations of the sovereign rights of Christ are as prevalent today as ever and there is need for continued vigilance. But might there also be dimensions to this expression that have fresh applications for us? What might it mean in a post-Christian, post-Constantinian world in which the pursuit of faith has become increasingly privatised and the notion of the Separation of Powers is axiomatic?[14] How do we live out this ultimate allegiance in a fragmented world of exclusively individual concerns, in which the highest goal is the pursuit of private happiness?

Because of who Jesus Christ is, how he lived, what he taught, how he died, the proclamation 'Jesus is Lord' sits uncomfortably with a life of public conformism and private devotion. If Jesus is Lord then the world around us will only find its fulfilment and redemption when it functions in ways that conform to his will. The loss of political power and influence which the Church in the West has experienced, and which has, perhaps rightly, been felt to be on balance a good and purgative experience, a liberation even, does also carry the danger that we will abandon the whole enterprise of working to make the kingdoms of this world the kingdoms of his grace. But to acknowledge the lordship of Christ is necessarily to seek a compassionate and just society - to labour for the release of captives and the recovery of sight for the blind. This acknowledgement necessarily, inevitably, presents a challenge to all forms of power that reduce the other. For those who follow Christ there can be no withdrawal from the struggle to redeem the structures of this world, which, for all their fallenness are still part of that real, created, experienced world that God loves and seeks to redeem.

For us in our generation success cannot look the same as it did for previous generations, who looked to see large numbers of people joining the churches and the policies of the nation being formed in conformity with the views of the Church. Can we find a new way to labour for the Kingdom of God, and to recognise and celebrate Christ's lordship when we encounter it? Our generation is challenged to consider what kingship might mean if it is not the

---

[14] These issues have been particularly explored by Stuart Murray, see his *Church after Christendom* (Milton Keynes: Paternoster, 2004).

same as domination.[15] How might the community which lives in and through Christ express the sovereign claims of Christ in ways which add to the freedom and potency of the individual rather than subverting it? It seems to me that the two poles of this expression give us two encouragements to move from the position of back foot dissent – the awareness of what it is we oppose and the courage to oppose it – to a position of front foot dissent.

The King's Church

If Christ is King, then we are called to live out the gospel in the hope and expectation that we will be able to change the world around us for good by the power of the Holy Spirit. This new emphasis in dissent, which has come to us in London particularly through the black Pentecostal churches, seems to me to be far more pregnant with hope for the future of the Christian community than the more pessimistic and disengaged pursuit of holiness which has sometimes prevailed among us.[16] The expression 'the crown rights of the Redeemer' is, after all, a resoundingly positive statement. It declares what Christ is, and only by deduction what other expressions of power are not. It declares that Christ is King in our lives and in the Church. Indeed it is Christ who has crown rights in the entire world. It is this Christ who will gather all things into the harmony of his rule and bring all things to redemption by his self-abandoning love. A church that lives out its allegiance to such a King will have a very different character to the Constantinian and pseudo-Constantinian model that has characterised so many centuries of Christian history. But it will not be privatised.

What might such a church look like? The alternative to universality would seem to be intensity. But intensity too can lead to a usurpation of the rights of Christ. Small, intense and devout communities can become self-engrossed, indifferent to the fate of those who do not share their experience, who are not part of the

---

[15] It is here that the best insights of feminist theology can help as we consider how God's power might be more observed in creativity than in control. See e.g. section 3, 'Practical consequences', in Ann Loades (ed.), *Feminist theology. A Reader* (London: SPCK, 1996).

[16] In 2007 the London Baptist Association's Pastors' Consultation focussed especially on what dissent might mean for our generation. With new forms of ecumenism emerging among us, the work of Les Isaacs and David Shosanya with Street Pastors and with Nims Obunge and the Peace Initiatives, there seems to be a much more confident stance towards contemporary society, and the conviction that we are obliged and empowered to impact our society for good.

self-selecting congregation. We can end up replacing the crown rights of the Redeemer with the crown rights of the community – a constant danger for Baptists. Where might we find an appropriate and life-giving intensity, a serious living out of allegiance to Christ which subverts all that is destructive of life in the society around us?

Obeying Christ
In the first place the proclamation of the crown rights of the Redeemer calls us again to that ultimate allegiance which, being owed to no-one else, is most definitely owed to Christ. We are called to follow Christ - to obey Christ. We have not claimed for ourselves a freedom to use or fritter away our lives as we see fit, free from all interference from outside; a kind of ultimate self-government. We have on the contrary claimed that we do have an ultimate allegiance, that we are indeed answerable. Not for us the comfortable excuse that the gospel imperatives are counsels of perfection, not to be expected of ordinary human beings. The commands to love our enemy and do good to those who hate us, not to lay up for ourselves treasure on earth, to forgive our brother from the heart, not to pass judgment, to welcome little children as we wish to enter the Kingdom of Heaven, to obey the commandments, to render to Caesar the things that are Caesar's and to God the things that are God's, to take up our cross and follow him, come to us with ultimate seriousness. Not for us a caste of a sanctified few who do holiness on behalf of the rest. Everyone who makes this proclamation takes upon themselves the yoke of a disciple of Jesus and is called to learn his ways and to obey his commands. That this way of life is singularly difficult, impractical and unworldly is utterly irrelevant. It is to Christ that we owe our allegiance – not to the easy, the practical or the worldly. Christ has crown rights, absolute rights.[17]

And as in our personal lives, so also in the life of the Church. If individual Christians are called to live in this self-abnegating way, so is the Church which is the body of Christ in the world. The Church too is commanded not to lay up treasures on earth, is warned about building bigger barns, is warned about the lust of the eyes, the lust of the flesh and the pride of life. The Church too must love her enemies and must be prepared to lose herself if she desires to find herself. There is a huge challenge

---

[17] [Editor: Cf. the essay by Colwell in this volume.]

here for the modern evangelical community. Has the Church embraced the command to lose herself or to lay down her life? Or have we acted as if in the Church there is a sacred heritage that must be guarded and preserved by us at all costs, and as if our highest call in ministry is the growth and expansion of the Church? But we do not believe in the crown rights of the local congregation or even of the whole Christian Church! It is Christ alone who claims our wills. It will only be in giving away herself that the Church will finally become that redemptive presence, that hope for the world, which the body of Christ should be.

The Redeemer
This brings us to the second emphasis in our phrase. It is the Redeemer whom we declare to be our king, the one who came to seek and save those who were lost, and who meant by lostness every form of lifelessness - sickness, marginalisation, exclusion, alienation, sin and death.

There is in this wonderful title a hope which was not laid hold of in the battles of the sixteenth century when the expression was forged. When Knox and other reformers spoke of the blasphemous usurpation of God's rights by the kings, or more especially queens, of their generation, again and again their thought was rooted in the Old Testament. The model of power and kingship with which they worked had far more to do with David than with Christ. But if it is the Redeemer who claims our ultimate allegiance, our understanding of how God exercises his power in the world and in the Church is transformed. To assert the crown rights of the Redeemer is to submit the whole programme of the Church and our own personal lives to the call, which overrides all other calls, to be agents of his redemptive grace. Of all the many things that the Church can become absorbed in - many of them entirely appropriate and necessary in themselves - none must ever take precedence over the command of redemption.

We are not called to be the moral policemen of the world. We are not called to corner the market in world faiths. We are not called to live beautiful and sanctified personal lives, remote from the world around us. Our calling is to recognise and collaborate with God's redeeming, transforming, life-giving love and grace in our world. Any congregation that proclaims the crown rights of the Redeemer and lives in accordance with that proclamation becomes redemptive as it uses all its substance, all its energy, all its emotional and spiritual strength, to reach those who are lost, pouring itself out even to death for the transformation of the world. This must involve many forms of engagement in the world, with its structures, its laws, its hopes and aspirations. It also necessitates a continual struggle with the world's cultural and political idols. It requires a way of life that is seen by the world to be odd, subversive, irritating. But the motive will always be compassion and concern rather than judgment, the instinct engagement rather than withdrawal. In the words of Yoder,

> For the people of God to be over against the world at those points where 'the world' is defined by its rebellion against God and for us to be in, with, and for the world, as anticipation of the shape of redemption, are not alternative strategies. We are not free to choose between them, depending on whether our tastes are more 'catholic' or more 'baptist', or depending on whether we think the times are friendly just now or not. Each dimension of our stance is the prerequisite for the validity of the other. A church that is not 'against the world' in fundamental ways has nothing worth saying to and for the world. Conversion and separation are not the way to become otherworldly; they are the only way to be present, relevantly and redemptively in the midst of things.[18]

It is unlikely that communities or individuals who live in the kingdom of the Redeemer will gain much influence in the other kingdom or become hugely powerful from a human point of view. You do not get rich by giving away what you have. In this sense community success, influence and prestige are presumably not matters of great significance. On the contrary, a church that lives in obedience to the Redeemer is likely to live and die largely unnoticed as it does its task of seeding the world with hope and grace.

But because we believe in Christ who is King, we live in the conviction that this way lies glory and we trust that the revelation we have in Christ is a true revelation of the God who will bring everything to a triumphant conclusion. Hence the spirit of the Church cannot be one of pessimism towards the world. In refusing to seek success along the lines of domination it does not express a culture of martyrdom or of despair. On the contrary, such a church must be full of the energy and optimism of those whose King

---

[18] John Howard Yoder, *Body Politics* (Waterloo Ont: Herald Press, 1992) 78.

reigns, the King whose programme has been proved to be victorious even over death. In choosing the quiet ways it is not lacking in ambition but it is looking for those successes that produce blessing, hope and new life in the world around. Sometimes those successes will bring converts into the Kingdom to share the task in hand. But the success of such a church will reach far beyond its own company as in multifarious and creative ways it seeks to overcome evil with good.[19]

Our fine old phrase, which - though not Baptist in origin - has become so by adoption, still presents an uncompromising challenge, not just to any other blasphemous form of domination but also to the heart of the Church. As we familiarise ourselves with a landscape in which the Christian community occupies a very marginal place, it continues to thunder the truth on which we stand – that Jesus is Lord. And in its focus on the Redeemer, it calls us afresh in that landscape, to be busy about the task of feeding the hungry, clothing the naked, welcoming the stranger, visiting those in distress, preaching the gospel, and, as heralds of the Kingdom which is surely coming, living out that life of allegiance in which lies the hope of our world.

---

[19] See the concluding application of Nigel Wright's *Power and Discipleship*, 34-37.

Select bibliography of the writings of Nigel G. Wright

You are my God: A Study Guide to the Passover Psalms (London: Bible Society, 1982)

Moving On: The Church (London: Scripture Union, 1983); also published in Arabic and Latvian

The Radical Kingdom: Restoration in Theory and in Practice (Eastbourne: Kingsway, 1986)

The Fair Face of Evil: Putting the Power of Darkness in its Place (Basingstoke: Marshall Pickering, 1988); published in the USA as *The Satan Syndrome: Putting the Power of Darkness in its Place* (Grand Rapids: Zondervan, 1990)

A Theology of Mission (Didcot: Baptist Union, 1990)

Mission i Morgens-dagens Menighed (Copenhagen: Baptist Union of Denmark, 1992)

Lord and Giver of Life: An Introduction to the Person and Work of the Holy Spirit (Didcot: Baptist Union, 1990)

Challenge to Change: A Radical Agenda for Baptists (Eastbourne: Kingsway, 1991)

[with Thomas A. Smail and Andrew Walker] *Charismatic Renewal: The Search for a Theology* (London: SPCK, 1993); published in the USA as *The Love of Power and the Power of Love* (Minneapolis: Bethany House, 1994); second expanded and revised edition 1995

Makt och Lärjungskap: En frikyrklig teologi om förhallandet fösamling-samhälle (Orebro: Orebro Missionskolas Skriftserie Nr 8, 1993)

The Radical Evangelical: Seeking a Place to Stand (London: SPCK, 1996)

Power and Discipleship: Towards a Baptist Theology of the State (Oxford: Whitley Publications, 1996)

Disavowing Constantine: Mission, Church and the Social Order in the Theologies of John Howard Yoder and Jürgen Moltmann (Biblical and Theological Monograph Series; Carlisle: Paternoster, 2000)

New Baptists, New Agenda (Carlisle: Paternoster, 2002)

A New Agenda for Tomorrow's Church: The Burleigh Lectures for 2001 (Adelaide: Burleigh College, 2002)

A Theology of the Dark Side: Putting the Power of Evil in its Place (Carlisle: Paternoster & Downers Grove: IVP, 2003)

Free Church, Free State: The Positive Baptist Vision (Milton Keynes: Paternoster, 2005)
God on the Inside: The Holy Spirit in Holy Scripture (Oxford: Bible Reading Fellowship, 2006)

www.ingramcontent.com/pod-product-compliance
Lightning Source LLC
Chambersburg PA
CBHW071441150426
43191CB00008B/1196